THUG
PREACHERS

THUG
PREACHERS

The Unspoken Truth of Pastors Who Rule
Through Fear, Bullying and Intimidation

Frank Jackson

XAVIER PUBLISHING HOUSE, INC.

Thug Preachers
The Unspoken Truth of Pastors Who Rule Through
Fear, Bullying and Intimidation

Author, Frank Jackson

Title Concept Andrea L. Cates
Executive in Charge of Editing, Annese E. Jackson
Cover Design by Xavier Publishing House, Inc.®
Production Associate, Eneyo J. Jackson
Interior Design, Amanda MacCabe
Post Production, Alero R. Jackson

Published 2016 by Xavier Publishing House, Inc.®
Munster, Indiana USA

First Edition 2016

ISBN-10: 0996881204

ISBN-13 978-0-9968812-0-3

Library of Congress Control Number: 2015919813

For information about bulk order special discounts contact:
Xavier Publishing House, Inc.® at xavierpublishinghouse.com
or
Frank Jackson World Ministries, Inc. at frankjackson.org

Preface — Note to the Reader

While it may look like just another book on preachers, most readers would have no idea how many long years of daunting work went into the making of "Thug Preachers." Looking back, it's staggering to think about how many years we worked, how many countries we visited, how many churches we attended and how many people we interviewed, while amassing research information, facts, and figures for this book.

Thug Preachers is the result of more than four decades of research, covering five continents. It is not intended to target the few celebrity ministers who are the object of other publications by other authors. The problem addressed in this book is much older and much broader than all the celebrity preachers combined. Truthfully speaking, I'm not so sure that all the ministers who have been targeted by other writers, even belong on the dirty preachers list.

The purpose of Thug Preachers, is neither to attack, nor propose to expose anyone, but to help unsuspecting victims of pulpit abuse and manipulation realize that there is hope. Of course, this cannot be effectively accomplished without providing detailed intelligence on how unscrupulous religious leaders operate, and how they mislead and take advantage of unsuspecting members, even within their own congregations. It also addresses the extreme emotional, mental, physical and financial damage they cause.

Thug Preachers speaks directly to past, present and future victims of church abuse, and offers healing from the damage and scars sustained from months, to years of abuse. I'll even tell you how to overcome your past, and how to take charge of your future through His power and grace.

Most of the stories reported here are based on events that took place somewhere in the United States, but the same kinds of atrocities could happen in Europe, Asia, Africa or most any other part of the world.

Also, as a matter of clarity, my own personal Christian walk and ministry experience have not been mistake free. Like any honest pastor would have to say, I've certainly made my share of mistakes as a Christian, as a leader, and as pastor. Although, I address some of those issues in this book, to publish an itemized list of my individual errors would offer no useful benefit to the reader.

Nonetheless, this book isn't about revisiting the errors of our past, but ensuring and reassuring that those problems remain in our past, and not appear in our present or our future. It is also about the church of Jesus Christ moving forward in the victory that only His Holy Spirit can grant us.

As you might suspect, the powers of darkness and the enemies of God have fought the production and release of Thug Preachers in unimaginable ways. During the writing of this book, I underwent eight different surgical procedures, including... brain surgery.

Just months before the release of Thug Preachers, I suffered what the doctors called, a massive Pulmonary Emboli (PE). Each doctor who saw me that day, said I was fortunate to still be alive. Doctors who have met me since the PE, tell me the same thing.

My wife, Annese "Liz," and I knew we were on a mission for God, and we both knew this powerful book had to be completed and released. We saw this as just another futile attempt of Satan to stop Thug Preachers from being published.

As I laid there on a gurney that was too short for my 6'3" statute, the doctors were discussing that the clots in my lungs might rupture, causing me to drown in my own blood. That was a victory that God wasn't about to let the devil achieve.

While yet in that, less than comfortable, ER bay, Liz and I touched and agreed in faith. After two days in the ER, they finally moved me up to a regular hospital room. They still weren't sure if I would make it, but Liz and I were sure. Later that night, as I laid on my hospital bed in the absolute darkness of a cold, unlit room, I slowly opened my eyes toward heaven. Then, I opened my mouth and declared— *"I shall not die... But Live!"*

"I shall not die, but live, and declare the works of the Lord."
Psalms 118:17 (KJV)

I believe that God resurrected me from my death bed to complete this book. As you read this book, I pray you will be blessed. To get it to you, almost cost me and my family the ultimate price... "My life."

Author

Warning – Disclaimer

The book, "Thug Preachers" provides general information on the appalling mistreatment perpetrated by some individuals against others in some religious or church environments.

It is presented with the understanding that neither the publisher nor author is engaged in rendering psychological, counseling, legal, or any other professional services through this book. The publisher and author realize that dealing with the aftermath of any form of abuse can vary from one individual to another. If counseling, psychological, legal or other expert assistance is required, the services of a competent professional should be sought.

It is not the intent of the author to reprint all the information that is otherwise available to authors and publishers, but instead to compliment, amplify and supplement other texts. You are encouraged to read all the available material, learn as much as possible about the many forms of church abuse, and tailor the information to your own individual needs.

The reports here are based on true accounts of actual events. None of the stories used are hypothetical. Some are occurrences that I have witnessed in my travels. Other stories are reported as conveyed directly to me from individuals who are survivors of the ecclesiastical hooligans who are the subject matter of this book. They are reported here as to the best of my own recollection.

Most of the names of any individuals and organizations have been intentionally omitted from this publication. Any identifying references to organizations, churches, pastors, parishioners or members of the general public is unintentional, and purely by coincidence.

The author and publisher of Thug Preachers positively recognize that God mightily uses both men and women in His Kingdom Building program. Therefore, we seek to recognize and acknowledge the ministerial call of God on both genders alike.

So, please note that in the interest of readability, most clerical leadership references to either gender are intended to imply both male and female.

No parts or sections of this book may be reproduced in any form, stored in any type of retrieval system or transmitted in any form by any means including but not exclusively electronic, mechanical, photocopy, recording or any other form without prior written permission of the author/publisher, except as allowed by the United States of America Copyright laws.

It is with exceeding great joy and the deepest of honor that I respectfully dedicate this book to the memory of my own personal mentor and father in the gospel ministry... Bishop H.W. Goldsberry, D.D.

Special Thanks

Generally, only one name appears on the book, even though many individuals are responsible for its inspiration, content, conception and creation. As much as I wish it were possible, in the interest of confidentiality, I am unable to name the many contributors involved in the production of Thug Preachers.

However, to those who entrusted to my stewardship, their deepest secrets and most painful experiences; to all the people whose stories and experiences have made this book both necessary and possible, I am both grateful and humbled.

To those who believed in me, when I no longer believed in myself, to those who prayed with, and for me when I was too broken to pray for myself; and to those who saw worth in me when all I saw was worthlessness, I say, "thank you. I will always treasure you, your steadfast belief in God's hand upon my life, your understanding of my shortcomings, and your priceless friendship."

Moving on, I realize that working with me on any project, especially a project for God, requires that the individual understands how meticulously particular I can be. My sincere thanks to my phase one interior designer, Amanda MacCabe of the United Kingdom, for her commitment to the first phase of Thug Preachers.

I would like to say thank you to the very special members of my staff who were instrumental in facilitating the various studies, inquiries and investigations we conducted while amassing research data for this book.

I am very fortunate to have been blessed by God with a family of professionals who possess the expert skills needed to work closely with me on my writing projects. Having said that, I would like to express my appreciation to my eldest offspring, Andrea L. Cates, for her sensitive and wise advice concerning the painful matter of abuse within the church; and also for her brilliant involvement in the titling of Thug Preachers.

To my son Eneyo "Josh" Jackson, I would like to say, thank you, for the times when you stepped up and made yourself available, just when I needed your help the most. Special thanks to my daughter, Alero "Bekah" Jackson, for her relentless dedication to the grunt work in the second phase of interior design. Thank you Bekah for a great job of post-production page formatting and clean-up editing of Thug Preachers.

And of course, a huge "Thank you!"…and a great big kiss to my incredible wife, and Executive in Charge of Editing, Annese "Liz" Jackson, for her ongoing support, perseverance and publishing expertise. Mere words cannot express my heartfelt gratitude for her invaluable help in directing the entire tedious and laborious editing process of Thug Preachers.

Finally, I am deeply indebted to the enormous hosts of experts, clinical professionals, college and university professors, clergymen, Christian educators, Bible scholars, orators and authors (past and present) throughout North America and from around the world, who played a gargantuan role in my far reaching research, in preparation for the production of Thug Preachers.

Frank Jackson

THUG PREACHERS

The Unspoken Truth of Pastors Who Rule Through Fear, Bullying and Intimidation

Table of Contents

Table of Contents

Table of Contents

WHY I WROTE THIS BOOK...

I wrote this book because, the matter of abusive pastoral leadership has become a widespread problem in Christian churches around the world. The one place where believers in Christ should be able to feel safe, is the Christian church. Sadly, for reasons, too numerous to fit onto these few pages, this problem is not decreasing. In fact, it seems to be growing more each year.

I wrote this book because, of the millions of pulpit abuse victims, who can benefit from it. Although, my prayer is that preachers will read it, and be blessed, this book is mainly directed to, and jam-packed with solid information for, the actual victims of the abuse perpetrated upon them by a pulpit thug.

I wrote this book because, of all the many pastors who presently participate in the misleading, thug form of church leadership. It would be wonderful if all ministers would simply practice and teach obedience to the words of our Lord and Savior, Jesus Christ, but that isn't our reality. I earnestly believe that many of these pastors are truly called of God. However, they are leaders who know to do right... but choose to do wrong

I wrote this book because, I realize that there are countless preachers out there, who would have a very different outlook on the pastoral ministry, and on their responsibilities to their congregations, if someone took the time to reach out to them.

I wrote this book because, I hope to provide help, advice, encouragement and guidance for the sincere pastor who may be genuinely seeking counsel and direction regarding his or her own issues and problems as a minister.

I wrote this book because, research reveals that, on average, about 1,500 pastors leave the ministry each month. It breaks my heart to know that good, seasoned, anointed preachers and teachers are leaving the pastoral ministry due to spiritual burnout, contention in their churches or moral failure.

I wrote this book because, I was once one of those pastors. I understand and relate to all three reasons. Thank God, these are all conditions that can be treated and corrected. I also know what it's like to feel abandoned by those whom, you sacrificed the most for. My dear brothers and sisters of the pulpit have given of themselves for so many years. Now, who will be there for them?

"I wrote this book because I care!"

Frank Jackson, Author

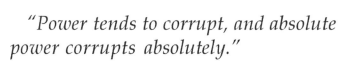

"*Power tends to corrupt, and absolute power corrupts absolutely.*"

Lord Acton 1887

Chapter One

BLIND OBEDIENCE?

*Does the Bible really teach that church members
are obligated to blindly follow and obey pastors
who rule over them?*

Acontroversial matter at the forefront of the church, is the subject of obedience to pastors and church leaders. Ask just about any pastor or parishioner, if the church member should unquestionably obey the wishes and demands of the pastor and in nearly every case, the answer will be a resounding "yes!" In this opening chapter I'll talk about where this thinking and teaching comes from, and why it continues to exist in the present day church.

While it may be hard for some to understand, the church is indeed a work in progress which has not yet reached perfection. Actually, I believe there may be many things about the church that Jesus would fix had He not given us the freedom to govern ourselves, and to choose the direction of our churches and organizations.

> The result of strong church leadership is often a strong church body. Fix the head, and the body will usually follow.

Most pastors are quick to say, the problems of the church lie within the members of the congregation. They vent about how much better the church would be if they had more dedicated members. I don't agree. I believe when it comes to the church, the problem is rarely limited to just the members of the church. Most always, the best way to correct problems in a church is from the top down. If the head is sick, the whole body is off beat and out of step.

"Why do you insist on being battered? Why do you continue to rebel? Your head has a massive wound, your whole body is weak."

Isaiah 1:5 (NET)

The result of good church leadership is usually a strong, spirit-filled church body. If we fix the head, through the grace and power of God, the rest of the body can be strengthened and restored.

THE USE OF THE WORD CHRISTIAN IN THIS BOOK

As a matter of clarity, I believe it is important to explain the purpose behind my use of the word "Christian" in this book. I realize that it is not documented in scripture whether the disciples and other followers of Christ referred to themselves as Christians. What we do know is the word "Christian" is found only two times in the King James Version of the Bible, while the word "Christians" is used just once.

According to the New Testament, the word Christian was a label first introduced and given to the disciples of Christ at Antioch. However, the Bible does not say who it was that called them by that term.

As far as the interpretation is concerned, some scholars say the intended meaning of the word Christian is, to be "Christ-like, or like Christ." Others say Christian means or implies, follower of Christ. Still, others give a host of other, seemingly spiritual meanings to the term Christian.

Although the word Christian has become popular in the Christian church, the Bible does not offer a specific meaning for this word. It also does not say whether the disciples ever called one another by the term Christian, as is common among today's followers of Jesus Christ.

> *"And when he had found him, he brought him unto Antioch. And it came to pass, that a whole year they assembled themselves with the church, and taught much people. And the disciples were called Christians first in Antioch."*
>
> Acts 11:26 (KJV)

> *"Then Agrippa said unto Paul, Almost thou persuadest me to be a Christian."*
>
> Acts 26:28 (KJV)

> *"Yet if any man suffer as a Christian, let him not be ashamed; but let him glorify God on this behalf."*
>
> 1 Peter 4:16 (KJV)

So as not to set off a theological war, please accept the following disclaimer—

The two words, "Christian" and "Christians," are used in Thug Preachers only as a point of reference. The intent here is to neither endorse nor denounce their usage. Nor, is it intended to offend any group of people. I chose to use these words mainly because they are terms that most people in the English speaking world are familiar with. Therefore, I use these words for this reason, and for this reason only.

3

AUTHORITARIANISM
Public Enemy Number One

Perhaps, one of the greatest enemies of the present day Christian church is a non-biblical system of church leadership known as "authoritarianism." You will probably never hear this word used in the church world. In the church you are more likely to hear terms like tough love, strong leadership, obedience to God and a host of other expressions which might be used to avoid declaring or calling attention to the fact that one individual may be exercising control and manipulation over the entire local church and the people of God.

An example of this is seen in the way many church pastors regularly use the Bible verse... 1 Samuel 15:22 to manipulate and control the church. When he wants to coerce the church into blind obedience, he rants and raves about how "Obedience is better than sacrifice!"

"Does the Lord delight in burnt offerings and sacrifices as much as in obeying the Lord? To obey is better than sacrifice, and to heed is better than the fat of rams."

1 Samuel 15:22 (NIV)

That's true. It does say that, but the obedience mentioned in this passage of scripture is not in reference to the church obeying the pastor. The Bible clearly speaks about the church (pastor included) obeying God, not mortal man.

Authoritarianism is a very oppressive and disturbing form or framework of social, political or religious structure characterized by absolute submission to authority. In other words, it requires that people (usually the followers of a society, organization or church) submit themselves to a single individual or governing board.

Authoritarianism is inconsistent with individualism and democracy. In a democracy, the declared wishes or votes of the majority determine the direction of an organization or government.

4

The direct opposite of democratic is monocratic. The word, mono tends to suggest or mean one. In a monocratic environment, one person may decide the fate of the organization and everyone in it.

We can find authoritarianism in just about every religion in the world. I'm sorry to report, it is one of the most common, and most accepted brands of leadership in the Christian church, everywhere. In fact, many sincere and honest (but yet authoritarian) pastors are not even aware of the presence and regular practice of authoritarianism in their own churches.

> **Authoritarianism is found in nearly every religion in the world. It is also one of the most accepted forms of leadership in the Christian church.**

Now, some readers may already be tempted to toss this book aside, because they are having difficulty understanding its' chief subject matter. Others, are on the edges of their chairs, hungry for the information this book offers. For those readers who may not understand words likes "authoritarianism," I believe by the end of this book you will feel and speak like an expert on the matter of democracy, monocracy and "authoritarian leadership" within the church.

The issue of authoritarianism is, perhaps one of the fastest growing problems in Christian churches throughout the United States and around the world. For generations, church pastors have been prancing around the pulpit, thumping their Holy Bibles and dogmatically shouting out to the congregation how God has commanded the church to obey their pastor.

I'm sure there will be acquaintances and friends of mine who may be tempted to believe this book is a poke or a jab at them, but they would be wrong. I wish this problem was limited to just a few preachers that I might know at the personal level, but it's much broader than that.

As much as I wish it were true, no single preacher owns the legal rights to authoritarianism or the officially registered trademark for monocratic leadership. If authoritarianism was limited to just one of my friends, I would not have had a reason to write this book.

Be that as it may, most authoritarians are single-minded individuals; focused on themselves. No matter what the situation or conversation, it will always come back to them. When they come across something that has been said or written by church members or colleagues in the ministry, they normally draw the conclusion that it is about them. In their minds, everything is about them. It's always about them. This type of assuming can cause great distress for the church. It forces the members to walk as though they are treading on eggshells.

Unfortunately, most traditional, hard-nosed preachers will not recognize themselves as authoritarians until they read this book. Their first inclination will be to deny. This is the kind of person who will read about the wrongful and hurtful actions portrayed in this book and say, "There's nothing wrong with that; I do it all the time!" That's exactly how a lot of people decipher right from wrong. If they themselves are doing it, then it must be okay.

Years ago, preachers used to choose which sports were acceptable, and which ones were damnable. For example, if a minister liked and played baseball, it was considered a fun sport. On the other hand, if he has never played nor understood the game of golf, he might preach about the evil corruption of golf. If he liked and played basketball, it was a great sport for enjoyment and fitness. But, if he wasn't a bowler, he saw bowling as corrupt and sinful.

They even came up with a scripture to support their views on these evil sports. They often preached from the first five words of 1 Timothy 4:8.

"For bodily exercise profiteth little..."

1 Timothy 4:8 a (KJV)

I suppose the same could be said for the sports that they enjoyed, as well. But, even if we ignored that one point. It is almost as if they were saying bodily exercise is wrong, but it's okay to kill yourself with a fork and knife at the dinner table. An unhealthy diet and lack of exercise are far more damaging than a basketball. I would imagine that this kind of reckless preaching and teaching might have played a major role in church people dying early from sicknesses and diseases that can easily be controlled with diet and exercise.

Here in the Apostle Paul's first epistle to Timothy, he says to his son in the gospel, he wasn't saying there was nothing to be gained from physical exercise. What Paul was saying was, "Physical exercise produces very little profit in comparison to what you can profit when you concentrate on building yourself up spiritually." What he wanted the church to know was, if you had to choose between physical exercise and a strong body in this present world and spiritual growth and development, along with eternal life in the world to come… choose life.

Some authoritarian pastors will see themselves in this book, but they probably will not take responsibility for their actions. It is not the nature of a die-hard authoritarian to be remorseful for what he has done. It doesn't matter if the authoritarian one is the head of the household or the head of the church, they will inevitably try to pass the blame to someone else.

When they do wrong, their apology is tainted. It will sound much like the abusive spouse or mate who says, "I'm sorry for hurting you. It's just that I love you so much, but you make me so angry." They go on to say, "I never really meant to hurt you, but you made me do it." Yep! To the abusive person it is always someone else who is responsible for what he or she did wrong.

Kind of like when we took my godson with us on a youth retreat many years ago. I don't really remember, but I suppose he may have been about nine or ten years old at the time. While on that trip his behavior was less than acceptable.

So, on the way back home his mother called to see how things were going, and we told her about his behavior. She asked to speak with him. As we got closer to his house we noticed him sitting in the back seat crying. I asked if something was wrong. He said, "Yeah. My mother says she's going to whup me when I get home." His godmother said, "Well you shouldn't have misbehaved. Without hesitation, he angrily quipped back, *"Naw! You should'na told on me!"* If only, you could have seen his facial expression.

That quick response coming from a child was amusing, but I doubt if the amusement factor would have been present had he been fifteen or twenty years older. Today, prisons are filled with individuals who are not willing to acknowledge that it was their own actions that got them locked behind bars, not the actions of someone else. Sure, we all know that there are men and women who are unjustifiably imprisoned, but there are more who are there as the result of their own behavior, than not. The sooner they realize it, the closer they come, to experiencing true repentance for their actions.

Dictatorial pastors are like children who refuse to be accountable for their actions. They will accuse members of the church of talking too much, spreading rumors, leaking information and causing dissension in the church. They become angry, and their wrath is fierce.

Even if some pastors do recognize themselves in this book, most of them will avoid taking responsibility for their actions by pinning the blame on someone else. I suspect the number one person to blame will be me for snitching on them. I'm sure they'll figure out a way to accuse me, just like my godson accused his godmother. I can almost hear them now... *"Jackson! You should'na told on me!"*

THE TRUE MEANING BEHIND PASTOR OR MINISTER

By in large, countless religious leaders have subscribed to the non-biblical philosophy, that "their followers" must obey them and submit to their rule over the church simply because of their pastoral label. Not because they are called and anointed of God or, because they are educationally or spiritually qualified. Not because of their years of experience, or because of their years of proven leadership, expertise and dexterity... but only because of their status or title.

This goes on even in the case where the title is a self appointed one. Perhaps, this notion is derived from what just might be one of the most misinterpreted passages of Biblical scripture:

> *"Obey them that have the rule over you: for they watch for your souls."*
>
> Hebrews 13:17 (KJV)

Very few church members and preachers recognize that the word "minister" as recorded in the New Testament actually comes from the Greek word, *"diakonos."* When properly translated this word simply means "servant." Nowhere in the entire New Testament is the Greek word, *"diakonos"* translated to insinuate ruler or monarch.

> *"But Jesus called them unto him, and said, ye know that the princes of the Gentiles exercise dominion over them, and they that are great exercise authority upon them.*
>
> *But it shall not be so among you: but whosoever will be great among you, let him be your "minister" – and whosoever will be chief among you, let him be your servant: Even as the Son of man came not to be ministered unto, but to minister, and to give his life a ransom for many."*
>
> St. Matthew 20:25-28 (KJV)

Here in the King James Version of the Bible, we can see that the *Greek word diakonos* was translated to say, minister. This interpretation seems to suit the thinking of more ministers than you might imagine. However, when we integrate both Greek and Hebrew research into our Bible study, we're able to get a better understanding of how some words with multiple meanings weren't always given the best translation from the original Greek to the King James Version of the Bible. The same could hold true regarding several other English translations of the Bible.

Below, we read the same passage of scripture from the twentieth chapter of St. Matthew, but this time from the New American Standard Bible. Here, in this version of the Bible the Greek word *diakonos* is accurately translated to mean servant.

"But Jesus called them to Himself and said, "You know that the rulers of the Gentile lord it over them, and their great men exercise authority over them.

It is not this way among you, but whoever wishes to become great among you shall be your "servant" (Greek: diakonos) *and whoever wishes to be first among you shall be your slave; just as the Son of Man did not come to be served, but to serve, and to give His life a ransom for many."*

St. Matthew 20:25-28 (NASB)

Jesus speaks out against the leaders dominating and unjustly exercising authority over the more vulnerable ones. He goes on to say, *"But it shall not be among you."* We see it throughout the Christian church. Overbearing preachers who have no burden for God's people are found everywhere.

They believe themselves to be authority figures or rulers over the people of God. The truth is, as pastors, none of us was called of the Lord to be rulers over the people of God. We were called to be examples of Christ.

Seven Commands to Pastors—

Peter sheds even greater light upon the subject of the minister's true role in the Church of Jesus Christ:

"To the elders among you, I appeal as a fellow elder and   a witness of Christ's sufferings who also will share in the glory to be revealed:

Be shepherds of God's flock that is under your care, watching over them – not because you must, but because you are willing, as God wants you to be; not pursuing dishonest gain, but eager to serve; not lording it over those entrusted to you, but being examples to the flock. And when the Chief Shepherd appears, you will receive the crown of glory that will never fade away."

1 Peter 5: 1-4 (NIV)

THE SEVEN PASTORAL MANDATES FOUND IN 1 PETER 1-4

1. Be a good shepherd.

2. Watch over the flock.

3. Be willing to serve.

4. Resist the temptation of yielding to greed.

5. Be eager to serve.

6. Never exercise dominion over those whom God has placed in your trusted care.

7. Teach and lead them by example, what God would have them to be.

In this passage, the word elder comes from the Greek word, *"presbeuteros,"* which means presbyters, bishops, pastors and overseers of the church. Here, the Apostle Peter warns against Pastors and Elders in the church lording over those that God has entrusted them to care for, and to serve.

As you read this chapter, please understand, church authoritarians are not necessarily bad people. Of course, they are all wrong for what they do, but the act alone does not constitute "mean spiritedness or ill intent." I know, to some of you it may seem as though I'm letting the fish off the hook, but rest assured. That's exactly what I am "not" doing. However, I do want to ensure that Christians reading this book don't feel inspired to spearhead a witch hunt or to launch a mutiny within the church.

There are good, God-fearing ministers in the church, who have not yet been enlightened as to the revolting wrongfulness of authoritarian leadership. In fact, many of them think they're doing God a favor by practicing what they believe to be "tough love." There are many sincere pastors who think this is just how it is supposed to be. They believe themselves to be the embodiment of God's purpose in the church.

"AS A TWIG IS BENT..."

I'm sure most of us have heard the quote, *"As a twig is bent, so grows the tree."* Take a very small, young, immature, flexible tree and bend or shape it in a particular direction. Next, tie it with rope or twine so that it holds that form. As it matures into a full-grown tree it will maintain that early shape. Even if you remove the twine, it will be permanently twisted or bent into that crooked shape.

> Pastors from an authoritarian background are more likely to continue the cycle of control and pulpit abuse.

So it is with people. While there may be cases where a loving and caring pastor may be authoritarian, he may be sincerely leading just as he has been taught to lead. Statistics prove what we already know. Many children who are bullied, grow up to become bullies themselves.

It also holds true that children who are the product of a strict authoritarian or abusive home are more likely to grow up to create a strict authoritarian or an abusive home environment for their own families. I'm sure at one time or another, we've all heard these words from an authoritarian parent, "This is how I was raised, and look at me. I turned out just fine." For the most part, what they're saying is, "This is all I know."

It's pretty much the same with pastors and overseers. Ministers and church leaders who were trained and mentored in a strict or authoritarian church environment are very likely to continue the fiendish cycle of church authoritarianism when they become the pastor of a church or overseer of several churches. As in the case of the young tree, even if you remove the twine they will hold that form. Forming young trees isn't just about training a tree to hold a crooked shape. You can also train a crooked tree to grow up to become straight and erect.

When my family and I lived in the Arizona desert, we had a young tree in my front yard that kept bending to one side and toppling over. We kept standing it back up. We even tied twine and attached the twine to stakes driven into the ground, hoping to force it to stand straight. We had a few strong winds come through, and our little tree supported by twine withstood the tests. Liz and I both thought the problem had been solved.

The twine and stakes worked fine; that was until a severe storm hit the desert. The next morning I went to the window and saw that tree lying horizontally on the ground. The roots were ripped out of the soil. Someone suggested that because the roots were ripped out the ground, there was no chance of saving that tree. Liz and I wondered if it needed to be disposed of.

We decided to give it one last shot. We had a landscaper come out. He replanted the tree into the earth. Next, he pulled the tree into a straight and erect position. Then, he gave it external support by placing straight pieces of lumber on four sides of it. As the struggling young tree fought to return to its' original form, he bound those straight pieces of supporting lumber and the tree together.

Soon after, when heavy storms blew through my front yard, with the support of those straight pieces of lumber, that tree stood upright. The leaves and branches may have taken a beating during those storms, but with a support system in place, that tree refused to give up any ground.

Eventually, the wayward tree began to show signs of maturity. It soon matured to the point where we knew it was safe to remove the lumber support from around it. Finally, even though the support system had been completely removed from around it, that tree was able to stand tall and straight on its' own. When future storms came, it proudly stood there and faced those storms by its' own strength.

I don't believe in tossing preachers out like last Sunday's newspaper, just because they might be out of step with scriptures. Some thug pastors are guilty through ignorance. Just like my little tree, they just need help and support. Yeah, maybe they are showing strong signs of leaning too far in the wrong direction.

This isn't necessarily because they are deliberately malicious. Sometimes, it's because they just believe in their hearts that this is the way it is supposed to be. This is how they were shaped and formed in the ministry, and even when the twine was gone, the twisted form held.

These wonderful brothers and sisters of the pulpit may have not yet fully received the biblical principle that the way to exaltation is through self humility.

> *"Therefore humble yourselves under the mighty hand of God, that He may exalt you at the proper time."*
>
> 1 Peter 5:6 (NASB)

What they have been taught is that the word "rule" in Hebrews 13:17 is a mandate from God for pastors to rule over or dictate to the flock. To them, it's just being a good Bible-based pastor. I'm sure most of us would agree that far too many people become parents long before they are prepared for the very demanding responsibility of parenthood.

Likewise, too many aspiring pastors fail to adequately prepare for the challenge. Very often, their whole concept of the pastor's role is based solely upon what they have learned from other pastors whom they have admired. Whether right or wrong, it's all they know.

THE PROBLEM

I earnestly believe that many church pastors would never have started out this way had they been properly taught or better prepared for the ministry in general. Had they known better, they would have done better. I'm sorry to say, many of them didn't know better. So, the problem they are now confronted with is the same problem the white minority was faced with in South Africa, not too long ago.

This minority group controlled nearly all of South Africa. Even though they made up only about 20% of the national population, they believed South Africa belonged to them. However, the approximately, 80% majority of black and colored South Africans performed nearly all the physical labor tasks.

Now, here was their dilemma:

The 20 percent minority enjoyed about 80 percent of the wealth of the land... while the 80 percent majority lived on, and provided for, and fed their families on the remaining 20 percent of the revenue.

14

There were laws in place that ensured the continuance of this policy. This unjust system is known as "apartheid." Generally, whenever members of the controlling minority spoke to the media, most of them admitted that they believed the apartheid system to be wrong. However, they also admitted that though they felt there was a need for reform, they found it difficult to give up a lifestyle that so greatly benefitted them.

The same is also true with enlightened pastors who have discovered that an authoritarian system in the church is wrong. Any church system that so greatly requires so much from so many, to benefit so few, cannot be right. It is a fixed order that is diametrically opposite to the teachings of Jesus Christ. Even for a genuine man or woman of God, it is not easy to give up a system of leadership that provides such bountiful rewards for the pastor and his or her family. It's even tougher for the charlatan.

> *"It is easier for a camel to go through the eye of a needle than for a rich man to enter the kingdom of God."*
>
> St. Mark 10:25 (NASB)

Continuing the Cycle of Abuse—

Sadly, members who may have migrated from other churches don't make it any easier for these confused ministers. In, many cases, some of their members are actually former members of other authoritarian churches and have undeniably been indoctrinated in favor of authoritarianism.

So, even though they are being abused, they too are convinced, that this is just good old fashioned pastoring. Surprisingly, many church people actually appreciate this style of leadership, and wouldn't have it any other way.

> *"The prophets prophesy falsely, and the priests rule on their own authority; and My people love it so! But what will you do at the end of it?"*
>
> Jeremiah 5:31 (NASB)

THUG PREACHERS by Frank Jackson

It's kind of like abused women who have learned to adapt to abusive treatment in their relationships. After having been in an abusive relationship for so long, in time a woman may not be able to appreciate a healthy relationship or a good man in her life. She may even admit that her reason for not being attracted to a good man is, "He's too gentle, and too nice." She often says is that she needs is a bad boy or a thug. The rougher, the better.

However, when she gets her prized bad boy, she continually complains about how emotionally, mentally and physically abusive he is. What she has failed to realize is, generally his abusive nature and indifference toward her (and often, toward the children in the relationship) are what makes him a bad boy. Needless to say, it goes with the territory.

Some years ago, an attractive young Christian woman had several young men in the church competing for her attention. Her problem with them all was they were too nice. They didn't seem to care about anything but what she wanted. She didn't like that.

There was one young man in particular who wouldn't give up. He was an established Christian who loved the Lord and the Word of God. He also had solid career goals for his life and for his family to be. He had three solid goals in life. Pleasing God, pleasing his mate and providing for his future family in as significant a way as possible.

Nevertheless, like so many other young women, she was unable to appreciate a man whose happiness came through pleasing her. He was too caring. She found that to be very boring. According to this young woman, she didn't want a man who gave into her on everything. She dropped him and found herself her heart's desire— A Bad Boy!

They got married, had children and lived happily ever after, right? WRONG! You were partially right, though. They did get married, and they did have children... lots of them! However, their life was far from happy. It was a life of poverty lined with physical and emotional abuse, diminished self-esteem and misery, for her and the children.

As you might have suspected, her bad boy was completely insensitive to the plight, and to the needs of his family. He was all messed up! He was busy playing the field, with no thought of what was going on with his wife and kids. He didn't care if the baby was sick, or if his children had food or milk, or whether they had a roof over their heads. What he did care about, as they got older, was swindling them out of every penny they had, down to the shirts off their backs.

Most (if not all) of the young men she rejected because they were "too gentle," went on to live healthy, family oriented, productive and prosperous Christian lives. By the way, the one who she thought was too loving and too caring, went on to become a Christian millionaire.

Another thing, women have a hard time leaving bad boys. They claim to love him too much. They also seem to believe deep down, he really does love her. They try to convince their relatives and friends that he just has a lot on his mind right now.

This is the same mind-set we find in the church. They see a thug presence in their ministry and find it somewhat appealing. They like his rough style. They are convinced that this is their pastor's way of showing his love for them.

For similar reasons, individuals who are immigrants from churches headed by bad boys find it difficult to respect a good, meek and Holy Spirit led pastor. They often mistakenly suspect his meekness and humility to be an indication of weakness in leadership ability. The more self-centered, pride driven and egotistic a pastor is, the more some people are likely to gravitate toward him.

Highly celebrated preachers who allow people to lift them to power can be swiftly brought down. One thing I have come to learn over several decades in the gospel ministry is, self-humility is the premise for divine exaltation.

> *"For everyone who exalts himself will be humbled, and he who humbles himself will be exalted."*
> St. Luke 14:11 (NASB)

In an era of celebrity preachers, humility is hard to come by. Often, when we look at the behavior of high minded church pastors, we see the heart of common street thugs. They may be wearing a preacher's robe or a clergy collar, but at their very core, is a deep-seated spirit of pride and malicious control. They are proud of their earthly accomplishments, and they live for the praise of others.

These men and women clearly understand and enjoy what they are doing. They are on a mission to build personal empires under the pretentiousness of "Kingdom Building." They are calloused and without conscience. They will trample upon any and everyone who gets in their way. They will use and misuse the people who love, depend upon and trust them the most.

They are the ultimate bad boys and bad girls of the modern day church. They are often remote, while other times organized. *They are the pulpit's— "Thug Preachers."*

Church Abuse Is Not Gender Based—

Abusive church leadership is not based on gender, just as domestic abuse is not a gender driven transgression. Of the 2.5 million reported cases of domestic violence and abuse in the United States alone, nearly half of those cases involve women abusing men. Only God knows how many unreported cases exist. Several of these cases have resulted in the loss of life. Domestic violence and abuse against men have become a global household problem.

Therefore, it should come as no surprise that there are women pastors in the Christian church who may be greater offenders than some of the men. It should also come as no surprise that in scenarios where a pastor is a kind person, church member abuse might still take place.

Truth be told, it isn't always the pastor that the church has to worry about. Sometimes, it is the pastor's spouse that they should be wary of. In fact, though no one wants to talk about it, some pastors are victims of their spouse's abusive and controlling ways at home.

I know of a few cases of domestic abuse taking place within the first family's home. These are both men and women first spouses who physically and emotionally abuse their mates. While, it's kept hushed, it happens all the time. Some domestically abused pastors have been living this way for so long that they have learned to accept and adjust to the treatment. Many have reached a point to where they don't even realize they're living under abusive conditions.

Research tells me that first ladies of the church are far more problematic than first gentlemen of the church. We've all witnessed it. A strong enough first lady will find a way to control her home, the church and even the homes of the church's members.

Trusting and naïve people make the mistake of thinking that if the pastor is a good person… the pastor's spouse and children must also be good people. That could be far from the truth. Many pastors are unequally yoked in their marriages, and the children of pastors can sometimes prove to be just as monstrous as the first lady or the first gentleman.

Some pastors' spouses are openly brutal toward members of the church. Not only do these spouses believe they are entitled a respect that falls barely shy of worship, they also believe the church should submit to them, simply because of who of who they are married to. Domestically abused pastors will sometimes sacrifice their members to keep the peace (this is probably a misuse of the word "peace") in their own homes. For the pastor to remove himself as the barrier between the member and the first lady is the equivalent of feeding a lamb to the wolf. The lamb is ripped to shreds, and the wolf goes on the prey for another lamb.

More times than I can remember, I have heard former members of various churches talk about how kind and spiritually nurturing the pastor was, but they still left the church. Through gentle probing, I have learned that there is a high percentage of people who jump ship, not because of a controlling pastor, but because of a controlling pastor's spouse. Unfortunately, there are controlling pastors' spouses who can sometimes be greater authoritarians than their mates can, but through the grace of God, you can survive this experience.

THE FIRST FAMILY OF THE CHURCH

Well, it's time to meet the first family of the church. I hope you're ready. As a matter of clarity, I think I should begin by explaining the most acceptable titles used for the pastor's family, and what these titles mean. Let's start off with the most familiar title, other than the pastor himself. The title "first lady" is normally used in reference to the male head pastor's wife.

On the other hand, most people don't really know what to call the head female pastor's husband. Here, the term "first gentleman" is typically used and accepted. And, of course, the "first family" of the church is the pastor's immediate family. That would mean, the first son, the first daughter or (collectively) the first children of the church, are all the children of the head pastor of the church.

Now, as far as member exploitation is concerned, any member of the pastor's family could be found guilty of misusing members of the congregation. The children of first families have been known to use (or misuse) their family status to manipulate, swindle, threaten, assault, or even terrorize members of the church.

Generally, because so many of the members are very gracious to the pastor (especially the sincere pastor) for the impact he has had upon their lives, older children of the pastor will sometimes borrow money from members with no intentions of ever paying it back. Out of gratitude to their loving pastor, the member will often dismiss the loan or decide to consider it a blessing to the pastor's family.

There are first ladies and first children of the church who suffer from a preconceived notion that as members of the pastor's family, they deserve special treatment. They believe they are entitled to higher privileges and greater immunity than the common members of the congregation are.

So, they will at times place unreasonable requests on the parishioners, or, they will ask for outrageous favors. One such case involved an elderly woman who was experiencing serious emergency medical issues. Frightened, she contacted her daughter to take her to the hospital, but the first lady had her to inform the ailing senior that her daughter was busy chauffeuring the first lady around as she ran her regular errands.

The members will normally accept the misuse by the pastor's family because they appreciate the pastor and his ministry. Of course, for some of us, we realize that the correct response to manipulation by anyone is to simply say, "No." It's too bad that some people have difficulty saying that. For them, it is less confrontational to accept the abuse.

> **For many faithful members of the church, malicious individuals from the pastor's own family could prove to be the ultimate deal breaker.**

This is especially true when the member comes from a horrible background. This kind of member feels obligated to the pastor and his family. This type of individual will usually credit the pastor with changing or saving their life. They think they owe their life to the pastor.

They really want him to know how much they appreciate all he has done for them. In their minds, giving back to the pastor by way of his blood-sucking family is the least they can do.

Without guilt, shame or embarrassment, the first family targets them. Often, the pastor is so busy taking care of the business and the needs of the church that he is unaware of the pandemonium that the members of his family have unleashed upon the church.

I am aware of certain scenarios where pastors discovered that their teenage or young adult child had been taking advantage of some of their fellow members. A few of these men and women of God openly denounced the actions of their son or daughter.

There was a situation where a pastor's son had been borrowing money from several of the members of his father's church. He continued to borrow without ever paying anyone back. Because those members didn't know how to say "no" to the son of their pastor, they continued to allow themselves to be misused and abused by the first family.

When the pastor discovered what his son was doing, he openly announced that his son was using his first family status to con the members out of money. He also insisted that the members stop lending money to his son to the point of letting them know that if they continue, they can expect to go unpaid.

Generally, dedicated members will remain faithful to their church or ministry until they either, die or depart the faith. As you might already know, it isn't unusual for members to maintain their loyalty to the church, even after having departed the faith. However, when it comes to a "deal breaker" even faithful members might choose to break ties with the church that they love so much.

Let me explain what the expression, "deal breaker" actually means. Deal breaker involves a specific provision in a binding contract. Here's how it works. When the provision or specified clause of the contract has been violated, that particular provision may be just cause to end the entire contract.

Meanwhile, back at the church, the loving and caring pastor may be the ministry's drawing card. He may be the number one reason for hundreds, or even hundreds of thousands of people flocking to, and supporting the ministry with their valuable time and finances. Nevertheless, for some members of the congregation, the insensitive, overbearing and manipulative members of the pastor's own family could very well be the ultimate deal breaker.

"*Reading the Bible will help you get to know the word, but it's when you put it down and live your life that you get to know the author.*"

Steve Maraboli

Chapter Two

KING JAMES IS NOT
THE AUTHOR THE HOLY BIBLE

*The King James translators were not the holy
men of scripture who were inspired by God
to write the Holy Scriptures*

You may have noticed that I've been quoting from the King James Version (KJV) as well as other English translations of the Bible. Now, before you stone me, you should know, I love the King James Version of the Bible just as much as anybody else. If I have learned nothing else from the church, I've learned that there are members of the church who believe the King James Version of the Bible to be the air tight Word of God.

I also believe the KJV Bible to be the Word of God. However, I also realize, of the many accurate English translations available, the KJV is only one of many English translations of the Bible. Others are present day translations of the Word of God, just as the King James Version is.

Years ago, when I first set out to learn the Hebrew language, my instructor, Dr. Oliver Thigpin was insistent on one thing. Dr. Thigpin would say, "You have a responsibility to translate from Hebrew into the best English grammar you know."

That's exactly what the Bible translators have done. The "thou's" and "thee's" of the King James era, would no longer be acceptable or practical phraseology in the twenty-first century. Sure, it sounds impressive to hear God speak this way in a motion picture like the Ten Commandments, but that's Hollywood. They want the movie to sound authoritative, believable and dramatic. King James (KJ) speech achieves that end.

Now, I'm not naïve regarding this matter. I realize there are religious cultures who commonly speak in KJ as a way of life. An example of this would be some Amish communities. I'm not knocking them, or their practice. I'm just saying, as holy as KJ may sound, King James is not the heavenly language.

Have you ever noticed that some ministers only prophesy in King James? They start out speaking in an unknown tongue; and usually it is. Suddenly, the tongues stop! There is silence. Now, for the next few seconds we have what we used to call in FM radio broadcasting, "a relaxed FM pause."

Then, from out of nowhere this preacher breaks out in a dynamic "Hollywood style," King James sounding (supposedly) prophetic announcement. An announcement that he wants you to believe is divinely inspired. Usually, he's just trying to get attention or impress people. Often, all that he is doing is quoting a scripture… such as 2 Chronicles 7:14.

You can do it too. Go ahead and start reading the following verse in your best King James sounding voice. Read it as though you have been commissioned to prophesy to the nation.

"If my people, which are called by my name, shall humble themselves, and pray, and seek my face, and turn from their wicked ways; then will I hear from heaven, and will forgive their sin, and will heal their land."

2 Chronicles 7:14 (KJV)

Wow! Can you see, how empowering that can be to a well-meaning, but fake prophet? Unfortunately, it is more misleading than it is empowering. Here's why it's misleading. Well, we know that's it's a Bible truth, and it is God's holy Word and promise to Solomon, concerning the Israelites.

However, it was not intended for the United States, Great Britain, Japan, Kenya, Australia, Egypt, or any nation other than Israel. And, by the way... the house that God chose to sanctify and place His name on forever, was the temple that Solomon had built in Jerusalem, not the Christian Church. I'll bet you're asking, what about the part where God said He would heal the land, right? That's easy. In verse 13 He had just told Solomon:

"When I shut up the heavens so that there is no rain, or command the locust to devour the land, or send pestilence among my people..."

2 Chronicles 7:13

Of course they would need healing. God is talking about a draught, a famine and a plague. Man, the livestock are going to be sick, the ground is going to be sick, and the people are going to be sick! You bet, they were going to need healing, and in a big way. This is why God promised, under certain terms, "He would restore them to prosperity and "heal their land." This is a promise of physical restoration for Israel, not a promise of spiritual revival.

Can it be applied to us? Well, let's think about that for moment. It was to a nation, not to a church, nor to an individual. And it was to certain people; chosen people; the Israelites; not the religious world. It was about a specific temple, not just any church. The language used, was covenant explicit. It had to do with a specific covenant between God and Israel; and no one else. There are parts

27

of the Bible that are to everyone, but this passage clearly speaks to Israel. However, there are so many wonderful promises in the Bible,

> Currently, there is a "King James Only!" movement building. The crusade is comprised of various organizations from around the world.

that do apply to us; promises just as great as the promise to Israel.

Now, let me get to where I was actually trying to go with all this teaching on 2 Chronicles. I kind of got a little carried away. But, here's my point, wouldn't you think that God would have known the Biblical history behind the seventh chapter of 2 Chronicles, before He gave the preacher this prophetic message to deliver to the whole Christian church, or to a local church body?

They may even announce something that we all already know, like… "God wants to save someone today!" Or, "God wants to bless you this morning. Lift your hearts in worship and His Holy Spirit will move in our service and pour you out a blessing that you won't have enough room to receive." Really? Now, How deep was that?

The KJ overtone helps the prophecy to come across more dramatically, and (to some) more believable. They believe KJ is God's language. His official language! People seem to think "This has to be God taking control of the preacher's speech. After all, if it's the preacher talking, why would he be speaking in God's language?"

It doesn't stop there. Did you know that, currently there is a "King James Only" movement circling the globe? The movement consists of multiple organizations dedicated to preserving the KJV of the Bible as the only accepted English translation. Crusaders in this movement believe the KJV is the only "Bible" recognized by God. It's almost as if they're suggesting that all the other versions are counterfeit or fake Bibles.

According to reports from Wycliffe Bible translators, Bible translating is an ongoing process. Recent information shows that portions of the Bible have already been translated into 2,817 different languages. Of these, 513 languages have a complete Bible, 1,294 have the New Testament and 1,010 others have at least one book of the Bible.

28

More languages are continually being added. Based on data released by the American Bible Society, there could be about 900 English translations and paraphrases of the Holy Bible.

Like many of you, the King James Version is actually my favorite English translation of the Scriptures, but that's not the point! Regardless to whether I stand at the podium to speak or sit down at my desk to write a book or presentation, I try as best as I can, to reach as many people as humanly possible. Modern English translations are easier for a lot of people to understand.

To many pastors, non-King James Versions of the Bible are offensive. I'm not sure if it's because these pastors aren't as Biblically secure as others might be, or if it's some other reason. But so many preachers seem to be afraid of anything that isn't King James.

It blows my mind that there are church pastors and overseers who actually forbid the members of their congregations to read any other version than King James. Now, if you really think about it, the problem isn't which version of this Holy Book people should be reading. The problem is in getting folk to read the Bible at all… Any Version! I really don't care which accurately translated version of the Holy Bible people choose to read, so long as they're reading it!

To be honest, at the young age of 19, when I started in the ministry, for me it was the King James Version or nothing. I used to refer to other versions as funny books. Over the years, I've learned that we must be careful not to confuse the King James translators with the holy men referred to in 2 Peter 1:20-21.

What's unfortunate, is some people still believe, King James actually sat down and single-handedly wrote the Bible. I wonder if it would bother them to know that King James didn't write the Bible.

> *"Knowing this first, that no prophecy of the scripture is of any private interpretation. For the prophecy came not in old time by the will of man: but holy men of God spake as they were moved by the Holy Ghost."*
> 2 Peter 1:20-21 (KJV)

Dr. Joe Paprocki (a minister and teacher for thirty-plus years) talks about a disgruntled adult student in one of his classes.

Her complaint was that there is too much confusion these days over various translations of the Bible. Paprocki says she angrily blurted out, "We should just go back to the original English manuscripts to see what Jesus really said!" Dr. Paprocki lightheartedly said, it was going to break the woman's heart when he tells her that Jesus didn't speak in English!

While speaking at a major church conference, a nationally known preacher openly and harshly condemned modern Bible versions. But once he got into his message he was counted to have paraphrased the scriptures 32 times, while repeatedly saying, *"A better translation would be..."* Then, he would paraphrase the many passages he'd be referring to.

EXAMINING THE WORD "RULE"

I actually love the King James Version of the Bible, but the truth is, the KJV of the Bible does have some poor translations in it. An example of this can be found in one of Paul's letters to Timothy, the apostle talked about the elders who rule well.

"Let the elders that rule well be counted worthy of double honor, especially they who labor in the word and doctrine."

1 Timothy 5:17 (KJV)

In this verse, the word "rule" comes from the Greek word "proistemi." The Apostle Paul's choice to use "proistemi" follows the metaphorical use of the Greek term with meanings such as "to lead, conduct, govern or preside." When we read that same scripture in the New International Version of the Bible, we see a different translation for the word the Greek word..."proistemi."

"The elders who direct the affairs of the church well are worthy of double honor, especially those whose work is preaching and teaching."

1 Timothy 5:17 (NIV)

To the power hungry preacher, this translation may be a real bummer, but it shows us that God is more concerned with us tending to the affairs of His church than He is with us ruling over one another. Christian leaders who rule (or lead) well, do so by delegating, appointing and directing… rather than by demanding, commanding, and dictating.

Many scholars believe the Bible to have been compiled by as many as forty different men from various walks of life. It contains the most powerful words ever written. To fully satisfy the directives of the Lord, it is crucial that we understand what God's word has to say about the church, the leaders of the church and the members of the church. Any misunderstandings in passages like Hebrews 13:17 can really cause a tremor in the heartbeat of the church.

Ask any preacher what" Hebrews 13:17 means to him or her, and two things will almost always roll off their tongues. Those two things are "obey" and "rule over." Many preachers would like to believe that their role in the church is to rule over the members. On the other hand, they also believe that the role of the members of the church is to obey the one (the pastor) who rules over them.

THE GREEK INTENT BEHIND THE WORD "OBEY"

Let's examine the deeper intended Greek meaning behind "obey" and "rule over." In Hebrews 13:17, we find that the word obey is translated from the Greek word *"peitho."*

The Greek word "peitho' appears more than fifty times in the New Testament. The first New Testament appearance of this word is in St. Matthew 27:20.

> *"But the chief priests and the elders persuaded the crowd to ask for Barabbas and to have Jesus executed."*

St. Matthew 27:20 (KJV)

Unmistakably, the most common Biblical translation of this Greek word in the King James Version of the scriptures is, persuade; persuaded; persuadeth… and so on. Vine's Expository Dictionary of New Testament Words reveals that *peitho* means "to persuade, to win over to, or to listen to and to obey. However, the obedience suggested is not by submission to authority, but the result of persuasion."

31

The point to be made here, is that mechanical obedience is the intended implication behind Hebrews 13:17. Yes, God's flock should always be open to being persuaded (*peitho*) by its shepherds. However, mindless slave-like obedience is not the relationship presented in the New Testament between leaders and those led.

Let's look at just a few (out of many) scriptures where the Greek word "peitho' is used in the New Testament.

> *"Knowing therefore the terror of the Lord, we persuade (peitho) men..."*
>
> 2 Corinthians 5:11 (KJV)

> *"For do I now persuade (peitho) men, or God; or do I seek to please men?"*
>
> Galatians 1:10 (KJV)

> *"For I know whom I have believed, and am persuaded (peitho) that he is able to keep that which I have committed unto him against that day."*
>
> 2 Timothy 1:12 (KJV)

These scriptures plainly show that the obedience suggested in the Greek language is not by submission to authority. It is a submission brought about through mature, responsible persuasion. Here are a couple of other verses where the word "peitho" is used for persuade.

> *"Now when the congregation was broken up, many of the Jews and religious proselytes followed Paul and Barnabas: who, speaking to them, persuaded them to continue in the grace of God."*
>
> Acts 13:43 (KJV)

> *"Paul entered the synagogue and spoke boldly there for three months, arguing persuasively about the kingdom of God."*
>
> Acts 19:8 (NIV)

This is an example of the Apostle Paul "reasoning" by way of discussion with the people in the synagogue. He wasn't ordering anyone around because of his higher credentials. He simply persuaded (peitho) them.

When the members realize that their pastor is not just there to glorify herself in her position... or to build the biggest and grandest church in town, just to own the bragging rights, they are much easier to persuade.

The Apostle Paul wasn't persuasive just because he was a great teacher and a powerful preacher. Paul was persuasive because he himself was absolutely persuaded by God.

"For I am persuaded, that neither death, nor life, nor angels, nor principalities, nor powers, nor things present, nor things to come, nor height, nor depth, nor any other creature, shall be able to separate us from the love of God, which is in Christ Jesus our Lord."

Romans 8:38-39 (KJV)

When the congregation is convinced that their pastor isn't just there to make a name for himself, but that he is fully persuaded by God, they are more likely to be persuaded by him. Who can forget the shocking words of King Agrippa to the Apostle Paul after Paul's great witness for Christ? Agrippa confessed that Paul had nearly won him over to the Christian faith.

"Almost thou persuadest (peitho) me to be a Christian."

Acts 26:28 (KJV)

It's important that the church leadership you are following is leadership that you trust. It's difficult to submit to, or allow yourself to be persuaded by leadership that you do not trust.

THE ACTUAL GREEK WORD FOR "OBEY"

Now, surprisingly, in the Greek language there actually is a word for "obey." But it is not "peitho." The Greek word for obey is "hupakouo." This word was first introduced in St. Matthew 8:27.

33

"And the men marveled saying, 'What manner of man is this, that even the winds and the sea obey (hupakouo) him!"

St. Matthew 8:27 (KJV)

"Hupakouo" appears a total of 21 times in the New Testament and has the word obey as its' root. Whenever "hupakouo" is used in scripture, it is properly translated as obey, obedience or obeyed, and there is never any doubt as to its' true intent or meaning.

"Children, obey (hupakouo) your parents in the Lord: for this is right."

Ephesians 6:1 (KJV)

"Even as Sara obeyed (hupakouo) Abraham, calling him lord: whose daughters ye are, as long as ye do well, and are not afraid with any amazement."

1 Peter 3:6 (KJV)

The sea obeyed Christ, children are instructed to obey their parents, and Sarah obeyed Abraham calling him lord. But nowhere in the Bible is the word "hupakouo used in reference to church members obeying a pastor.

No pastor has the right to command the members of the church, as Jesus commands the wind and sea. Moreover, church members should not be expected to, mindlessly obey their pastor as children are expected to obey their parents, or as wives are admonished to obey their husbands.

The Greek word "peitho" (meaning persuaded) is never used in this manner. Rather, the Greek word "hupakouo" is used instead for mandated obedience.

GOD DOES NOT REQUIRE MINDLESS OBEDIENCE

Any minister who looks to Christ as his example should understand that blind, mindless obedience to a man or woman is not what is depicted in Hebrews 13:17. The Apostle Paul told the Corinthian church that he did not wish to control their walk with God.

"Not that we have dominion (over you) and lord it over your faith, but (rather that we work with you as) fellow laborers (to promote) your joy, for in (your) faith (in your (strong and welcome conviction or belief that Jesus is the Messiah, through whom we obtain eternal salvation in the kingdom of God) you stand firm."

2 Corinthians 1:24 (AMP)

True men and women of God have no desire or inner yearning to control or dominate their brothers and sisters in Christ. What they do have, is a sincere desire and inner yearning to help them make the best choices in their spiritual quest and to reach their full potential for the Lord.

So, when a preacher, teacher or anyone else, tries to use one or two poorly translated scriptures as a basis for building the foundation for their belief, in an attempt to control you, watch out.

Honestly, I don't care which version of the Holy Bible you read or study… or even preach from. That's between you and God. I'm just happy that you read (and preach from) the Bible!

Whenever, any preacher teaches against using any version of the Bible other than the King James Version, take it with a grain of salt. They've got people thinking, when they get to heaven, God is going to start talking to them in King James.

Remember these words, King James is not, and never has been the official voice for the Holy Trinity. Nor, is King James the official language of God.

Society offers two major categories of hard thugs, and dreadfully—

"Both categories exist in the pulpit!"

Frank Jackson

Chapter Three

UNDERSTANDING
THUG PREACHERS

*You might as well know who you've allowed to rule
over you, because they sure know who you are*

In this chapter you'll get to know and better understand
the thinking behind the actions of pulpit hoodlums.
Risking, appearing redundant throughout this book, I will
remain true to my continued Christian, ethical, and professional
responsibility to ensure that you recognize that when I speak of thug
preachers, I am not referring to the millions of true men and women
of God working in the Lord's service around the world.

I am speaking exclusively of a select group of men and women in the ministry, who operate under the pretense of chosen and ordained vessels of the Lord. These unsavory church leaders, pastors and overseers should never be confused with God's genuine, superlative assemblage of caretakers of truth. For they are indeed, God's real protectors of the true gospel.

UNDERSTANDING PULPIT THUGS

Society offers two main categories of hardened thugs. Both categories stand behind our pulpit podiums each Sunday. It is important that we realize that there are actually two very distinct categories of thug preachers operating in the Christian church.

First, there is the "Reclusive Thug" who generally operates independently. The reclusive thug is not a part of any mainstream religious organization or movement, but tends to operate in his or her own religious sphere.

Next, there is the "Gangster Thug" who hardly ever operates alone, but is usually a part of an organized church system. That organized church structure can easily be a large, long standing, orthodox denomination or simply a small short-lived religious sect.

To get the greatest benefit from this book it would be good for you to understand the mind-set of both types of thug preachers. You should know that they are both after your hard earned money, your commitment to blind obedience to them, and your invaluable time. These preachers are determined to recruit you into their churches "by any means necessary!"

You're probably thinking, only an idiot would fall for the games that some these preachers play. And of course, you're much too smart for that. If this what you're thinking, let me warn you. The fact that you are an intelligent individual is not automatically an indication of your invulnerability to thug rule. I would caution you against thinking that you are immune to the lethal sting of pulpit scorpions. But, at least you're in good company. There are millions of highly intelligent people in abusive churches worldwide, who still have not yet figured it out.

THE ROCK STAR FACTOR

Unfortunately, authoritarianism clouds and distorts the believer's perception of what a true Christian leader is supposed to be. This is why millions of parishioners see the pastor as somewhat of an illustrious celebrity; sort of the way much of the world views a rock star. Rock stars are extremely powerful personalities in our present society.

Just as rock stars are highly regarded by society, pastors also are highly regarded by society. The members of the congregation want to be associated with them. The neighbors want to be recognized by them and eagerly wave to them as they drive through the local community. Political officials compete for their support. Even people who don't like them desire to be connected to them.

Pulpit thugs have the "rock star" factor. There's no doubt about it, there have always been religious leaders who have lived the life of a rock star, long before rock music or rock stars even existed.

Rock Stars Have Fans—

Like a rock star, some ministers have an enormous fan base. Some of the biggest rock and pop stars have hundreds of millions of fans. A huge pop star said, the thing that made it so tough for him as a child, was that he grew in front of a hundred million people. Countless pastors have dozens to hundreds, to thousands, to even millions of fans.

Rock stars usually do whatever they choose, whether moral or immoral and their die-hard fans will continue to support them. Thug preachers who commonly draw more focused attention to themselves than to Jesus, count on their fans to support them the same way.

Rock Stars Have the Power to Influence—

They have the power to persuade fans. Some kids would have never experimented with dangerous drugs had their idol not been openly proud of being a junkie. Kids do it because their rock star idols are doing it, and to a kid, their idols seem to be having a lot of fun. If a rock star tops the charts with a song about rebellion, drugs or suicide, people who love them are often tempted to do it.

39

The charismatic religious leader, Reverend Jim Jones, influenced hundreds of his parishioners to follow him when he relocated from Indianapolis, Indiana to San Francisco, California. Later, he again influenced about one thousand of his members to join him in moving again. The move this time was from California to Guyana in North Eastern South America. While in Guyana, Jones influenced all but a handful of his disciples to take part in a mass suicide pact. Over nine hundred people, including 200 children, died on that horrible day.

Clearly, the Jim Jones massacre and diabolical murder scheme was extreme, mainly because he was able to persuade such a massive number of people to die at one time. Still, it isn't unusual to find individuals on a smaller scale who are willing to do anything the pastor commands of them, even if it goes against the Word of God and defies human logic. The bottom line is this. It doesn't matter whether their intentions are good or bad, religious leaders are some of the most influential leaders in any society. This is true everywhere in the world.

The meek, but strong-willed leader of Indian nationalism in British-ruled India, Mohandas Karamchand Gandhi, was the role model for civil justice fighters on all parts of the globe. By way of non-violent civil disobedience, Gandhi led India to independence. His influence was the inspiration for Dr. Martin Luther King, Jr., and civil rights and freedom movements worldwide.

Even with Gandhi's non-violent example of bringing about peace and justice, I'm not so sure that, Nobel Peace Prize winner, Dr. King, would have been as persuasive had he not been such a well-spoken member of the clergy. I thank God that Dr. King's power to influence brought about a positive change in America, and for the good of the world.

I also wonder if Dr. Billy Graham would still be able to fill 60,000 seat stadiums if he had not been such an influential religious leader. Incredibly, at the end of each crusade the world has witnessed several hundreds of people come forward nightly to accept Jesus Christ into their lives. It is up to the leader to choose to use his or her influence in positive or negative ways.

Rock Stars Have Groupies—

Rock stars also have a gigantic following of groupies. These are very zealous fans (usually girls) who go all out just to get close to the various well-known celebrities, hoping to engage in some form of sexual activity with the celebrity. These celebrities are athletes, politicians, entertainers, broadcasters, actors or anyone who may possess, power, fame or fortune; even ministers.

For example, all very popular rock stars have members of the opposite sex (and at times the same sex) scheming and conniving just to be near them. Some groupies will literally sell their souls to spend the night with a rock star. In general, groupies are female. When men do the same thing, they are not usually called groupies. They are considered weird and they are .labeled as stalkers.

Years ago, during a nationally televised interview, a major former rock and roll star confessed, that at the end of his performances, he always knew there would be at least one groupie waiting backstage in his dressing room. His aids would randomly pick someone out of the large, screaming crowd of groupies. Whoever was picked won the opportunity to spend a few sensual hours with a rock star.

What I thought was odd, was the artist said he never knew whether the groupie waiting in his dressing room would be a man or a woman, but that didn't matter to him. These were people who he knew he would never see again. So, during that period in his life, things like gender didn't seem to matter. Fame, money, groupies and the power to influence are attractive to a lot of people. Yes indeed, to a lot of people, human idols seem to have it all.

Many years ago, Basketball Hall of Fame superstar, Magic Johnson, announced that he had been diagnosed with the Human Immunodeficiency Virus, commonly known as HIV. There were those who thought he should have kept that information to himself. I don't agree. I think what he did was difficult, but brave.

The problem was he had allegedly, had sex with over one thousand young women. As I recall, most of them were groupies who he would never see again. Still, Mr. Johnson wanted them to know that they had reason to be tested for HIV.

This was his only guaranteed way of getting the word out to all of them. His courageous act may have saved hundreds of lives; maybe even thousands, when you think of the indirect spread of the HIV disease.

> Men who are in spot-lighted or symbolic positions seldom have to search for women. Women search for them.

There is definitely no scarcity of groupies in the world. Another basketball legend tops the charts as far as I'm concerned. This Naismith Memorial Basketball Hall of Fame superstar never married or had children, but he is purported to have had sex with over twenty thousand women. The fact that he found time to play basketball at any level is mind-boggling to me.

Men in spot-light or symbolic positions seldom have to search for women. Women search for them. Preachers are no different. However, in the church, women who are drawn to preachers might be viewed as loyal supporters or admirers, rather than groupies. Both male and female alike, admire and gravitate toward church pastors and talented preachers; especially male preachers.

They are admired for what they symbolize. To some, they symbolize or represent God's power and strength. To others, they represent a father or mother figure. Some will even see the pastor as their own personal guide to the Kingdom of God.

While there will always be those who have their own perception of the preacher, the truth is, the preacher is just a man or woman like anyone else. Now, so long as you understand that, it is perfectly okay to admire God-fearing preachers for their stand for God. This can be a healthy admiration. It gives you a target to aim for, but never lose sight of God, and never become a worshipper of the pastor.

Don't become an unhealthy admirer who tries to establish relationships with preachers for all the wrong reasons. Unhealthy admirers are just naturally attracted to the perceived power symbolized by preachers.

Pulpit thugs exploit that natural attraction, and use it to their own advantage. There are those pastors who do things to enhance their intrinsic magnetism. This could include even cosmetic surgery. They also make it a point to dress and smell good, and tease fans, just as a rock star sex symbol might do. It's good for their huge egos. Of course, they usually prefer to call it confidence rather than ego.

This is the same as playing with fire; the larger the church or ministry, the longer the list of unhealthy admirers. The problem with these toxic admirers is they are always around, and they are always relentless.

Unlike groupies who follow entertainers, relentless admirers of pastors pose a greater risk for unwholesome relationships to develop. Although many groupies follows stars from one town to the next, most groupies interaction is one time only. Church groupie interaction often leads to relationships.

Fortunately, for the most part, whether the pastor succumbs to a groupie is in the hands of the pastor. While we may hear preachers commonly say, "She seduced me." Or they might say, "She came on to me," it is the preacher's responsibility to say "no." In secular professions, it is the legal obligation of the professional to exercise professional restraint. That same level of professionalism should be adhered to within the church.

Rock Stars Have Unimaginable Materialism—

It's hard for some people to even imagine the level of wealth some rock stars achieve. Some rock stars and recording artists are the true "rags to riches" story. Like rock stars, many preachers enjoy immeasurable materialism and unbelievable wealth. In the United States, it is possible for a minister to go from rags to riches, literally!

There are countless cases of impoverished individuals who go into the ministry solely for financial gain. Unbelievably, many of them ultimately reach six and seven figure incomes; and beyond. This is not to say that all preachers in this category are thugs. I'm just reporting on the monetary possibilities available to men and women of the pulpit.

Rock Stars Have Popularity—

Furthermore, like a rock star, many preachers are held in high esteem; often higher than that of Jesus Christ. They have oversized egos and enjoy a form of fan driven diplomatic immunity, which I cover in more detail later in this chapter.

Rock stars usually have people tripping over one another just to get close to them. They do whatever they choose to do, not matter how illegal or immoral it is, and their fans are okay with that. Fans want to touch them, any way possible.

The rock star lifestyle can sometimes, present a challenge to the preacher. For many, it is difficult to say "no" to the lucrative dividends. These imposters are neither rock stars nor true representatives of God. They are nothing more than a bunch of out of control thug preachers hiding behind the pulpit podium!

COMMON TRAITS OF THE RECLUSIVE AND GANGSTER THUG

As we cover this topic, I would like for you to know that, while clearly all pulpit gangsters are thugs, all pulpit thugs are not necessarily gangsters. Although, both goons have a lot in common, there are also very apparent differences that distinguish one from the other.

However, before we talk about the evident differences that separate them, let's first examine the reclusive pulpit thug and carefully identify the distinguishing characteristics and dissimilarities that set them apart from one another.

Both Live for the Praise of Man—

Thugs have an inner craving to be praised by other people. This why they make sure that their religious service and notable deeds are done openly. They want their good works to be seen by as many people as possible. Jesus calls this hypocrisy.

They boast about their large donations, the people who have been helped by them and their contributions to society.

> *"For they love to pray standing in the synagogues and on the street corners to be seen by others."*
>
> St. Matthew 6:5 (NIV)

According to the New Testament, as Jesus preached, the crowd grew into the thousands, to the point where people were pressed together, with some stepping on the toes of others. Out of concern for His disciples, Jesus warned them to be careful as to not be contaminated by the leaven (the phoniness) which puffed up the Pharisees.

> *"Meanwhile, when a crowd of many thousands had gathered, so that they were trampling on one another, Jesus began to speak first to his disciples, saying: 'Be on your guard against the yeast of the Pharisees, which is hypocrisy.'*
>
> St. Luke 12:1 (NIV)

As you can see, counterfeit preachers are not new on the Christian church scene. They've been around since the beginning of Christianity.

Both Claim to Be God's Representative—

Thugs tend to establish themselves as God's "Official" ambassador to the Christian church. Ironically, they all seem to claim a deeper spiritual understanding and closer relationship to God than their pastoral counterparts do. Additionally, they focus on teaching about their own ideologies, rather than the will of God.

When we read the words of the prophet Ezekiel as he cried out against the religious leaders of his time, we realize that authoritarianism and church abuse may be as old as religion itself.

> *"You have not strengthened the weak or healed the sick or bound up the injured. You have not brought back the strays or searched for the lost. You have ruled them harshly and brutally."*
>
> Ezekiel 34:4 (NIV)

Even back then, trusted leaders cruelly disregarded the needs of those who God had placed under their watchful care. Ezekiel's strong reprimand was clearly directed at overseers who used their positions of spiritual authority to rule, exploit and manipulate the people of God in favor of their own selfish purposes.

This type of thug preacher teaches that it is wrong for you to have a secret between you and the Lord. They would have you to believe that God will never speak directly to you or to any other Christian leader about you without first speaking to your home church pastor about whatever it is He is dealing with you on.

So, when God speaks directly to your heart or through a true man or woman of God, you will inevitably find yourself going to your pastor for approval. Because of their claim of official authority, in the eyes of the church, this somehow gives the pastor the right to decide what you should or should not do.

Thug pastors will have you to believe that they can do whatever they like without repercussions; or that they are immune to penalties for wrongful conduct. They are very convincing when it comes to warning the laity about the perils of disagreeing with them.

What they want you to believe is, to hold them accountable for their behavior violates a directive from God. When they are called into accountability for inappropriate actions, they often quote from the book of Timothy as a means of backing people off.

"Rebuke not an elder."
1 Timothy 5:1 (KJV)

People are afraid to challenge these pulpit hoods, because they are taught, to do so could prove to be detrimental. Pastors frequently use Biblical quotes such as, "Do not touch my anointed ones" to create a fear in the minds of the people.

"Do not touch my anointed ones; do my prophets no harm."
1 Chronicles 16:22 (NIV)

Now, if you're thinking that I don't believe God means what He says in this scripture, you're mistaken. I absolutely believe He does. I Get it! I just don't believe that most of the people running around using this verse, are God's anointed ones. I'm doubtful that most of them have even been called to pastor. That's the first thing. You can't just make yourself God's anointed. He has to do it!

46

Next, I don't believe He intended for preachers to use Him as their attack dog when people take issue with them and all their dirty deeds. Just because you're a preacher doesn't mean, whenever someone disagrees with you and your wrongful actions, you get to tell the Lord... ***"Sic 'em God!"***

Where pastors have an edge on diplomats is, while most heads of state are free to do pretty much whatever they choose, while outside their home country, they may have to conform when they return home. Pastors on the other hand, can generally do whatever they choose, even while at home or away. They can commit immorality, claim immunity and continue as though nothing happened.

Both Claim to Hear From God—

Pastors often intimidate pew members by claiming to have an ever-connected ear to the mouth of the Lord. The members tend to believe that anything that God wants them to know will come through their pastor. If God does not speak it to their pastor first, they think it cannot possibly be from God. On the other hand, members believe whatever the pastor says to them must have come directly from the mouth of God.

Many times, information shared between two or more members of the congregation is believed to have been shared in strict confidence. When in fact, it is somehow reported to the leadership. Thug leaders can now use this information to cause their members to believe that they (the pastors) possess a supernatural and deeply spiritual connection with God.

The pastor will usually not let on that she has been previously made aware of this hidden secret. Then suddenly, at the right moment she may call this person out during the service. To substantiate her claim of divine hookup, she will openly reveal to this very nervous individual the acutely secret and extremely confidential information that God has (supposedly) just revealed to her through the Holy Spirit.

Of course, when this great revelation miracle is performed in front of the entire congregation, the church is even more convinced that this woman is truly led and sent by God to watch over and direct their lives.

Both Claim to Speak for God—

Now that the congregation is convinced that this imposter is a true woman of God, she is free to move on to the next step. The people have accepted the belief that she hears directly from God, At this point, it isn't hard for her to persuade them that not only does she hear from God, but she also has the authority to speak for God.

With the unsuspecting member now having been singled out in front of the whole church, and with the pastor having shared this hidden secret that (in the members' minds) could only have been revealed by God, she is now able to tell the individual what he or she should do with their life.

This thinking of "divine connection" gives the pastor the influence necessary for controlling every aspect of the member's life. They are convinced; she not only hears from God, but "she now speaks for God. To disagree with the pastor, is to disagree with God!"

The church can now easily accept the phony notion that she (the pastor) has exclusive and direct authority from God for controlling nearly every area of their lives, including their homes, and their marriages. To be clear, this fake phenomenon is not confined to the pulpit. It takes place just as frequently behind closed doors, such as in the pastor's office, over the phone, at an arranged meeting, etc.

Now that the pastor is recognized as the reigning voice of God in the church, the members are taught that to be sure of God's direction for their lives they must rely upon the pastor for final confirmation. After all, this highly praised pastor or great woman of God (as they are often reminded) has been sent by God to watch over them and to direct their lives.

The pastor might even claim that what he says, especially when in the pulpit, is not his own words, but God speaking through him. So, for a member of the church to disagree with the (often, unreasonable) demands of their church pastor or overseer is considered to be the same as disagreeing with God. What has always amazed me is how pulpit hoodlums can claim to speak for God, but they seldom say what God is saying unless it benefits their own selfish agenda.

As a matter of clarity, I must state that I am not saying that members of the local church congregation should not trust the seasoned judgment of a true man or woman of God. I believe that God does use His ministers to lead and guide the flock. I have experienced hundreds (perhaps thousands) of times when God has given me a word of wisdom for someone.

The key difference is, whenever a true man of God has an opportunity to share a message from the Lord with an individual, it will be consistent with the Word of God. Furthermore, he won't try to cram the message down the recipient's throat. Yes, he is obligated, by God to discreetly, deliver the message, but he is neither obligated nor ordered by God to force, intimidate or manipulate the receiver into acting upon the message.

Whenever a pulpit thug comes to you with a (so-called) prophecy or message from God, he gives the impression of rejoicing with you when you immediately accept it and act upon it. However, if you hesitate, or question his words, or refuse to act upon the message given, he may become irritated, annoyed and very aggressive in forcing the issue.

Whether out in the secular world or in the church world, thugs don't like their actions or words being called into question. They are intolerant of individuals who may have a different opinion or viewpoint on issues. They see this difference in opinion as hostile and threatening to their empire. Ever notice sometimes, when a member of the congregation disagrees with, or questions the pastor, that preacher can go from zero to sixty in a matter of seconds.

Let us examine what just happened; not only have you questioned his authority, but you also rejected a directive from the pastor that would have benefited him more than it would have helped you. First, you stepped on his ego. Then, you deprived him of an opportunity to swindle you out of something that he felt entitled to; even if it was just your open acknowledge and validation of his divine appointment. When a minister can become enraged concerning advice that he says is from the Lord, be on guard.

> *"Then the Lord said to me, "Those prophets are prophesying lies while claiming my authority! I did not send them. I did not commission them. I did not speak to them."*

Jeremiah 14:14 (NET)

Both Claim to Have a Vision From God—

You might wonder what would make intelligent, full-grown adults follow such cult-like theological indoctrination and accept this childlike treatment. Here's where it starts. All pulpit scoundrels claim to be on a divine mission to fulfill a greater vision given to them by God.

I suppose the single greatest reason people follow these leaders of distortion is, they believe what these preachers tell them concerning the great vision that God has given solely to this one pastor. Usually, it is a mysterious plan that allegedly, only this particular he or she is qualified to unravel, and to understand. To know the vision, you will just have to just trust whatever the pastor tells you it is. Moreover, whenever they do share information about the vision, it is usually done on a "need to know" basis only. Generally, one "need to know" reason is when they need money to fund this divinely mysterious vision. When they need to raise money, they will share the vision.

I'm reminded of a true story of the pastor of a well-established denominational church who wanted to purchase land upon which to expand the church's ministry. He met with the bank and later arranged a meeting to inform the church's board of directors, many of whom were in upper corporate management in their regular lives.

When they asked him to help them understand why he wanted to purchase this property, he became very angry and shouted, "Because God told me to do it! I don't have to answer to you or tell you anything! God told me to do it, and that's all you need to know!"

So, realizing that he was treading upon eggshells, one board member said, "That's fine. I think this just might be a good idea, but to get the loan approval, I'm sure you didn't say to the bank what you just said to us. Pastor, all we're asking is that you tell us what you told the bank to convince them to grant the loan." The pastor angrily responded, "I answer to God, and God only! I don't have to explain anything to any of you!"

> *"They are prophesying to these people false visions, worthless predictions, and the delusions of their own mind."*
>
> Jeremiah 14:14 (NET)

He who controls the information fed to the mind controls the mind... And he who controls the mind, controls the individual.

Most pulpit scoundrels claim that they are out to fulfill a God-given vision; a vision which the laity, and perhaps, even leaders of the church are spiritually incompetent to comprehend. This is the reason, so many of them claim they must handle information with such secrecy. In a crude kind of way, what they're saying is, "You're all too stupid to understand what God is telling me about the business of the church."

Both Fight for Control of Your Mind—

Almost everything in the thug preacher's teaching and preaching boils down to one thing. The pulpit hustler wants to control your mind. They know if they control your mind, they control you, and possibly your family.

This accounts for why so many thugs try to keep you from exposure to the teaching and preaching of other ministers. It is important that you only receive the information that they want you to get. They deliberately control the information presented to their church members, because they know that whoever controls the information fed to the mind, controls the mind. And, he who controls the mind, controls the person.

Authoritarian pastors also control your time. Time control serves as a means of keeping the members completely wrapped up in the local church environment. They go out the way to keep their members absorbed with special programs, anniversaries, birthday celebrations, fund raising drives, excessive meetings and a host of other activities. Their hope is that the members are too busy and too exhausted to think about anything else.

Generally, time control also aids in keeping members away from family and friends. They know and fully understand what abusive mates have known for generations; if you control the relationships, you keep the person away from the caring advice of others. Once they have control of the mind and the relationships, you'll hear thug preachers talk about what they will, or will not permit their members to do. Pastors regularly discuss how tight of a grip they have on their members, as though they are talking about their children.

One such pastor was bragging to a group of gangster pastors about how he doesn't permit his members to visit other churches. There is another pastor who says, before his members can leave his church to join another church, that member and the pastor of the other church must both come to him to get his permission. One pastor even said, his members must get his permission before offering help or assistance to other members within the same church.

In many churches, the members are not even allowed to come together to study the Bible, unless it is done in a thug controlled environment. What this means is the thug must approve the location, which is usually the local church or pastor's house. The thug also gets to decide who may attend and who will be allowed to speak. Normally, the study has the thug or a thug appointed leader as the teacher.

It is not, unusual that the teaching is one way only, without others being able to offer their own opinions. In certain situations, members may be permitted to ask questions, but they are not permitted to offer comments. This is the pastor's way of purposefully controlling your knowledge of God, the Bible, and your Christian responsibilities. Surprisingly, for millions of people, their gospel is whatever the preacher tells them.

The Apostle Paul knew that there would always be greed-driven preachers who were willing to create their own version of the gospel, to control the minds of the people of God. Because Paul believed so strongly in the gospel of Christ, he declared to the church of Galatia that if an angel from heaven (or even if he himself) came to them with a conflicting teaching, may they be condemned to hell.

> *"I am astonished that you are so quickly deserting the one who called you by the grace of Christ and are following a different gospel – not that there really is another gospel, but there are some who are disturbing you and wanting to distort the gospel of Christ.*
>
> *But even if we (or an angel from heaven) should preach a gospel contrary to the one we preached to you, let him be condemned to hell!"*
>
> Galatians 1:6-8 (NET)

Both Possess Overwhelming Power to Influence—

In both the civilized and the uncivilized worlds, religious leaders within all faiths and religions, enjoy an indescribable power to influence their followers. To the unscrupulous church pastor or overseer, the church is his kingdom, and the lowly misinformed members of his congregation are his loyal subjects. As the result of poor Biblical teaching (usually by design), the church members remain his loyal subjects and the pastor remains their trusted ruler.

The thug preacher, who now has spiritual control of your mind, knows that if he is in total control of what you believe spiritually, he can control much of what you will do naturally.

> *"While Pilate was sitting there on the judge's seat, his wife sent this message to him: 'Don't do anything to that man, because he is innocent. Today I had a dream about him, and it troubled me very much.'*
>
> *But the leading priests and elders convinced the crowd to ask for Barabbas to be freed and for Jesus to be killed. Pilate said, 'I have Barabbas and Jesus. Which do you want me to set free for you?' The people answered, "Barabbas."*
>
> St. Matthew 27:19-21 (NCV)

53

We can tell from this passage of scripture that even when faced with overwhelming reasons for making a good choice, thug preachers have the power to influence a person in favor of doing that which is clearly wrong. Because of a very disturbing dream that Pilate's wife had just had, she pleaded with her husband to have nothing to do with the death of Jesus Christ, "because He is an innocent man."

That was good advice that went unheeded. Pontius Pilate had the power to release to the multitude, one prisoner of their choice. Pilate presented two very different prisoners to the people. One was Jesus, a just man. According to the words of Pilate, Jesus was also known as the Christ. Without a doubt, His claim to be the Messiah was no secret. It was also no secret that He had committed no acts worthy of imprisonment; let alone, execution. Yet, here He is, in a contest to determine whether He would live or die.

The other prisoner was a hardened, murderous criminal, whose name was Barabbas. When asked by Pilate, which prisoner they would have him to release, I'm sure Pilate thought the decision would be a quick and easy one.

Pilate must have been, cleverly, thinking to himself, "Man, this a no-brainer. Of course, the crowd will choose Jesus, and my hands will be clean. Why wouldn't they choose Jesus? Between Jesus and Barabbas, they have to choose Jesus! They have no choice." At least, that's what Pilate thought.

However, based on St. Matthew's New Testament report, the unbelievable happened! The religious leaders got the crowd worked up, and persuaded them to choose the murderous Barabbas over the faultless one. Just days earlier, those same people hailed Jesus as the son of David and the Messiah. But, today... they preferred a serial killer to the Messiah.

Although, the chief priests and elders had no authoritative power to order the people to ask for Barabbas over Jesus, they were successful in persuading the multitude to ask Pilate to release a notorious murderer back into society to kill again. This put the plans in motion to slaughter the innocent, sinless sacrificial lamb. What an unimaginable power religious leaders have; the power to influence people to do what they would ordinarily not do!

Some pulpit thugs don't limit their influence to what goes on in the church, but they also influence what goes on in the homes of some of their members. Thug pastors may even decide what their members can (or cannot) watch on television. They control what members can read and how they must discipline their children.

Thugs sometimes influence what members should wear and to what degree they should honor or respect the wishes and feelings of their spouses. Incredibly, there is a whole list of other areas of control too unbelievable to mention in this book.

Both Use Power as a Natural Aphrodisiac—

With a reputation as a ladies' man, former U.S. Secretary of State Henry Kissinger once said, "Power is the ultimate aphrodisiac." For many preachers and control freaks of every kind and nature, and from every walk of life, Kissinger's quote seems to be spot-on.

If you pay attention to what I say in this section, you should be able to see how church pastors are turned on by their power over the people. Church leaders are no different from others who are addicted to, and intoxicated by, the use of power over individuals.

There are the preachers who can only express their true nature through power or control over someone else. It is what stimulates the forced rapist. Experts on the mind tell us, the rapist is not turned on by the idea of sex, but his stimulation is the result of the reality of his own exertion of power over his victim.

All around the world, there are millions of employers, politicians, judges, surgeons, celebrities, police officers, teachers and preachers who experience that same rush every day when they dominate another individual. They get high on power, and will struggle emotionally if they are forced to live without it.

In high school sports, I have witnessed power intoxicated coaches keep a senior player benched unjustifiably for most of that student's final season. This unfortunate abuse of power against students takes place in high schools all across America. This is a cheap power play. Some might wonder, "What's the big deal? It's only a game." Well, you might think that, but abusers of power are a bit more calculating than that.

Here is how it works. When high school coaches fail to play team members who are in their senior year, it usually deprives that student of the possibility to earn a college or university athletic scholarship. Moreover, because it is the students' last year in high school, they aren't afforded another opportunity. They don't get a do-over.

In my opinion, this alienation by out of control coaches has nothing whatsoever to do with sports. I believe they do it because they know they can get away with it. Just like the abusive husband, or boyfriend, or wife... or girlfriend for that matter. They abuse, mainly because they are calloused people who believe they can do so without the threat of penalty.

The abuse that takes place right in front of a crowd of people produces the most exhilarating form of intoxication to an abusive individual. There's the thrill of being able to wield this much power, while knowing that those who witness your actions will say nothing, and those who govern over you will protect you from the equality and fair justice seekers of the world.

When a church, institution or organization fails to impose and enforce a zero tolerance policy against the violation of one's civil rights and religious freedoms, a grave injustice is present in that environment. There will always be people of every age, religion, gender and national origin who take advantage of a corrupt freedom to abuse someone who they perceive as different, weaker or more vulnerable than themselves.

Abusive police officers love being able to openly beat another human being senselessly. This was the case with Robert Leone who was charged with breaking the "fist" of a Pennsylvania state trooper with his (Leone's) face. As far as I could tell, it's possible that Mr. Leone may have been punched, kicked, stomped and struck with weapons hundreds of times that day. One of the officers actually jumped from atop a car onto Mr. Leone's back with both feet, while he was already face down on the ground, being brutalized by several other officers.

This crime against humanity didn't just happen behind closed doors. While, it is reported that Leone was beaten by the

Pennsylvania State Police on at least four separate occasions that day, it is also reported that at least two of those beatings took place right out in the open, in front of civilian witnesses. Fortunately, someone had the foresight to video record some these horrible criminal violations of a civilian.

Contrary to what you might be tempted to think, I don't believe this senseless crime was racially motivated. Both, Leone and the offending state troopers, were all Caucasian. This atrocity would have definitely constituted an excessive use of force against any man. But, it is even worse here, because Mr. Leone suffered from a serious medical disorder that may have impaired his mental judgment.

I don't believe the offending officers were motivated by anything other than power and control over their weeping, moaning, pleading and helpless victim. Unfortunately, the only ones who could have stopped these four senseless beatings were the other officers at the scene. It's too bad that they either chose to either, participate in the beating, or to turn a blind eye.

It is the same for high school athletes who are victims of abuse. Usually when their ill-treatment takes place, it isn't done behind closed doors, but in front of hundreds, even thousands of people. Teammates see it happening. Other students, parents, teachers, the athletic director, members of the school's board of directors and the school principal all witness it. After all, it's not their child. Why should they get involved?

They all observe this sinful injustice against a student, and no one steps forward to say, "This is wrong!" Especially when gender, religion, national origin, race, physical or mental disability, socioeconomic status and age are involved.

This blatant form of abuse is the kind of freedom that power drunken preachers enjoy. They thrive on the power to abuse another human being; a creation of God— "Right out in the open, and no one is going to do or say anything about it!" Everyone sees it, but they pretend not to notice… or they blame the victim.

What a slap in the face that is to all the Robert Leones, and to all the millions of church members who go through unspeakable abuse during church service, right in front of the masses, while no one does anything about it. No one steps forward to say, "This is wrong!"

Actually, it works in reverse. In some of the rare cases where someone does step up in an attempt to stop the injustice against an individual, usually that person who tried to help falls under attack by the perpetrators, or by their supporters.

Both Enjoy the Protection of Diplomatic Immunity—

Diplomatic immunity is a term used to imply, that ambassadors and other representatives of a foreign nation are not subject to the laws of the nation to which they are assigned. It is an exemption, which excuses diplomats from taxation, searches, arrest, etc.

This loophole in the law is enjoyed by political officials and their dependent families under international law and is usually on a reciprocal basis. In other words, if you will turn your head to my unlawful deeds while in your country, you will be afforded the same luxury when you come to my country.

Diplomatic immunity allows international officials and heads of state to get away with unspeakable things that might be considered criminal in the common or the regular non-diplomatic world. Foreign diplomats and representatives have sometimes gone unpunished for serious crimes after claiming diplomatic immunity.

The main purpose of diplomatic immunity is to protect diplomats from harassment or arrest by their host government. It should never be used as a protective shield so diplomats could break laws at will.

What's interesting is, in the United States of America, our own leaders and heads of state are subject to the laws of our land. The U.S. president can face impeachment if he breaks U.S. laws, as evidenced by President Richard Nixon regarding the Watergate scandal. Or, if he violates the presidential code of ethics, as in the case, of President Bill Clinton, concerning the oval office indiscretion.

A foreign diplomat can (technically) be accused of the same misconduct while visiting the United States. However, a visiting head of state is given a break that our presidents are not entitled to in the U.S. The foreign dignitary may claim protection under the banner of diplomatic immunity, while our dignitaries cannot.

Preachers are much like these foreign leaders. How many times have you seen where ministers have committed horrendous acts of misconduct while the church looks the other way? These preachers continue in the ministry as though nothing has happened. There are many pastors who enjoy a common form of ecclesiastical diplomatic immunity.

Thug preachers will have you to believe that they can do whatever they like, without repercussions; or that they are immune to penalties for their misconduct. In part, they are right. They may skate through, and around man's law, but when it comes to God, a reckoning day is just ahead.

They are very convincing when it comes to warning the laity about the perils of disagreeing with them. What they want you to believe is, to hold them accountable for their behavior (or misbehavior) violates a directive from God. When they are called into accountability for inappropriate actions, they often quote the Bible verse, 1 Chronicles 16:22.

> *"Do not touch My anointed ones"*
>
> 1 Chronicles 16:22 (NIV)

Another Bible scripture that you will hear thug preachers frequently use out of context is 1 Timothy 5:1.

> *"Rebuke not an elder."*
>
> 1 Timothy 5:1 (KJV)

Additionally, they focus on teaching about their own ideologies, rather than the will of God. When we read the words of the prophet Ezekiel as he cried out against the religious leaders of his time, we realize that authoritarianism and church abuse may be as old as religion itself.

59

"You have not strengthened the weak or healed the sick or bound up the injured. You have not brought back the strays or searched for the lost. You have ruled them harshly and brutally."

Ezekiel 34:4 (NIV)

Even back then, trusted leaders cruelly disregarded the needs of those who God had placed under their watchful care. Ezekiel's strong reprimand was clearly directed at overseers who used their positions of spiritual authority to rule, exploit and manipulate the people of God in favor of their own selfish purposes.

"Most people don't care who's in charge, as long as someone is."

Tanya Huff

Chapter Four

THE RECLUSIVE THUG

How the reclusive thug's system of
"Absolute Control" is set up and managed

ꓔ

Just as I've stated in chapter two, while the reclusive (or independent) thug and the gangster thug may have many things in common, each one will have their own traits, which tend to distinguish one from the other. Even then, it may yet prove to be problematic for some to differentiate between the two. Please bear in mind, while all gangsters are thugs, all thugs are not gangsters.

To be specific, most gangsters will have many (if not all) of the ruthless traits of a reclusive thug, but most reclusive thugs will usually have only a few of the traits of the organized gangster thug pastor.

An example of this would be in how they (very differently) set up their systems of control. In this chapter, we will look at how the reclusive thug preacher's system is set up and how it is managed. In later chapters, we delve deeply into the gangster thug preacher's system of total authority.

In the interest of ease of speaking, from this point forward I may simply use the word "thug" when referring to the reclusive thug preacher. When I use the word "gangster," I am speaking specifically of the gangster thug preacher. The next four chapters should prove to be more enlightening on this subject.

Usually Nondenominational—

Unlike the gangster, the reclusive thug pastor, more often than not, flies solo. That's what makes him reclusive. As a rule this type of thug is not a part of any known denomination, nor does he wish to be. Reclusive thugs exist in a bubble like ambiance. They have no mandated traditional or historical system to follow. Their dress code is whatever suits their individual personality, or whatever they feel like wearing on a given day. This could range from a T-shirt and blue jeans to a custom designed and finely tailored European suit.

Very often, the reclusive leader is the founding pastor or senior overseer of a nondenominational or interdenominational church. Christian ministries and churches established by these pastors usually suffer from "Founder's Syndrome" (FS). By Founder's Syndrome, I mean that the church's Statement of Faith, Church Doctrine or Mission Statement, tends to be whatever the pastor believes; and is subject to change without notice.

The problem with FS is the church has no existing platform upon which to build, as with established denominational churches. Therefore, the pastor has nothing more than his own training, background, experience and personal thoughts from which to draw. There are many situations where this has led to unspeakable results.

Of course, it would be unfair, untrue and ridiculous to group all non-denominational church pastors and leaders together. I know several nondenominational pastors who have strong

Bible-based churches. Some even come from very well established denominational churches, while others come from rock solid nondenominational ministries, very much like their own. In fact, I even know of strong and anointed pastors who have come from somewhat questionable churches.

Just as compassionate individuals can come out of abusive homes, great Christian leaders can come from bad churches. It is as though the lesson they learned from their previous pastor was, "How NOT to pastor a church!"

The bottom line is, there are Spirit-filled and Spirit led men and women of God, serving in the role of pastor of nondenominational ministries and churches everywhere on the planet. These are the pastors who God is using to bring about spiritual healing to broken people. It is important that we do not judge wrong, the integrity and sincerity of these good leaders. We should not hold the actions of a few ruthless pulpit hustlers against these true ministers.

Non-accountability—

Reclusive thugs usually frown at the idea of accountability, but they thrive in an environment of non-accountability. They like the power of being able to stand before the congregation to announce their own decisions and planned agenda for the church, without having to consider the opinions of board members, church leaders or anyone else in the church.

In fact, most reclusive thugs don't even have a "real" board of directors. What many have, are a few family members positioned as members of the board of directors. Often, the board will consist of the pastor as president, his wife as treasurer and his son or daughter as secretary. This satisfies the state's mandatory minimum criteria for a not-for-profit organization. This is pretty normal when setting up a new corporation. However, leaders sometimes forget to broaden the church's system of government as the church grows.

Other reclusive thugs will have a governing board similar to that of the founding gangster thug. This is where the directors are no more than a small group of members from the church (usually appointed by the pastor) who the pastor knows for sure will definitely not question his actions; nor will they hold him accountable for suspicious behavior. For the most part, the thug truly enjoys not having to answer to anyone.

Moreover, the thug and the gangster will both possess the same level of hard-nosed rascality, but they tend to operate somewhat differently. Despite the different ways in which they operate, to the injured party there is no difference. The pain of control feels the same.

> *"We are not trying to dictate to you what you must believe;*
> *we know that you stand firm in the faith. Instead, we are working*
> *with you for your own happiness."*
>
> 2 Corinthians 1:24 (GNT)

In this letter, what Paul is saying to the Corinthian church is, "We are not trying to control you or dictate what your actions must be. We are all laborers together, working in your best interest. We have no desire to come to Corinth to rule over your faith, but to help you." The motive of all true men and women of God should be to help the people of the Lord, not to dominate or rule over them.

THE THUG'S BATTLEGROUND

The thug's battleground is usually inside his church building. Although, he is comfortable fighting from his office or anywhere else in the building, he fights best from the mighty, impenetrable pulpit fortress. Thug preachers feel a sense of security while in the pulpit. They feel protected.

It is the same feeling a person who engages in road rage gets while inside their vehicle. They feel empowered to say and do things that they would never say or do if they were outside their car. They hide behind the steel and glass barrier between them and the individual who is the source of their rage.

Thug pastors are pathetic cowards who lack the spiritual adequacy, divine wisdom, sensitivity training or genuine desire to lead God's people in the Word… and the will of God. So, they have made a conscious decision to manipulate their own church constituency into following the demands, lusts and will of the pastor, rather than follow the Word of the Lord.

Public Chastisement—

Thugs commonly use the church pulpit for public chastisement. When the pulpit thug is displeased with the actions of a member, rarely will the so-called correction start out with the pastor approaching the member first. In fact, what reclusive thugs will do is wait until the church service is in full swing. Then, they find a way to launch an all out attack on a poor unsuspecting member sitting in the pew. This attack can result in public humiliation, open chastisement and embarrassment.

I'm not sure why, but many reclusive thugs seem to get some sort of a rush or satisfaction out of publicly destroying the self worth of their members. I suppose, in their own pathetic way they feel a sense of empowerment.

Sadly, but typically when this act of abuse occurs, the poor unsuspecting member is caught completely off guard. Watch the pastor's body language during these disgraceful outbursts. Notice how they seem to straighten their bodies and stick out their chests. To a dictator pastor, this is a proud moment. What a great feeling of absolute power they enjoy.

I was sitting in service one Sunday morning when the lead pastor of that church made an altar call for people needing to receive spiritual help from God. One of the elders of the church had been sitting in the audience with his guest. At the point of the altar call, the elder brought his guest forward. While waiting for the pastor to make his way to them, noticeably praying, the elder placed one of his hands supportively on the shoulder of his guest,

When the pastor finally made it to where they were standing, he did something awkwardly strange. Instead of praying for the guest, the pastor had someone to pass him the microphone. Then, seemingly from out of nowhere, he verbally attacked and humiliated the poor elder in front of the guest and the entire church body.

I got the impression that the pastor was upset because he did not think the elder was faithful enough. He kept shouting,

"You're supposed to be an example in this church. I'm your pastor and you know you haven't been calling me like you're supposed to. As an elder in this church, you're supposed to call me every day!"

Man! I was completely blown away. I thought, "Wow! What was that all about?" The elder was visibly embarrassed by the open rebuke. The fact that a pastor feels the need to know your daily whereabouts categorically shows hints of insecurity and thug leadership. Who has the time to talk to anyone other than his or her own family, every day? By the way, with all the attention shifted to the elder, I don't remember if the pastor ever got around to praying for the stunned visitor who came forth to receive prayer.

I have heard a significantly high number of pastors boast that God has appointed them as ruler over their local church. They say this is their reward from God for their faithfulness to the ministry. The scripture they commonly use for this is St. Matthew 25:23.

> "His lord said unto him, Well done, good and faithful servant; thou hast been faithful over a few things, I will make thee ruler over many things: enter thou into the joy of thy lord."

St. Matthew 25:23 (KJV)

Notice, in this passage the word lord with a small or lower case "L" comes from the Greek word, "kyrios." According to Vine's Expository Dictionary, there are several times when the word kyrios is used in English translations. The essential meaning of this word is, "He to whom, a person or thing belongs, about which he has the power of deciding; master, lord."

Other corresponding usages include:

1. The possessor and disposer of a thing.

2. The owner; one who has control of the person, the master in the state: the sovereign, prince, chief, the Roman emperor.

3. Is a title of honor expressive of respect and reverence, with which servants greet their master.

This is just another example of how frightened and insecure pastors are willing to do just about anything they think is necessary to maintain control over their members. I have also heard many ministers refer to this verse, but most fail to quote it in rightful context.

For example, you might hear the preacher say, "The Lord says, if you're faithful over the few, I'll make you ruler over many!" The implication he is making is, because he has been faithful over the church when it was small, the Lord God almighty has appointed him ruler over the members of a much larger body of people.

This scripture passage is not about ruling people. Jesus was speaking a parable about the Kingdom of Heaven being like a wealthy man who was about to go on a journey. As their lord and owner, the man summoned three servants to meet with him. Their lord divided his wealth between his three servants. One was given ten talents, one was given two and a third man was given only one talent.

The servants who were given the ten and two talents quickly invested them and produced a return on their investments. The third servant who was given one talent lazily buried his one talent and produced nothing.

When their lord returned, he found that the two servants had doubled their investments, while the one with only a single talent proved to be disappointing and untrustworthy. As a reward for their faithfulness, the master gave the responsible servants greater responsibilities. They had proven they could be trusted.

Now, if you were paying attention, the word lord is not with an upper case "L" but a lower case letter. This parable is about a slave master, not our lord and savior Jesus Christ. The New International Version of the Bible says the same thing as the King James Version, but in a more relevant and easier to read translation.

> *"You have been faithful with a few things; I will put you in charge of many things. Come and share your master's happiness!"*
>
> St. Matthew 25:23 (NIV)

The master rewarded the two dedicated servants for taking such diligent care of his business while he was away. The lazy servant was rebuked for being undependable and untrustworthy. Because most church people are not avid students of the Bible, preachers can tell them anything and they will usually believe it.

Open Ridicule of Members Over Pulpit Insecurities—

Thugs are insecure and paranoid about members leaving their churches, and with good reason. Reclusive thug pastors tend to have more of a transient following than gangster pastors do. This is especially true with some of the smaller independent churches. This could be attributed to the fact that because members have no one to turn to for guidance when the thug lets loose on them, people will often just leave the church in either frustration, shame or fear.

When it comes to some of the larger nondenominational or independent churches, they usually seem to have the necessary magnetism to maintain a sizeable congregation. On the other hand, denominational churches are often able to hold on to members who are faithful to that particular denomination. This is regardless to who the pastor is, or whatever may be going on in their particular church. It's similar to politics.

There is a true story about a U.S. presidential candidate's sister who said she is proud of her brother. However, she went on to say she would not vote for him because he is running on the Republican ticket, and she's a Democrat. Members will remain with the neighborhood Baptist, or Methodist, or Lutheran... or whatever pastor, because he happens to be of their denomination. However, when it comes independents, their pastors tends to be the attraction, rather than any denomination.

In a foolish attempt to keep members from leaving their church, naïve pulpit thugs usually inadvertently drive members further away from the church. Reclusive thug preachers are notorious for openly scolding their more faithful, dedicated or passive members, especially if they have missed a recent church service, meeting or event.

For example, a young born-again woman shared this true report with me. She was a member of a medium-sized urban church. She had influenced several young people to join the church. Ironically, many of them were already members of other churches in that city.

At her invitation, they started out as visitors, resulting in several of her guests decidedly moving their membership to her church. The pastor loved her for what she was doing to help build the church membership. He called it, "a great work for the Lord."

> **Some pastors are insecure, because they know that what they are feeding their flock is 100% Junk Food!**

One Sunday, she took one of her previous guests up on an invitation to visit their church. The following Sunday, during the service at her home church, from the pulpit her pastor openly humiliated her for visiting another church.

Later, she went to him privately to tell him that she didn't think what he did was appropriate. His response was, "When you went to visit that church, you hurt me. You hurt me really bad. You shouldn't have gone to visit another church."

He went on to say to her, "You're a drawing card for me. A lot of people have come to this church because of you. I can't have you going around visiting other churches." She replied, "Yes, people do come here because of me, but I can't continue to invite people to my church if I can't ever accept their invitation to visit their church."

Her pastor said, "I know what you're trying to say, but I didn't give you my permission to visit somewhere else. You have to get my permission before going to anybody's church!" She didn't leave right away, but the young lady eventually did leave that church. These insecure preachers lack confidence, mainly because they know better than anyone else, that what they have been feeding their flock is pure, undiluted, 100 percent "junk food."

> *"After they had eaten, Jesus said to Simon Peter, 'Simon, son of John, do you love me more than these others do?' He answered, 'Yes, Lord, you know that I love you.' Jesus said to him, 'Take care of my lambs.'*
>
> *A second time Jesus said to him, 'Simon, son of John, do you love me?' 'Yes, Lord,' he answered, 'you know that I love you.' Jesus said to him, 'Take care of my sheep.'*
>
> *A third time Jesus said, 'Simon, son of John, do you love me?' Peter became sad because Jesus asked him the third time,*

> *'Do you love me?' And so he said to him, 'Lord, you know everything; you know that I love you!' Jesus said to him, 'Take care of my sheep."*
>
> St. John 21:15-17 (GNT)

What a magnificent moment this must have been for Peter. This is confirmation of Jesus reinstating Peter as one of His specially selected group of disciples. He asked Peter three times if Peter loved Him. On the third time Peter was a little concerned. He may even have wondered if Jesus was alluding to something that he wasn't aware of. So, he responded, *"Lord, You know everything."*

This may have been the answer Jesus was looking for. Jesus does know everything. Peter then said to Jesus, *"You know I love you!"* What Jesus said to Peter on that day in Bible history, was what He is saying to all caretakers of truth today, "If you really love me, take care of, and feed my sheep."

The food with which shepherds are to feed the flock of God can be none other than the Word of God. In 1 Peter 2:2, Peter declares that Christians are to desire the sincere milk of God's Word.

It is the shepherd's responsibility to provide the purest milk available. Without spiritual milk, a newborn cannot develop to the point where he is able to handle or process solid food or strong doctrine.

> *"You have had enough time that by now you should be teachers. But you need someone to teach you again the first lessons of God's teaching. You still need the teaching that is like milk. You are not ready for solid food. Anyone who lives on milk is still a baby and is not able to understand much about living right. But solid food is for people who have grown up. From their experience, they have learned to see the difference between good and evil."*
>
> Hebrews 5:12-14 (ERV)

What the thug pastor fears most is that one of his members will stumble upon a true man or woman of God bearing a message from Heaven and— *he's busted!* He is afraid that once you taste of the real Word of God (the sincere milk) you will begin to grow up.

One Sunday morning, I heard a pastor say to his congregation, "If you like the cooking at home, why would you want to eat anywhere else?" He went on to use that as an analogy to support his views on why his members should not want to visit other churches, or to hear other ministers teach or preach.

Of course, he does encourage them to support the hand full of loyal ministers on his staff, who highly praise him. Also, the few visiting ministers who he carefully selects to speak to his congregation. This type of pastor teaches that everything you need from the Lord is right here, inside these four walls.

I don't support church hopping, but in reality, this preacher is frightened. Let me tell you why he's frightened. He knows that once you have tasted and experienced a good, spiritually balanced, Biblically nutritional, "life changing" meal, you can no longer be satisfied with a steady diet of junk food. That's what he fears most!

It is this fear that will cause thugs to stoop to any level to keep a member; particularly if that member has a skill or talent or if she is a strong financial supporter from which the pastor and his "family church business" can profit.

Pastoral Scheming and Conniving to Maintain Membership—

Several years ago, a pastor arranged to meet with a spirit-filled young woman from his church, to tell her what God had revealed to him about her. Fortunately, the young woman was foresighted enough to take another minister and his wife into the meeting with her. During this pretense meeting, the pastor prophesied (or "prophe-lied") to the young woman that God had revealed to him that she was to marry a particular young man from that church.

She told the pastor that she had no romantic interest in this young man. The pastor told her that she may feel that way now, but God wanted her to act on this prophecy. He went on to predict that if she obeyed this word from the Lord, she would discover that her feelings regarding the young man would change. She replied, "If this truly is the will of God, then I will wait until God speaks to me too. Until He does, I have no interest in a relationship with this man."

Sometime later, the pastor gave the exact same story (involving the same young man) to another female member in his church.

73

This young woman just happened to be the younger sister of the first woman he had prophe-lied to. Apparently, being a false prophet doesn't do much for your intellect. Little sister also refused to act on his fairy-tale prophecy. Both sisters realized that this was no more than another diabolical scheme manufactured by their pastor to keep them connected to his congregation.

This was his way of keeping members from leaving the church. The pastor's logic was simple. When a church-going woman marries a church-going man, customarily the wife joins her husband's church. He was afraid of that happening. But as you might suspect, with open arms, he gladly welcomed members from other churches.

Now, you would think by now, this pastor would have given up on trying to marry this young man off… wouldn't you? Well, he didn't! I have no idea how many women had to endure this prophetic gibberish. After much time had passed, a newly saved young woman made an engagement announcement.

She said her pastor had called her into a private meeting to share with her, God's plan for her life. Although the two sisters told her about their experiences with the pastor and his deception, she trusted her pastor. She went on to marry that exhilarated young man. After three children and several years of marriage, he left her for another man. She was devastated. He was still exhilarated.

> *"Many false prophets will come, and cause many people to believe things that are wrong."*
>
> St. Matthew 24:11 (ERV)

It wasn't until that pastor had become deathly ill that he confessed that what he had done to this young woman was wrong. Sure, he retained a member, but he destroyed a life. Thugs can be very calloused and fully prepared to disregard the feelings of anyone in reaching their goals.

Because people represent money to the thug, they have an awful lot riding on their ability to maintain a sufficient membership. For many, this is their livelihood. They're trying to either reach, or stay in that place where they can call themselves full-time pastors.

Pulpit thugs destroy many lives, while trying to build and maintain the church membership. They will say and do just about anything to get or keep a member.

THE THUG'S MESSAGE

The central theme of thug pastor's message is "Blind Obedience." Indisputably, the thug pastor is the ultimate authoritarian. We can see an example of this in the way he uses 1 Samuel 15:22. When he wants to encourage his church to blindly obey his wishes, he'll rant and rave about how... "The Bible says, obedience is better than sacrifice!"

That is true. It actually does say that, but the sacrifice mentioned in this passage has nothing to do with the church obeying the pastor.

> *"Does the Lord delight in burnt offerings and sacrifices as much as in obeying the Lord? To obey is better than sacrifice, and to heed is better than the fat of rams.*
>
> 1 Samuel 15:22 (NIV)

This scriptural passage says nothing at all about obeying the pastor. It speaks in direct reference to obeying God. Here, it says that the Lord is more pleased with your obedience to Him, than He is with all your offerings and sacrifices.

Let us approach this matter of blind obedience from a perspective of sheer logic. There are many instances where spiritually ignorant men and women simply decided to set themselves up as pastors. Frequently, there has been no formal training involved, but they do bear the title of pastor. Now, here's the question. "If they were spiritually ignorant before they made themselves pastors, what did their new title do to enhance their pastoral dexterity or their spiritual knowledge base?" *Not one single thing!*

The point is, if yesterday before you added a title to your name, you were unqualified to lead the members of the body of Christ, you are still unqualified today! God doesn't care about your new title. Logically speaking, no believer of Christ should be expected to obey this individual blindly. Titles are not the anointing of the Holy Spirit. Nor do titles give you years of seasoning, development and experience.

In his message, the thug pastor consistently abuses and misuses the Word of God. I have noted below, just a few (out of many) elements you can expect from a thug preacher's message.

Weak Biblical Support—

Here is a short list of things that you can expect to find in the thug's Sunday morning message. Reclusive thugs seldom start out with any formal pastoral training. Hence, it makes sense that, typically they are novices concerning the Bible and the ministry of our Lord. They tend to preach against educating one's self in the things of God. They devaluate college and university degrees; even seminary training. They often speak of divine revelation, to imply that their message comes directly from the Lord, not necessarily from the Bible. This is just a cheap excuse for being spiritually and Biblically unequipped to lead God's people in the way of righteousness.

> *"Do your best to win God's approval as a worker who doesn't need to be ashamed and who teaches only the true message."*
>
> 2 Timothy 2:15 (CEV)

It is the thug's goal to prevent people from appreciating the benefits of taking responsibility for their own Christian education. If he can keep them blindly groping around in ignorance, they will lean on and trust his guidance for their spiritual lives and well-being.

> *"My people are destroyed for lack of knowledge."*
>
> Hosea 4:6 (KJV)

Do I believe that ministers must have degrees from institutions of higher learning as a criterion for preaching the good news of Christ? Absolutely not! However, I do believe that ministers should receive some form of ongoing training, Biblical learning, or even personal mentoring from an experienced minister, in order to live up to the words found in 2 Timothy 2:15.

While it is true that there are some independent church pastors who possess amazing knowledge of the Bible, and even more amazing abilities in presenting their sermons, many reclusive thug pastors possess very little actual Bible knowledge. Because so many reclusive thug preachers are lacking in their knowledge of the Bible, they are limited, to preaching about the things in life that they are most familiar with.

This is why they talk so much about movies, TV shows, actors, athletes, politicians and other celebrities in their Sunday morning messages. Some preachers know more about Brad Pitt, than they know about Jesus. Or, they know more about Denzel Washington, than they know about the Apostle Paul. Consequently, they preach what they know.

Sure, they may be able to find a few popular Bible verses to sling around, and some inspiring lyrics from a couple of familiar gospel songs, but that does not constitute sound doctrine. Frankly, I don't think they are interested in sound doctrine. I suspect they are more interested in passages of the Bible that they can misuse and misquote in their quest to exploit the people of God.

Typically, the reclusive thug isn't much of an expository or textual preacher. He's more of a topical preacher. He finds it easier to preach from a Bible verse, or brief passage of scripture, or even a stimulating non-scriptural based topic, theme or subject.

When he reads his opening scripture, you would be wise to pay close attention. Mainly, because this may be the last and only time you will hear this scripture during his entire sermon. Next, he will usually announce an exciting title for his message. Often, it will be based on a popular song, or a current and popular phrase that may be going around in the church or the secular world.

Selective Preaching—

Reclusive thugs often do what I call, "selective preaching." To be clear, selective preaching does not necessarily have to be a bad thing. For the preacher who has difficulty presenting an organized sermon or staying on track, selective planning and preaching can actually be a blessing to her pulpit ministry.

THUG PREACHERS by Frank Jackson

I'm sure we've all sat under the preaching of a good, Bible teaching minister who made us glad twice. She made us glad when she began her power-packed message, and she made us glad when she finally ended it. Unskilled preachers often have trouble closing out the sermon. Therefore, these ministers would do well to be selective in what they present in their messages and how they plan to end it. With good selective preaching, the minister is able to make sure that she is delivering the highest quality of Bible-based preaching that she is capable of delivering.

> The reclusive thug's method of selective preaching is not the same as strong, healthy Bible-based preaching.

However, this is not the selective preaching I am talking about. The reclusive thug's method of selective preaching has nothing whatsoever to do with presenting a strong Bible-based sermon. He doesn't care if his message is well structured. He doesn't even care about whether he ends his sermon in a timely fashion unless his church is so large that he has to have multiple duplicate services.

Now, I know I said many thugs have very little knowledge of the Bible, but don't be fooled. There are also some thug preachers who possess an incredible command of the scriptures. These thugs deliberately avoid preaching on, or mentioning Biblical passages that declare what God really expects of us as Disciples of Christ.

They refrain from teaching too heavily on Christians trusting in the Lord, rather than man. They also don't talk much about God's wonderful plan of salvation. They selectively leave out scriptures that support "salvation by faith, not by works." They understand that if the members earnestly dedicated themselves to our Lord and Redeemer, it could negatively affect the pastor's true agenda. They completely ignore deliverance and demonology.

The reclusive thug primarily focuses his preaching on messages that are deliberately and very cleverly designed to promote unconditional loyalty to him and the church. This is not the same as loyalty to God, but he would have you to believe it is all the same.

"There is a way that seems right to people, but that way leads only to death."

Proverbs 16:25 (ERV)

Thug pastors will keep you so wrapped up with church faithfulness until you will be left with very little quality time (away from the church) to share with God or your own family.

Unreasonable Commitment—

In their quest to tie up your schedule, pulpit thugs insist on irrational dedication to them and the church. They preach about devotion to God, but if you listen closely and follow the steps in their teaching for building a closer Godly relationship, you will find that it always involves dedication that benefits the pastor and his church business. You may hear the thug preacher boast about his gifted ability to delegate responsibilities to others.

"They tie up heavy, cumbersome loads and put them on other people's shoulders, but they themselves are not willing to lift a finger to move them."

St. Matthew 23:4 (NIV)

Church people are just normal everyday people who happen to be members of a local church. So many of these people are carrying heavy stress loads already. They're trying to manage their family, their jobs, their schooling, the church obligations and so on. The point is, there are some dedicated, hard working members in the church who could really use a break once in a while.

Unfortunately, rather than lightening their stress, some pastors actually add to the already heavy stress of their loyal members. Oppressive preaching and teaching can push people to the brink of a nervous breakdown. Members are brought just short of making a blood commitment to the thug pastor and to their particular ministry.

One independent thug went so far as to have the members of his church stand and openly pledge lifetime allegiance to his church. When the pastor noticed that one of his elders was not standing, he openly confronted the elder. When asked why he was not standing, the elder responded that he could pledge to be faithful to God for the rest of his life, but he could not make that commitment to an organization. He went on to say, "None of us know what God's plan is for the rest of our lives."

With that having been said, the pastor suggested that if the elder was unwilling to make a lifetime commitment to their local church, maybe this is not the church for him. The pastor presented an ultimatum to the elder to either make a lifetime commitment or leave the church.

In sales, this is called the "takeaway" strategy. When a real estate sales representative cannot get a customer to make a final decision, she makes her client think he may lose the deal. She tells him that another customer is interested in that exact home. She explains that the other (imaginary) customer has already seen the house and fell in love with it. She reveals that the imaginary client is meeting with another agent later on to sign the purchase agreement.

The buyer now believes there is a likeliness that the home may be sold to someone else. So, at the realtor's suggestion, he decides to put a contract on the house right away, so as not to have this perfect home and great deal taken away from him. This is exactly how the "take away" is supposed to work.

Now, I don't think the pastor expected the elder to leave the church. I think he was trying to force him into a position where he had no choice but to follow the wishes of his pastor. He was using the "take away." This time, the "take away' strategy backfired on the thug pastor. The elder agreed to leave that congregation. Anytime someone is placing unreasonable demands on you or those around you, pay attention. It is incumbent upon you to make grown-up decisions. Do not allow anyone to bully you into making choices that are unreasonable, or that are not in your best spiritual interest.

Recently, many pastors have become very aggressive about covenants between the pastor and individuals in the church. What the pastor does is approach a leader or pew member in his church about entering a covenant together. The individual is led to believe that the pastor thinks so highly of him that he wants them to vow a special pledge to each other. Although, he may feel flattered and special, that member is only one of many members who are being approached concerning a covenant with the pastor. Each member thinks he has established a special, one of a kind relationship with the pastor. He now feels it is his sworn obligation to succumb to the frequent and unreasonable requests of his pastor and new covenant partner.

A Half-Truth—

There is one thing that the thug preacher knows and understands all too well. He knows that a half-truth is easier for people to accept than an outright lie. If there is an ounce of truth to what a preacher is saying, most followers will accept anything he says as truth.

Therefore, the thug uses the Bible in his preaching and teaching only because he has to. Often, the thug's preaching style is to read a scripture, to establish in the minds of the church, that it is God whose words they are hearing; not the preacher's.

Once he has fully persuaded the church that his preaching is Bible based, he can now freely transition into what he really rose to his feet to talk about. He uses the Bible as his platform because it implies a "divine truth" in his message, but his message is neither divine nor the truth. What he says when he gets deeper into his message may be far from divine… even further from the truth. He can now begin his usual ritual of bashing and humiliating individuals in the congregation.

Have you ever noticed the Bible smacker? As he's preaching, he holds his Bible in one hand and every so often he smacks on it with his other hand. Then there's the Bible waver, who holds his Bible up in the air and waves it around. A lot of preachers do this as a subliminal suggestion to the church that everything you are hearing is coming from that Bible that he's smacking or waving around. Very likely, if he were to open that Bible once in a while instead of just pounding on it or waving it around, he might be hard pressed to find much of what he's talking about in that book.

"Beloved, don't believe every spirit, but test the spirits, whether they are of God, because many false prophets have gone out into the world."

1 John 4:1 (WEB)

Kingdom Building—

Reclusive thug preachers spend a lot of time lecturing about "Kingdom Building." Now, you might be tempted to think they are genuinely concerned about building the Kingdom of God, but their actions speak louder than their words. Their words say Kingdom Building, but their actions say, "Empire Building." While preaching, he may say God's Kingdom, but he really means his own kingdom or empire. God's Kingdom is built through soul winning. Man's kingdom is built through materialism.

Investopedia is one of the largest, trusted and respected websites on the Internet created for investors (www.investopedia.com). It is entirely devoted to providing education on investing. Investopedia offers the following definition for empire building.

"Empire building is the act of attempting to increase the size and scope of an individual or organization's power and influence. In the corporate world, this is seen when managers or executives are more concerned with expanding their business units, their staffing levels and the dollar value of assets under their control than they are with developing and implementing ways to benefit shareholders."

★Quote from Investopedia

The managers depicted in this definition of empire building, are the perfect example of "Corporate Thugs." Corporate thugs are known for building their empires on the backs and shoulders of others. They are the masters of hostile takeovers. Their true loyalty (or lack thereof) is tested in the face of money, fame and power. To the corporate thug, everyone is dispensable.

Now, if you were paying attention, you would have noticed that the same traits could be found in pulpit thugs. They too, are trying to increase their power and influence. Like the corporate thug,

82

some pastors are more concerned with expanding their membership numbers, their leadership staff, and their finances.

They are less concerned with developing and implementing ways to benefit their congregations, the people who support them the most. Investopedia goes on to explain the adverse effect empire building can have on a corporation.

> *"Empire building is typically seen as unhealthy for a corporation, as managers will often become more concerned with acquiring greater resource control than with optimally allocating resources."*
>
> ★Quote from Investopedia

The spirit of empire building is seen in the reclusive thug's emphasis on the physical kingdom rather than the Spiritual Kingdom. What a big mistake that can be!

> *"For what shall it profit a man if he shall gain the whole world, and lose his own soul?"*
>
> St. Mark 8:36 (KJ21)

There's no denying it. Reclusive thug preachers are some of the best investors in the world. Sure, they may go about it the wrong way, but they are good at what they do. They invest your time, your energy and your resources... and they collect their dividends. Man, that's better than Wall Street! When it comes to the thug preacher, you make the sacrifices, and they reap the benefits. It can't get any better than that!

Arousal of Emotions—

From here the thug will move into the most enjoyable and entertaining part of the message. After all, he does want to end with the people feeling good. This is when he elevates the crowd to heights of enthusiasm. He really wants everyone to leave excited and raving over how well the pastor preached today.

As a rule of thumb, when he has concluded, you may notice that he hasn't talked much about sin, repentance, forgiveness, salvation, heaven or hell. What he has talked a lot about is your religious obligations and absolute obedience to your pastor. He has also talked about the bountiful blessings available to those who freely give their tithes and offerings.

The reclusive thug isn't interested in getting people saved through true spiritual awareness. He's too afraid that if his members become too enlightened, he may lose them. This is why slaves in the United States were punished if they wee caught reading or writing. Slave owners knew, if their slaves learned to read, they would eventually discover information that could lead to their freedom.

Like slave owners, the thug preacher is more interested in telling her congregants just enough to keep them coming back for more. This way, they will continue to build it, as she continues to maintain her material empire.

Finally, the thug takes advantage of this last and closing opportunity to remind you one more time of your obligatory loyalty to the church and to your pastor.

STAY ON GUARD!

There you have it, the reclusive thug's message, concisely. Of course, this generality is not intended to cover all reclusive thug preachers, but it should be enough to send up a red flag when you are exposed to churches where Jesus Christ crucified is not the central focus of the ministry.

"For the preaching of the cross is to them that perish foolishness; but unto us which are saved it is the power of God."

1 Corinthians 1:18 (KJV)

The most important thing any minister can talk about in his message is Jesus Christ crucified, buried and resurrected. Aside from the cross, there is no redemption. The way to God is through our Lord and savior Christ Jesus. There is no other way.

"Jesus saith unto him, I am the way, the truth, and the life: no man cometh unto the Father, but by me."

St. John 14:6 (KJV)

We are not denouncing genuine men and women of God, but we are denouncing rogue preachers who follow a carefully and thoroughly planned strategy to do wrong. They are masters at what they do, but it is not of God.

In the next chapter, I'll be explaining why so many men and women are attracted to a pretentious life, rather than a genuine one.

"For the love of money is the root of all evil: which while some coveted after, they have erred from the faith."

1 Timothy 6:10 (KJV)

Chapter Five

THE RECLUSIVE THUG'S LURE

*The real reasons as to why so many reclusive thugs
are attracted to the pastoral ministry*

W hile both the reclusive thug and the gangster thug may share an obvious commonality, their motivations for wanting to become a pastor may be very different. What do you suppose would make a man or woman relinquish the true blessings of the Lord to become a replica vessel of the Lord?

Well, for starters, some of them are messed up to the point where they themselves don't even know that they're messed up. I have often said, "The hardest man in the world to save, is a man who is not saved, but he thinks he is." In this chapter, I'll talk about some of the lures that have attracted and overtaken so many reclusive thugs.

Easy Start-Up—

Reclusive thugs are easily attracted to the idea of the minimal hassle or the hassle-free startup associated with setting up a new ministry or church. Unlike the gangster thug who may be stepping into an already established or existing ministry or church, the reclusive thug does not have to impress a church board of directors to get his job.

The idea of minimal investment is also attractive. They can start meeting in a home or a small donated or rented space and worry about expansion space as needed. They like the idea of being able to bring a few people together for Bible study and later turning it into a church.

Please understand, by no means am I suggesting that ministers forming and leading Bible study groups are thugs. It is quite the contrary. It is not uncommon for true men and women of God to set up Bible study groups with the intentions of starting a church. Many well known Bible-based churches have started this way.

In fact, the first church that I ever formed started out of a Bible study. What is interesting is I did not set out to start a church. I merely made plans to study the Bible in my home with my nephew, who at the time was a new convert. Others found out that we were planning to meet to study the Bible and asked if they could join us. Naturally, I consented.

Each week the numbers grew. Many of the regular group members were inviting guests to the meetings. As the numbers grew, more and more unbelievers were accepting Christ. Finally, we reached a point to where we had run out of space in my home. I had to use a public address system so participants in adjoining rooms could hear me. Individuals were being saved, a great many of them had no church home for ongoing training and leadership.

I prayed for direction from God, and not long after that, the new church was born. The first service resulted in 42 people becoming members of the church. Fortunately, through our Bible study, most of them had already become genuine born-again believers. We were blessed to be able to segue to a new church with people who we had helped develop a strong Biblical foundation.

> There are many people in the church are more comfortable with a pastor who has not lived a perfect life.

We knew what we had in these people. They were dedicated and excited about God, and His glorious Word. We could not have started with a better group of believers. From there, the church took off. If the Lord permits me to, I'll be speaking more about our church in an upcoming book.

I would like to point out, not all the Bible study participants became members of the new church. A few were already members of other churches. However, many of those people did continue to attend the Bible study, which continued even after the church was established. As for the Bible study participants who were from other churches, we never once tried to persuade any of them to switch their membership to our church. That wasn't our purpose.

No Background Check—

I have met numerous pulpit thugs who were real street thugs in the world. Many have long felonious backgrounds that would prevent them from landing a respectable, high income management position in corporate America.

So, it doesn't take a brain surgeon to see how this could make the pulpit ministry very appealing to a felon. Since, there is no background check, it doesn't matter if the thug has been convicted of armed robbery, embezzlement or murder. Under the protection of the Constitution of the United States of America, the thug is free to set up his or her own religious organization without the threat of retaliation.

Please know that having been convicted of a felony in his or her past does not necessarily disqualify an individual from being able to serve or lead the people of God. In fact, there are times when this may be the one thing that connects the pulpit with certain individuals in the pew.

When leaders who have lived criminal lives are willing to admit to their constituency, the errors of their own past, rather than glorify their past actions, the reaction is usually a positive one. Especially, when the preacher is a man. Although, most men in the church are usually accepting, the women in the congregation tend to be a little tough on a woman preacher who has lived a hard, or a street life.

Thank God, millions of people are inspired by ministers of this sort every day. I suppose they appreciate the fact that the pastor is not some sort of superhuman or supernatural being. To them, she is not just their pastor. She is a normal person who understands them and their tarnished past. They can relate to her, and she can relate to them. They positively believe she can identify with them, and that she understands their feelings, emotions and shortcomings.

Relaxed Educational Requirements—

No diploma? No education?… *No problem!* The ministry as a business entity is also appealing to the thug because of its lenient educational requirements. Generally, education is a non-issue for thugs wishing to start their own church or ministry. She can be a high school graduate or a high school dropout. It does not matter.

If she is the founder of her own church or ministry, her level of education probably is not a factor. I even know of at least one situation where the minister had never attended any school at all. Not even grade school.

Ministers don't really need to concern themselves with college degrees. There are more than enough diploma mills out there to turn every preacher in the world into a Doctor of something within 48 hours. For a fee, an online diploma mill will issue to you a college or university degree within 24 hours to 72 hours of the time you place your order.

You can choose your particular field of study and your level of higher education. Which means within a matter of hours you can receive a BS in Communications, or a Masters in Family Counseling, or a Doctorate in Divinity. The point is, you can get whatever degree you want from a diploma mill without meeting the traditional requirements or qualifications.

In fact, there are many pastors with religious studies doctoral degrees who have not completed elementary or high school, nor have they met the General Educational Development (G.E.D.) high school equivalency requirements. I have actually spoken with pastors who have doctoral degrees, but can't seem to remember the name of the school that allegedly issued their degree.

If you think it isn't that simple, try this experiment. Go online and enter "degree issued to pet" in your Google search box. What pulls up is a Google search list linking you to multiple reports of pets who have been issued a college or university degree by a diploma mill.

Don't be surprised if your pastor's doctoral degree is the product of one of the many online diploma mills. However, if that is the case, there is a bright side. Just think about it. From now on, when you go to your pastor for help, you at least have the comfort of knowing that he or she is just as qualified as a basset hound or a common house cat to guide you in all the important spiritual areas of the life.

Professional Counselor/Therapist Status—

I have often wondered about the advice given to people who have experienced major trauma, abuse, grief, domestic dysfunctionality, and anything else you can add to the list. How many times have you heard the words, "Seek the help of a counselor or talk to your minister," broadcasted over your radio or television? It is just expected by church society that a minister is a knowledgeable professional, equipped with the expertise to provide mental curative and emotional restorative counseling to individuals.

Since when did being a minister or pastor qualify you to counsel people on the major issues of their lives? I wish I had a dollar for every time people have told me they had received counseling about a serious matter, only to discover that the person who had counseled them was less qualified to counsel than the one receiving the counsel.

Unqualified church counselors have been responsible for the destruction of innumerable marriages, relationships, homes and lives. Literally, millions of people within the church have been duped into thinking that a minister's license or ordination comes with a Ph.D. type of proficiency in political, medical, social, religious and family counseling.

For the most part, people will trust the pastor's judgment and advice in pretty much every area of their lives. Sadly, this is a major blunder. Regarding untrained counselors, whether in the ministry or in the streets, the advice they give is based on nothing more than their own personal background, feelings, ideas and opinions regarding a particular issue.

A sense of superiority over the congregation has deluded the preacher into believing that he really is qualified to counsel on the issues of life. Untrained personal and family counselors are also a big problem in the church. Perhaps, bigger than most people realize.

"Untrained," does not necessarily mean uncaring. There are many good, caring pastors giving bad advice to their members. However, when the unqualified counselor is a thug preacher, the consequences can be even worse. When a thug gives counsel or advice to a trusting soul, he is almost always thinking of himself and his own agenda first.

Thugs love it when their members come to them for advice on monumental decisions in their lives. The thug will seize the opportunity to help bend the trusting member's decision so that it fits into the thug's own selfish purposes. Watch how some preachers teach their members concerning church faithfulness. They will advise their members that the church should come before everything and everybody, including the member's own family.

Now, we know God should always come first in our lives, but the church is not God. Another issue in the church world evolves around, whether married people should spend family or alone time at home with their families and spouses, or attend church every time the doors open.

There are many situations where a man (or woman) is a faithful church member. He never misses a single service, Bible study, choir rehearsal, business meeting or special event. His wife, who may also be a member (or one of the leaders) of the church, misses spending private time with her husband. Even though they are continually in church together, she misses quality time alone with him. So, she may suggest to her husband that she would like for him to stay home to spend some alone time with her tonight.

Now, an unqualified pastor or counselor might advise the husband that the devil is using his wife to hinder him from being faithful to God. I've witnessed this senseless advice being given, to both male and female. This can prove to be bad advice.

Not only can this horrendous guidance stir a hornet's nest in a couple's home, I know of many times where unqualified counseling eventually led to divorce. An interesting point to note here, is pastors are giving out advice that they know can destroy a member's marriage, while they themselves remain married through thick and thin.

Unfortunately, church members fail to comprehend, while God does call to faithfulness, that faithfulness is to God, not to a church or a pastor. That is of course, unless you are married to the pastor. Sure, any good member of the church should be a dedicated member, but that dedication should not be at the cost of your family.

A very faithful and wondrously saved woman in my church came through the door looking as though something was wrong. She started out by telling me she was having trouble in her home. She went on to say how the devil wanted her to stay home from church to spend time with him. This woman was faithful to everything that took place at the church. I asked her who she was referring to when she used the term, the devil? She said, "My husband."

She continued, "Pastor Jackson that devil tried to keep me from coming to church tonight. He wanted me to stay home with him." She then asked for counsel on what she should do about her problem.

I said, "For starters, you need to stop calling your husband the devil." She said, "But he's not saved." I told her, "I don't care if he isn't! He's not the devil. He's your husband!" She chuckled and said, Okay pastor, I understand. What else should I do?" I replied, "Next, you need to go home and spend some alone time with your husband." She said, "But Pastor, what about the service?" I responded, "We'll be just fine. Now go home take care of your husband… and by the way, thank God that it's you he wants to spend alone time with tonight."

She chuckled and said, "Thank you so much, Pastor Jackson." The following Sunday, I came out of my office and took my seat in the pulpit. When I raised my head, guess who was sitting there? That's right. I saw her husband sitting in the audience. He looked straight at me... and nodded to me with the biggest smile ever on his face.

> **Thug pastors are willing to sacrifice any member of your family, if it means they get to keep the rest of your family.**

The thug is calloused. If the husband of one of the members is able to persuade the wife to spend alone time at home with him, her pastor becomes concerned. To the thug this is an indication that she is following the wishes of her husband rather than those of her pastor. Thug pastors take offense to that. Often, there will be stiff consequences for her making this decision.

If the pulpit thug has to tear up your family to keep you faithful to the church, to your pastor, and to his or her spouse, so be it. Their thinking is, "Half of something is better than all of nothing." If they can't keep the whole family faithful and in their church, they'll take whatever they can get. They're willing to sacrifice any members of the congregant's family if they get to keep the rest of the family.

You would not trust an untrained or inexperienced dentist to perform a root canal or an untrained lawyer for legal representation; nor would you trust an under experienced physician for open heart surgery. So, why would you trust an untrained or inexperienced counselor for advice on matters that chiefly affect you, your life and your family?

When the thug needs professional help in his own life, he doesn't go to another thug preacher for guidance. Like most people who know better, thug preachers invest genuine quality time and effort in locating and researching the best available specialists to address their needs and the needs of their own families.

People in need of serious counseling should seek out qualified professionals for help. That does not mean you have to turn to the secular world for guidance. I'm sure there are thousands of born again Christian counselors available to prayerfully counsel and advise in uniformity with the Word of God.

Although, you do have to be extremely cautious, it is possible to find highly qualified "non-degreed" family and spiritual advisors. Many of these men and women of God possess vast knowledge and years of experience in providing the needed guidance for you and your family. Sometimes, the advice is as good, if not better, than that an institutionally trained advisor.

This skill may have been the result of the individual learning from a strong mentor, while observing the mentor at work. Of course, this usually involves the mentor pouring his or her vast wealth of counseling knowledge and experience into the protégé.

I was blessed to be able to study family counseling in seminary, but truthfully, I learned more from spending time with my pastor and other great counselors in the Christian ministry than I could have ever learned in the classroom. For this to happen, your mentor (or mentors) must be a seasoned expert, who possesses the inborn ability to duplicate himself in his understudy.

I cannot stress enough, the importance of you finding a good, qualified Christian counselor, should you ever need one. Your pastor may be offended by this bit of advice, but if she or he has a problem with you acquiring qualified help, you might want to start praying about whether you are under the right leadership. Remember, this is your life. Take charge of it. Bad advice leads to bad results.

Medical Advisor Status—

I am always amazed at how much trust people put in the medical advice that comes to them from their pastors. I have known people to die, simply because someone counseled them against trusting in the professional abilities of medical doctors. Often, when doctors diagnose conditions and recommend treatment, people will go to the pastor for his opinion regarding the doctor's advice to them on their medical issues.

Now, I realize there are some ministers who are also medical doctors. My very good friend from Chicago, the late, Dr. Carl B. Turner, was a profound minister and teacher of the Gospel. He was also a highly skilled OB/gynecologist and surgeon. Dr. Turner, a dedicated missionary doctor, had his life snuffed out, while working abroad on the mission field to save the lives of hundreds of others.

There are other missionary doctors, like the amusing, Dr. Steven Miller, the gifted orthopedic surgeon in Phoenix, Arizona, who could be talking about serving God through missions one moment, and suddenly, providing vital medical information just moments later. It just goes to show you, God doesn't make junk. These doctors have both served God at the very top of their fields, in their churches and on the mission field abroad. Dr. Miller is gifted in performing what other doctors might consider impossible surgeries.

Then, there is the very brilliant Dr. Horace E. Smith, the pastor of a high-spirited, 3,000-member church in Chicago. It is my understanding, that Dr. Smith is also an attending physician specializing in Pediatric Hematology/Oncology at Ann & Robert H. Lurie Children's Hospital of Chicago (formerly Children's Memorial Hospital). As it relates to his credentials, this is just the tip of the iceberg. Google his name and you will see an amazing man of God and a wonderful gift to health and humanity.

Of these three men, as of the writing of this book, Dr. Smith is the only one that I have not had the pleasure of personally meeting. However, I had the opportunity to visit his church recently. On that particular day, the building was overrun by very prominent church and political dignitaries. I watched as Dr. Smith, seemingly unbothered by the presence of so many religious notables, so effortlessly conducted the flow of the program.

Of course, if I were to continue, the list of talented medical professionals who are also in the service of our Lord, the names could fill this entire book. The point is, there are many Christian leaders who just happen to be excellent practicing physicians, as well. These inspired men and women of God are highly skilled and educationally qualified. They are trained to offer spiritual guidance, prayer and medical advice. When they speak, you should listen.

However, when the leader is not trained or educated in medicine, even though they may be great at offering spiritual direction, when they begin offering medical advice, you may have a recipe for disaster. One such case involved a young woman who endured incredible pain while the pastor's wife continued to stress that she should not see a doctor.

Now, by personal experience, I believe in God's healing power. Please know, that the woman giving the advice was not a thug preacher, In fact, I believed her to be a devout Bible centered, sincere Christian. Even though she had no formal medical training whatsoever, the family heeded her advice.

Consequently, the young woman died, leaving behind a brokenhearted young husband and a newborn baby. It was later discovered that the young wife and new mother had suffered from a very common medical condition. A simple, routine medical procedure might have saved her life. Obviously, the whole family and their church were all grief stricken.

To be clear, I believe in miracles, and our faith in God's ability to perform the impossible, is usually a prerequisite for miracles. Some people confuse faith with pride. They have been preaching healing for so long until they take it personal when members of their church want to visit a doctor for medical diagnosis or treatment.

They see it as a weakness and as a reflection upon the church, or upon their ministry, or upon their pastor's faith. When you mention seeing a doctor, what an arrogant pastor hears you saying is, "Pastor, I don't believe in you." A prideful pastor might pray for you and advise you to trust God, which is good advice. Too bad he doesn't always mean it. Very often, what he's doing is rolling the dice. If you live, he claims the glory. If you die, he blames your lack of faith.

THE FAMILY'S BUSINESS OR LEGACY TO PASS ON

Now, let's talk about the single greatest lure. As most of us know, some business people label their family businesses after themselves. You've seen names like Mrs. Field's Cookies, Simpson's Diner, Brown's Barber Shop, Johnson's Publishing Company, Martinez Auto Repair or Jacobson & Sons Moving and Storage.

Ever notice how some churches have the pastor's own name somewhere in the church's name? In the following example, I chose not to use real church names. If a name shown here in my example is the same as a known church's name, it is purely coincidental.

Churches bearing names like Murphy Temple, Johnston Church of God, Wellington Baptist Church, McGee Temple Church of God In Christ, Brown Gospel Tabernacle and Smith Christian Center are not as uncommon as you might suppose. This is no different than the businesses that we just talked about. Don't think for one moment this was by accident. Pastors commonly brand their churches with their own names.

This church is usually not just the pastor's ministry, but the family's "business legacy." Often, pastors will have a son or daughter who may be directing or singing in the choir. This younger one might even be completely uninvolved with the church. However, if the pastor begins to age or becomes ill, at some point he will announce that his son or daughter has received a calling to the preaching ministry.

Now, the pastor can begin the process of grooming his son or daughter to take over the church. It has happened in ministries from small to mega. Look at what has happened with some of the most widely known ministries on television and you will see this tradition in action. The larger the ministry, the more likely this will happen.

It doesn't seem to matter that a year ago, that son or daughter who is being groomed to take over might have been out getting drunk rather than attending Daddy's church. It also doesn't appear to concern anyone that there are more qualified and more seasoned elders in the church. It's the family's business. Thus, the business, the authority and all monetary proceeds, stay with the family. "It's a family affair."

Think about it for a moment. What other business do you know of, where people outside the family are willing to faithfully finance and build some other family's company, while knowing that they don't stand an ounce of a chance of ever becoming the president or CEO of that business, no matter how qualified they are. I can't think of any business, but the church.

Now, I do want to end this thought by saying, there are many instances where a son, a daughter or even the pastor's spouse, is called by God and fully qualified to succeed their incumbent parent or spouse, as pastor or leader of the church or ministry. In these situations, it would be unfair and unwise to hinder the will of God.

I also want to be clear on why it makes sense that some ministries should be named after the minister, especially when it comes to an evangelistic ministry. All ministries are not physical buildings where people regularly meet for worship. Billy Graham Evangelistic Association operates in auditoriums and stadiums all over the world.

Graham's radio and television broadcasts have been reaching millions of listeners and viewers for decades. Although he is no longer preaching in the Billy Graham crusades, if his name were not associated with this ministry, there would be no foolproof way to promote the ministry and its' crusades and radio and television broadcasts.

It would have been tough for worshippers to find him over the past fifty years or so. Sure, they could have given the ministry a neutral name like "Evangelistic Crusades," but that could be anybody. Ministers like Billy Graham are forced into linking their name to the ministry.

For ministries with a physical building, with an address, and regularly scheduled worship services, the problem of finding them, directing people to them is eliminated regardless to what name is on the building. You can just give out the address or even a marker or landmark (such as, across the street from Freeman Park or Regional Hospital) and people will find them.

There are also churches, schools and organizations that have been named in honor or recognition of great contributors to the formation or growth of a denomination, school or Christian organization. An example would be the Dwight L. Moody Bible Institute in Chicago, which by the way, started out as the Chicago Evangelization Society.

Historically, the Methodist movement was derived from the inspirational life and teachings of the eighteenth century, John Wesley. I don't know for sure, but several sources that I have read, say the Methodist churches claim about seventy-million adherents around the World. According to some of my sources, there are over 40 denominations that are the result of John Wesley's vision and hard work.

I have noticed that several Methodist churches bear the name Wesley on their sign. Clearly, there seems to be no intent to brand the church with the pastor's name, but only to pay respect to the founder of the overall Methodist movement. The same should be understood as it relates to the Moody Bible Church, the Moody Bible Institute or other such churches and institutions.

However, usually when thug pastors label their local church with their own name, the intent is usually to brand their personal empire or family business. They just need you and your monetary loyalty to finance their corporation.

On the other hand, the fact that a pastor has named the church after himself does not necessarily mean that he is a thug preacher. He may just like the name.

"No preacher, regardless of where he serves, is free to reinvent preaching."

Steven J. Lawson,
The Kind of Preaching God Blesses

Chapter Six

THE PULPIT GANGSTER

Religion, organization and a vastly wide system of
political and behavioral cover-up and denial

ן

Welcome to an impressive ring of systematized religiosity; much like the organized underworld. To be clear, by no means am I comparing the illicit aspects of organized crime to the pulpit. Sure, I've seen a number of pistol packing preachers over the years. A few of them were legal. Most of them were not. But, this isn't a comparison between the mob crime and the pulpit. I'm simply comparing the rigid "structure" of gangland to similarly structured church denominations.

For the gangster thug, ecclesiastical colleagues are an intricate part of this religious composition. Gangster thug pastors are normally part of a wider system of behavioral cover-up. Typically, they are elevated from an associate clerical position to the pastor or senior pastor position.

From there, some may even move upward through the hierarchy to a regional, district, state or national position. For some, the dream of securing an international spot is difficult, but very real. This could even lead to securing a chief overseer or presiding bishop's seat over an entire denomination.

Like the reclusive thug, many gangster thugs are magnetically attracted to the pastoral ministry for the glory, money, materialism, power and longevity; and because of its "family business" potential. Interestingly though, for the gangster there are some areas that are very different than for the reclusive thug. Topping the list, are tougher qualifying and educational requirements, along with a full background investigation, to include verifiable references.

Tougher Qualifications—

For the gangster, the requirements may not be as easy going as they are for the reclusive thug. Gangsters, for the most part are usually pastors within established denominations. So, typically they are hired by the church board to lead the church. Normally, a church board of directors will recruit, interview and try out the prospective pastoral candidate before he actually gets the job.

Often, the bar is set much higher than it may be set for the reclusive thug or independent pastor. The board members are primarily looking for four things in particular. They want someone who can preach well, someone who can build the membership, someone who can raise funds and someone who will respect and follow the wishes of the board of directors.

Educational Requirements—

While there may be a few denominations who aren't as concerned with the prospective pastor's educational background, there many other denominations who are very concerned.

The gangster's level of formal or higher education is sometimes a determining factor in landing him the position as pastor of a denominationally affiliated church. The board members are likely to inquire as to a candidate's educational background. Since he has invested so much time planning and preparing for such a time as this, most gangsters will easily conquer this hurdle.

He understands that formal education in some higher level of religious or theological studies is simply part of the qualifying process. So, he has probably already taken care of this requirement. In fact, I have seen pulpit gangsters with educational credentials that are so impressive that just about any church leadership committee and congregation would feel honored to call him or her their pastor.

At the very least, the pulpit gangster is in the process of completing their college, university or seminary requirement. Some denominations honor nontraditional degrees from diploma mills, while others require genuine degrees from recognized institutions.

Background Check—

While reclusive thugs may be able to start up and pastor a church with no background check whatsoever, the gangster's former life will likely be investigated. Many churches require that the candidate applying for the position of the church's pastor, submit to a background check. Of course, there may be a way around this. The candidate may able to get well-known pastors or overseers to furnish personal and professional references for him; in which case, extensive or in-depth probing into the applicant's (often tarnished) background may be deemed unnecessary.

EXCEPTIONS TO THE RULE

For some denominational churches, the criteria may be strict when searching for a new pastor, but there are some exceptions to this rule too. There are circumstances where the pastor is not hired by the church's board of directors. Some pastors actually inherit their pastorate. Heirs to the pulpit can come from many possibilities, but more commonly, they come from any one of the following three different likelihoods.

Bloodline Pastors—

Sometimes, a bloodline exception takes place when the prospective pastor is the son, daughter, grandchild, nephew, brother, spouse or some other relative of the incumbent pastor. Under these conditions, while qualifications may be important, they'll probably not be as important as the bloodline connection.

Remember, this is still the family business. In fact, you should not be surprised if you discover that the current pastor is a second or third generation pastor from the same family. As with Prince William, who was born and raised to take over the throne, the pastor's kin may have been born and raised to take over their family owned church.

Assistant Pastors—

Churches that abide by an older and more traditional leadership structure will probably have an assistant pastor working alongside the pastor. For traditional churches having several associate ministers, the assistant pastor is usually second in command, much like a vice-president. Most often, if the church does follow the old structure, when the time comes to replace the existing pastor, the board moves to have the assistant pastor installed as the new pastor.

More modern churches are likely to have a team of associate pastors, headed by the senior pastor or his first assistant. In these churches, the new pastoral replacement strategy varies. However, because blood is thicker than water, in recent decades bloodline heirs are trumping assistant pastors and first assistants when it comes to occupying the chief executive's seat in the pulpit.

Co-pastors—

Today's churches will likely have the pastor and his or her spouse working together as co-pastors. These are more likely to be independent churches, rather than denominational churches. This is kind of like having both husband and wife on the deed to the house. If one of them dies before the other, the house automatically goes to the surviving spouse.

Even though, there are times where the spouse is obviously unqualified to lead, some pastors have discovered that this is still a clear cut way of protecting the family business. What she may do is place her son or daughter in the pastor's seat, while running the church from behind the scenes. The main priority is to protect the family's interest. They can worry about the logistics later.

FOUNDING PASTORS

Gangster thugs can be either, founding pastors or successors to the pulpit throne. While it may be nice when it happens, not all pulpit gangsters are fortunate enough to inherit an already established pastorate. There are plenty enough gangster thugs who have started their own local church within a major denomination, or who became a part of the denomination after the local church was established.

Here, she is the first generation or the founding pastor of that particular church. If the gangster has had to start her own church, chances are she started her church the same as the reclusive thug.

Bible Study Group—

The church may have been born out of a Bible study or some other type of group meeting. Largely, pastors who start out this way have the group participants' best interest at heart. Some study leaders are highly competent as discipleship trainers, while others lack significantly in Biblical knowledge and leadership abilities. Most often than not, despite the study leader's shortcomings, this is where we can find some of the most sincere prospective pastors.

Instigated Church Split—

Some thug churches are the result of an instigated church split. You might be surprised to know how many gangster thugs have initiated a church split at their former churches to jump start their own churches. Gangsters are notorious for leading a mutiny against the pastor of the church where they themselves were once members.

Very often, the gangster who leads the mutiny against the pastor, is usually an associate or assistant pastor of that church. He will point out weaknesses or flaws in the leadership. Later, rumors about the pastor begin to circulate throughout the church.

The gangster will encourage certain key members of that church to follow him or her into the wonderful new and perfect church that God has (supposedly) directed him to start up. They speak of grandeur and new ideas. They create a buzz about the many top leadership positions that will need to be filled at the new church. So, people follow the aspiring pastor in his quest to build a perfect new church for the Lord, hoping that he will appoint them to one of those big positions that he keeps reminding them of.

CONSISTENCY IN DRESS CODE

Generally, pulpit gangsters who are part of a larger organization follow an official code of dress. Just as in the underworld, common street thugs will wear whatever they choose, but members of more sophisticated, higher level, well organized crime are typically meticulously well dressed. Street thugs may attend a meeting in a T-shirt, tank top, jeans, shorts, dress clothes, etcetera, while members of the organized world of gangsters are likely to show up to meetings in business suits or business casual attire.

Denominational pastors tend to come together in a uniformity or code of dress, with position and rank standing out. Most of the ministers in attendance might wear dark suits and clergy shirts with white collars. We can tell that these are church ministers because of how they are dressed. The higher ranking leaders are identifiable as principle officials by the variance in garb.

For example, in some denominations, when presiding bishops attend special services or ceremonies, they will wear a clerical suit or a "ceremonial" vestment. The clerical attire is composed of a black suit, a clergy collar and a scarlet or purple clergy shirt. If a bishop is on the organization's general board or is the presiding bishop, he must wear the scarlet clergy shirt whenever he wears the clerical suit.

The ceremonial vestments are composed of a purple or scarlet cassock (the color depends on the rank of the bishop in the church), a white surplice, a purple or scarlet chi mere, a purple or scarlet tippet, a gold pectoral cross and a clergy collar worn around the neck. Also, there are certain ceremonies or services where bishops are obliged to wear their ceremonial vestments.

I was very surprised at the words of a challenge presented by an official within a major denomination. He challenged the 250 bishops of his denomination to trade in their gold chains, crosses and rings, which he placed at an approximate value of "one million dollars." He suggested that the money could be used for education and missions, rather than adornment.

THE GANGSTER'S BATTLEGROUND

Unlike the solo flying reclusive thug, the gangster's battleground knows no boundaries. He is most comfortable fighting from the pulpit, the Bible study classes, his office, in front of the church building, at a member's home, in a business meeting... or anywhere else. Though he is willing to fight when and wherever the opportunity presents itself, he is most at home while in the pulpit; mainly because of its' associated empowerment. Not only does he enjoy the power, he also enjoys the adrenaline rush he gets when performing in front of a crowd.

Several years ago, a pastor was standing at the podium explaining his vision for the church. He shared how God had told him (so he said) to have each member to pledge $1,000. He then asked that every person who was willing to pledge $1,000 would stand up. Now he was able to zero in on yet seated members, targeting each one of them for public humiliation. He demanded that those who were not standing, openly explain to him why they could not give $1,000.

No reason offered to this preacher and his wife was acceptable. He then did what thug pastors normally do in this situation. He refused to move on with the service until everyone was in obedience (allegedly) to God. Remember, pulpit thugs claim to speak for God.

This pastor openly and harshly rebuked his (yet seated) members for not trusting God enough to pledge $1,000 to the church.

Next, the pastor started suggesting ways for them to get the money, to include borrowing money from a friend or relative, selling some personal items of value or taking out a personal loan from a bank, credit union or finance company. One by one, with tears streaming down some of their faces, the remaining seated individuals rose to their feet to pledge the $1,000.

This is an energizing moment to a pulpit hoodlum. In his mind, he must have been thinking, he was powerful enough to make these faithless people trust God. After humiliating his members, the gifted pastor actually went on to preach an incredible message. As embarrassed as they may be, many lay persons are at a loss as to how they should handle open harassment and humiliation from the pulpit. Thus, the vast majority of them humbly accept it.

THE GANGSTER'S MESSAGE

Unlike reclusive thugs, the gangster has probably studied homiletics and hermeneutics at a prominent Christian seminary. So, she will probably understand the science of Biblical interpretation and the art of preaching or sermon order and presentation. Clearly, she knows how to start, deliver and end her sermon on time.

More than likely, she will have a solid theological foundation. Chances are, she will not have to rely upon topical preaching as a crutch for every message. She is presumably qualified to present either textual or expository messages with ease. Her message is sure to contain calculated Biblical references, laced with a fervent delivery and an electrifying finale.

Yes, the gangster may definitely stand far above most reclusive thugs in trained preaching, but still there will be a common thread running through both of these thug pastors in their preaching. The underlying theme of her message, benefits her own personal agenda. There will be, on average, six major points the gangster pastor will make before she closes out her sermon.

Now, let me show you some of the fine print in the six key points of the pulpit gangster's message:

1. Absolute Authority

The cornerstone of the gangster's message is unquestioned "Blind Obedience." He accentuates that by teaching that the pastor should be consulted in just about every area of the members' lives, even when it is not of a church or spiritual nature. However, when it is clearly a church or spiritual issue, consulting the pastor is a no-brainer.

Allow me to share another true account with you. My family and I attended a funeral one Saturday morning. The pastor who delivered the eulogy was a powerful speaker. We decided we wanted to visit his church. So, right after our own church on the next day, we loaded up the family and drove across town to that pastor's church.

Arriving early, we sat in the sanctuary waiting for the service to begin. Once started, the service moved smoothly along like clockwork. When the pastor stood to preach, we were far from disappointed. What a great message! As he was wrapping up an incredibly inspiring sermon, I leaned over toward my wife and said, "Now, this is a profound message." She concurred.

No sooner than those words had departed our mouths, the pastor looked directly at us and shouted, "If you're here today and your pastor doesn't know you're here, you're wrong!" He went on to say, "You need to go home right now and call your pastor on the phone and apologize to him." Then, he yelled, "Unless you went to your pastor and got his permission to be here, you have no business being here!" Stunned, I thought, "Yeah, I hear you yelling preacher, but what if I am the pastor? Now who do I need to call?"

What really caught my attention was how enthusiastic the congregation seemed to be in supporting the pastor's authoritarian teaching. My wife and I were both reasonably sure that most of what he said was intended to send a clear message to his own congregation. I have shared this story many times with other pastors, and surprisingly, most of them agree with this pastor's point of view.

2. 100% Loyalty to the Pastor and to the Church

One sure way to get a gangster pastor up in arms is for a member to visit another church. Though they may not be as bad as the reclusive thug, pulpit gangsters still get a little nervous when their members visit other churches or sit under the teachings of other ministries. Gangsters are paranoid at the possibility of Word based ministers exposing them for what and who they truly are. So, it is imperative that they keep their members away from potentially sound doctrine.

Keeping members in the dark by keeping them away from other Biblical perspectives gives a preacher tremendous power over the member. In this setting, he can teach and preach any false heresy of his choice and the members will never know they have been hoodwinked. Historically, the single greatest method used to keep people enslaved has always been to deprive them of knowledge. If you keep them clueless, you keep them powerless.

> *"My people are destroyed from lack of knowledge. Because you have rejected knowledge, I also reject you as my priests; because you have ignored the law of your God, I also will ignore your children."*
>
> Hosea 4:6 (NIV)

In this verse of the Bible, God is clearly pronouncing judgment on both the present and the future generation of priests who refuse to teach the oracles of God. Knowledge of God can give new life, but the lack of knowledge concerning the Lord can prove to be fatal.

The gangster leader blatantly lives a double standard. He will go out of his way to organize drives, events and special programs to entice members of other churches to visit his church, but he pitches a fit if one of his members goes out to visit another church.

3. Doom to Those Who Leave to Join a Different Church

If you have never seen a pastor prophesy horror and damnation, just try leaving the gangster's church to join another church. This prophet of doom would have you to believe that this is practically the same as leaving the Lord. Gangsters do not take it lightly when a member leaves their church; especially to join another one.

Cult leaders would have individuals believe there is nowhere else they can go and remain saved. They teach, if you ever leave this "one true church" you may end up in hell. This is a fear-based control mechanism designed to keep you inside the cult. It also gives cult leaders tremendous power over their followers. When cult members believe that leaving the cult is the same as leaving God, or (sometimes) their last or only chance to succeed in life, they will submit to their cult leader, even when they disagree him.

Gangster pastors operate the same way. When a member leaves to join elsewhere, gangsters take it very personal. As in Dr. Jekyll and Mr. Hyde, they can instantly change from a father figure into your worst nightmare. It would not be unusual for him to mark those members as bad persons, and to turn the church against them. He will have nothing good to say about the ex-member. Using information obtained during counseling sessions, thugs point out flaws in the ex-member's commitment to God. Existing members are rebuked for associating with them. If this has ever happened to you, accept this as your confirmation that your choosing to leave might have been a good decision.

The gangster seeks to create fear in the minds of anyone who might be remotely thinking about continuing a relationship with the departing member. He wants to be sure that the ex-member does not influence other members to follow into probable enlightenment. Remember what I said in an earlier chapter, "If he can control the relationships, he can control the person."

You would think if a member of a church wanted to visit or join another church within the same (or similar) denomination or organization, the pastor would be okay with that. Wouldn't you? By in large, churches within a specific denomination should all be teaching the same doctrine.

Although he would have you to believe it is, this struggle is not about you leaving God. It is only about you leaving a local church group. If the pastor had Godly integrity, he would appreciate the fact that those members remained within the body of Christ. Deplorably, the pulpit gangster is not interested in your dedication to God, but to your lifetime dedication to the church and the church's pastor. Just as Paul warned the early Roman church, we must be careful not to bend the scriptures in order to persuade ourselves to accept the words of the creature over the words of the Creator.

"Who changed the truth of God into a lie, and worshipped and served the creature more than the Creator..."

Romans 1:25 (KJV)

In this verse, Paul speaks of wicked people who made a conscientious decision to regard the truth of God as a lie. By doing so, they found it easier to choose worship the creator, rather than the Creator. If we look around us, we see this same problem throughout the modern Christian church. Preachers are promoting themselves, and getting more attention than Jesus seems to be getting.

4. Our Grass Is Greener

There is another side of the gangster pastor who publicly criticizes members who decide to leave his church for another. When he goes before the congregation on Sunday morning, he sends a strong message to all visitors that, "the grass is greener over here." He's trying to draw members from other churches, even from within his own denomination.

He preaches to entertain and to impress, rather than to lead the lost to Christ. Therefore, he has to build his church by taking in members from other churches. This type of gangster is common. What this preacher is doing may be church building, but it is not Kingdom Building. We must not confuse shuffling people around from one church to another, with adding souls to the body of Christ.

Let me tell you about a gangster pastor who bitterly rants and raves about anyone wishing to leave his church. He makes it known that both the member wishing to leave and the potential new pastor must both approach him to get his permission. He also makes it clear that he will not be releasing any members of his church to join other churches.

114

This pastor has openly and spitefully targeted individuals who have wanted to leave his church for another. These attacks have even taken place during their Sunday morning services. This is his way of making an example of them, just in case someone else is also thinking about leaving his church.

Too often, people stay and continue to accept abuse, because they believe their pastor must release them before they can move on. Having gone to the pastor to be released, they now have a bigger problem. Because the pastor is offended by the notion that they even considered joining another church, he harbors resentment against that member. The resentment is often manifested as bad treatment of the member and the member's family.

Watch the pastor who screams the loudest about pastors needing his permission before receiving his members. He usually forgets his own creed of honor when he gets a chance to accept congregants from other churches as new members of his church.

5. The Pastor's Biases and Demands

This is where the gangster demonstrates his skillful ability to "freestyle." Anything that he is upset about comes up in this portion of his sermon. It also provides a great opportunity to plant or water the seed of church legalism. During freestyle, he can attack anyone in the congregation who has displeased him, and make it appear as though it isn't him, but it is God who is openly chastising those members of the church. At this point, the gangster might declare his political views, social biases, or likes and dislikes. He may even exercise his power of influence to persuade the congregation in support of his own interests.

6. The Close and the Appeal

Finally, while the musicians are playing, and with the arrogant poise of a hip-hop rapper, the pastor might break out into two or three lines of freestyle rhyming. He will then quote a few spoken lyrics from one of his favorite songs… and conclude with an appeal to the attendees to make a decision.

What that decision is, depends on the church or the pastor. It could range from joining that particular church to accepting Jesus Christ as Lord and Savior. I've seen people stand to accept Christ,

> One of the biggest flaws with the pastor's appeal after the sermon is, people are often confused about what they are being asked to do.

but rather than lead them to the Lord, the church accepts them into the church as a new member. This causes some people in the church to believe that joining the church is the same as being born again.

One of the biggest flaws with the commitment appeal right after the sermon is, pastors are not always clear about what it is they are asking the people to do. So, the confused individual isn't quite sure about what they are coming forward to do. Often, people don't know if they're being asked to join the church, or accept Christ, or both.

I've attended churches where the pastor asked the new prospect what it is they want to do in the church. If the person said they would like to sing with the choir, he would immediately send them to the choir stand to stand with the church's choir. If they wanted to be an usher, the pastor would send that person to wherever the ushers were at that moment. I'm sure you get my point.

Of course, the pastor usually knows nothing about these people. Sometimes, the church and their pastor are just happy to get another member and they want to lock them down with a commitment, such as the choir, the deacon board, the usher board, etc. Now, he can say to them, "I'm depending on you. Don't let me down."

Let me tell you about my oldest sister, who by the way, wasn't saved at that time. One Sunday morning, she went to visit a local church in her community. The people were very welcoming to her. So, when the appeal was extended by the pastor to join the church, she walked forward to become a member. After joining, unlike some of the pastors I just mentioned, this pastor didn't bother to ask her what she wanted to do in the church. He took it upon himself to issue to my sister, a fully recognized Evangelist's License.

How about that? She joined the church and became a licensed evangelist— *and she didn't even know what an evangelist was!* She also didn't know a single verse of scripture. In fact, I don't know if my sister ever learned a Bible verse during the entire time she was a member of that church.

As a Final Point!—

There you have it. The six most common elements you are likely to hear in a pulpit hoodlum's message. While some elements may seem to overlap another, each one is indeed a stand alone issue. Now, just because your pastor may have figured out a way to disguise some of these six key points as Old or New Testament teaching doesn't let him off the hook.

Let me close this chapter the right way. Your pastor may be sincere, but perhaps confused about her role as your pastor… and your role as her member. In which case, you're probably not being fed a steady diet of the key six points that I just talked about.

However, you are more likely to hear your pastor touch on some of those six points every so often. He is reluctant to make a full commitment to such strictured doctrinal teaching. Although, he's been taught that this is what he should be preaching and teaching, he's just not sure. He's not thoroughly convinced yet. To him, authoritarian rule in the church may look and sound normal, but it just doesn't feel right. Praise God! There is hope for this pastor.

"Character is what a man is in the dark."

Dwight L. Moody

Chapter Seven

THE GANGSTER'S CHOSEN ONES

*An elite team of specialists, who teach
and preach the pastor's agenda, cleverly
disguised as a vision from God*

ז

G angster pastors work with an elite team of hand-picked specialists who teach and preach their pastor's own agenda, cleverly disguised as a vision from God. These leaders are crucial to the pastor's success. However, they are not the ones who have the power to ensure the gangster's continued reign, irrespective of his lack of integrity or devious conduct. That group of leaders will be discussed later in this chapter.

Gangsters meticulously select their leaders directly from their congregational pool. They particularly choose men and women who are willing to give total and unquestioned allegiance to the pastor in return for positions of prominence and power in the church. Not always, but often these leaders become the abusive pastor's agents for controlling and manipulating the congregation. They are taught to use cunning and persuasive methods when it comes to membership indoctrination. The methods used, include but are not limited to:

NEW MEMBERS CLASSES

Some churches insist that their new candidates for membership attend a mandatory new members' class. This compulsory training is usually just a counterfeit Christian principles or new believers' foundation class. The chief reason for this farce is that it provides an opportunity for the leadership staff to indoctrinate new members. Some churches state that even though you joined their church during one of the regular services, you are still required to complete the new members' training sessions before your membership is official.

Often, it's a five or six-week indoctrination process, usually about the church, not God. It's conducted by specially appointed leaders. Yes, I said it! Appointed... not anointed. These leaders are usually associate ministers or deacons of the church. Let's review the typical new members education process found in some churches:

Week One: *"Pastoral Leadership"*

In the first session, you will learn everything they would like for you to know concerning the pastor of that particular church. By design, this session leader tends to teach more about the pastor than about Jesus. He or she talks much about how effective the power of God is in the pastor's ministry.

Week Two: *"Blind Obedience"*

This is where the associate ministers introduce undisputed allegiance to the pastor and church. They explain that God demands, that you are to be obedient to the pastor who has been chosen by God to rule over you.

Week Three: *"Stewardship"*

Here, you learn how your blessings from the Lord are tied into your monetary giving. You are taught to understand that your tithes and offerings are a major part of your Christian obedience.

Week Four: *"Faithfulness"*

Now, it is time to learn that nothing should come before the church or the pastor's beckoning and calling. You learn that the wrath of God may be unleashed upon those who miss the church's services or events. This also, is where the church leaders start dangling carrots in front of new members. They speak of levels to which God can elevate them if they remain faithful.

Week Five: *"Meet the Pastor and Pastor's Spouse"*

After being fed several weeks of the pastor's accolades, by the time new members meet the pastor his the first spouse up close and personal, they are in awe of him or her.

Congratulations! You are now fully recognized and accepted as an official member of your new church family.

Now, don't you just feel more knowledgeable about salvation, the Holy Spirit, Jesus Christ and God's Biblical principles… after successfully completing five weeks of new members' training classes? Of course not! Why should you? They didn't cover any of those areas during your New Members' Training.

Please don't think that I am opposed to new members' training. I wholeheartedly teach and believe in the concept of providing new members with an immediate basis for living and maintaining their relationship with the Lord. One of the best things a church can do for its' new members is to offer them a continuing six-week Christian foundation class, which has been conscientiously and deliberately designed and structured to give new believers an advantageous Biblical beginning.

Churches that provide this type of solid Biblical training have discovered that several existing members who thought they already had a good understanding of the principles of Christ, also benefited. New members' "fast track" training is indeed an important weapon against the devil, but unless it is designed to lay a concrete Biblical foundation, it serves no useful purpose.

WEEKLY BIBLE STUDY

Many times the Bible study is not a study of the scriptures at all. It is perhaps, more of an extension of the new members' classes. They call it "Bible Study" because, as I stated earlier, a half truth is easier for members to believe and accept than an outright lie. Again, with the Bible as the pretentiously established platform, here is where the associate ministers have an opportunity to sharpen their skills in manipulating certain passages of scripture to teach puppetry obedience to the pastor, stewardship of money and faithfulness to the church.

I've been invited to a few Bible studies where the only Bible present was mine. In the first Bible study that I ever attended of this type, they had been using the television show "Survivor" as the basis for their study. Somehow, they were able to find the story of Christ in this TV reality series. Each week they would come together to discuss the most recent episode of the show from a (supposed) higher spiritual perspective. Seemingly, they had convinced themselves that God was revealing to them some deep mystery that carnal minds were unable to see in this show.

I hadn't seen the show, but I had seen the Bible. I made the mistake of thinking they were interested in incorporating the Bible into their Bible study discussion. So, I addressed what I heard them say, but from a Biblical perspective. I quickly realized that I was messing up their Bible study by introducing Bible scriptures into it.

Other study groups use books written by Christian authors as the central theme for their study. That can be a good thing, but when it is done without the presence of the written Word of God as the final authority on the matter, it can lead to a nasty outcome.

THE GREATER HIERARCHY

Aren't you wondering how it is that a pulpit gangster can get away with so much deviousness within an organization or denomination that is supposed to have checks and balances? Well, please allow me to introduce at this time, their "protectors."

This group is composed of the top hierarchy leaders. These chief executives are the superintendents, administrators, directors, executive committee members, presidents, bishops and a host of other officials of the church. They are the true leaders who possess the power to bring a halt to the pulpit abuse within the organization. Yet it continues. Perhaps, because many of the leaders at the top are the examples that pulpit gangsters aspire to be like.

The one thing that most men and women in power want most, but need less— *is more power.* More power produces more opportunities to control more people. This includes some people who may have been the pastor's peers in earlier days.

Not all denominational officials are insensitive to the problem of pulpit gangsters sprinkled throughout their various denominations. I know of many true men and women of God in upper executive church leadership, who are appalled at the notion of thugs in the pulpit. In fact, many of them are speaking out against authoritarianism and fighting to bring about change. Too often though, in the face of such widespread abuse, these minority voices are but a faint whisper. Within nearly every denomination, the abuse must stop, beginning at the top. Then, and only then will the matter of thugs in the pulpit receive widespread attention.

JESUS' EXAMPLE TO PULPIT GANGSTERS

In the Gospel of St. Matthew, we can see how compassionate Jesus was about helping hurting people. This is the example for how our Lord desires and expects His true ministers of the gospel to react to people who are broken down by pulpit gangsters. Regretfully, instead of showing Christian compassion, other pastors and church leaders tend to further victimize the already weary abuse victim.

"When He saw the throngs, He was moved with pity and sympathy for them, because they were bewildered (harassed and distressed and dejected and helpless), like sheep without a shepherd."

St. Matthew 9:36 (AMP)

In this verse of scripture, we can see that Jesus was moved with emotion, because of the people who were being harassed and abused by the Pharisees. Abuse perpetrated against innocent victims by gangsters was even going on in Ezekiel's day. It has existed throughout the period of Jesus' earthly ministry, and it continues to exist today.

"None are more hopelessly enslaved than those who falsely believe they are free."

Johann Wolfgang Von Goethe

Chapter Eight

ENSLAVED TO PULPIT HOODLUMS

"You are slaves of the one you obey"

Romans 6:16 (NIV)

ome years ago, when my oldest son Joshua was very young, he was sitting in his bedroom reading a book that made a small reference to slavery. It was just a tiny mention, but it got his attention. He turned to me and asked, "Dad, in the old days, how was it that some people got other people to become their slaves?"

Now, there I was wondering if he was expecting an eyewitness report from me on the "old days" of slavery. With Joshua, we always had to be on guard regarding age. At that time, his perception of age and the eras was a tad bit off.

A few years earlier, while watching the "Flintstones" one afternoon, he turned to my wife and asked, "Mom, back in the old days, did they have ID stones for driver's licenses? Josh was pretty much like the little boy who asked his grandfather if he was on the ark with Noah. Naturally, the grandfather replied, "No, I wasn't on the Ark." In shock, the stunned grandson immediately asked, "Then, why weren't you drowned?"

Of course, when my son, asked me about slavery, I suspected he thought I was there when it all began. As I turned and looked down at the obvious bewilderment on his innocent face, he continued, "If someone walked up to me and said, *'You're my slave!'*...I wouldn't do it."

Well, I thought his question on the origin of slavery in America was a profound query, worthy of a profound answer. Since we were a homeschooling family, I decided to merge my reply into the academic curriculum for both Joshua and my 11 year old (at the time) daughter, Rebekah.

For the next six weeks, I was busy helping them understand how millions of people became enslaved and stayed enslaved against their own wills. During this process, I also made it a point to make sure they understood that many slaves believed that they were destined to live and die in bondage. They thought they were born to be slaves, and their owners were born to rule over them. They simply accepted what they believed to be God's will for their lives.

In the years that followed, I have reflected many times on Josh's question. When I began the process of writing this book, I had to revisit that question. I wanted to address the matter of enslavement and bondage as it relates to the church. I have prayerfully arrived at two definite conclusions. Before I share my conclusions, I should warn you of the devil's evil plot is to prevent you from receiving the message intended for you in this section of Thug Preachers.

What I talk about here is not easy to read. In fact, this entire book is tough for the average churchgoer to stomach. If by now, you haven't already begun to develop a dislike for me, this is probably where your disdain for me will begin. If you are a thug pastor or the friend of a thug pastor, I expect that some of you to despise me.

When I initially started writing this book, that used to bother me. I'm way past that now. At this point, I just write what He instructs me to write. I leave the rest to Him. The devil's goal concerning you and this book is to make you angry with me, and with the book. He'll make you angry enough to slam it shut, and to put it down. The devil does not want you exposed to this information because he works most effectively in your ignorance.

No, I'm not talking about academic or social illiteracy. By ignorance, I mean a lack of knowledge in a specific area. Or that one may be lacking in knowledge about a particular subject. Not only does the devil seek to keep you, the lay person, in the dark about this matter, he also seeks to keep preachers from seeing themselves in it.

I am fully aware that I am stepping into a hornets' nest with this chapter. To some of you, what follows may be the equivalent of blasphemy, when in reality what I talk about in this chapter can save you from a blasphemous practice.

SUBLIMINALLY, THE CHURCH IS TAUGHT TO GIVE REVERENCE AND PRAISE TO THE PASTOR

Here is my first conclusion. Because, pastors are held in such high reverence, most of my readers are likely to believe that this is an attack against genuine men and women of God, or even God's purpose for the church. That assumption would be incorrect.

To be honest, most parishioners fall just short of praising their pastors for blessings that have come from God. Modern preachers usually try to find a way to connect themselves to what God is doing for the members. They try to draw attention to themselves as though they had something to do with you being blessed.

When God heals you, your pastor should be happily rejoicing that the Lord has laid His hand upon you, and that He has accomplished the miracle of healing in your body. Unfortunately, blessings can sometimes evoke the opposite effect. I have heard preachers complain that the person giving testimony failed to give them their due credit. They want their names mentioned during the testimony, as being the pastor or evangelist who had prayed for that individual. I've even heard ministers angrily say, "They'd better not ever call on me for prayer again!"

This explains why so many of the testimonies go in the direction of praise and thanksgiving to the preacher. People have learned this is what pleases the minister. Listen to the testimonies aired from some of the biggest miracle and healing campaigns on television. You witness what appear to be great miracles from God, but when the people are called to testify, they mention the evangelists' names more than the Lord's name. Usually, the ones who do not exalt the evangelists are not shown on television.

The testimony goes like this, "I had cancer, and the doctor said I had three months to live, but Evangelist John Doe prayed for me and I've been healed ever since!" Alternatively, you might hear, "I didn't think my credit was strong enough for me to qualify for a home, but after Pastor Jane Doe prayed for me, the realtor called and told me that my loan was approved by the bank! Thank you, Pastor Doe. You are truly a woman of God."

Neither of these two testimonies earnestly glorifies God, but ministers really seem to enjoy this type of praise report. God provides the miracle and the minister receives the glory. This is what borderline blasphemy looks and sounds like. You would be wise to avoid it like the bubonic plague.

It is a sin to teach the people of God to praise man over God. It is an even worse crime against God for the preacher to "accept" praise and honor that belong to the Lord. It is equally wrong for the church to allow themselves to be persuaded to render unto man, that which belongs to God. In three separate books of the New Testament Jesus tells us to give God that which belongs to Him.

"They say unto him, Caesar's. Then saith he unto them, Render therefore unto Caesar the things which are Caesar's; and unto God the things that are God's."

St. Matthew 22:21, St. Mark 12:17, St. Luke 20:25 (KJV)

When mortal men and women receive praise that should have been uploaded to heaven, they begin to feel heavenly. Sometimes they forget that they represent the creator, Lord, master, healer and savior of all humankind. They start referring to themselves as healers and miracle workers.

As ministers, when it comes to miracles, all we have been commissioned by Him to do is pray for people. God is the only one who can heal and save from sin, but preachers are now starting to boast about their ability to get people saved. Personally, I believe the Word of our Lord Jesus, when He said that no one comes to Him except God draws them.

"No man can come to me, except the Father which hath sent me draw him."

St. John 6:44 (KJV)

So, conclusion number one finds the church soft worshipping the creature over the creator. I call it soft worship, because to many parishioners it all seems harmless. However, while this outlandish admiration may seem innocent to most of the members, it can easily cross the line that God has drawn in the sand by way of the first commandment in Exodus 20:3.

"Thou shalt have no other gods before me."

Exodus 20:3 (KJV)

THE CHURCH BELIEVES IT IS
THE PASTOR'S RIGHT TO DICTATE

Because, of this lighter form of pastor worshipping, the pastor tends to feel in charge; really in charge. As he begins to flex his muscles, the response from the church is better than he had expected. The people actually appreciate his ruler type of leadership. They see him as a strong leader. To them, this strength represents the power of God.

This is what most longtime churchgoers are used to. They say, "This is how it has been at all the churches where I have been a member. If it's not broken, why fix it?"

Both members and leaders believe it is the pastor's God given right to dominate, dictate to and control the congregation. Many members have a greater respect for a controlling pastor. Over time, the control can lead to any one of many forms of enslavement.

Way too many pastors make the mistake of imagining themselves to be on the same level as Jesus. They compare themselves to Jesus. Over the years, so many ministers have talked about how Jesus wore a costly robe that was woven from top to bottom.

They usually go on to say, if Jesus wore expensive clothes, so can they. Then they create a whole life of extravagance for preachers, because of that one robe. They rationalize expensive clothes, furs, boats, cars, multiple homes, exotic trips, etc.

They read how Jesus was treated and believe they are just as entitled as Jesus was. They seem to forget that to reign with Him, we must be willing to suffer with Him.

> *"If we suffer, we shall also reign with him."*
>
> 2 Timothy 2:12 (KJV)

Furthermore, the disciples didn't try to make themselves equal to Jesus in deity like today's preachers. Ridiculously, modern pastors live more luxuriously than Jesus ever did. They want to possess His glory, but refuse to bear His cross. They want to live in the mansion without having to experience the stable. At Calvary, the soldiers gambled over His robe. They wanted the robe, but not the crown of thorns.

Several years ago, a fellow minister and I were delegated to organize an international church conference for a major denomination. It was to be held in a major U.S. city. One of the first things we needed to do, was to meet with the church leaders in the targeted city. So, one Sunday when we arrived at a very large church in that city, we were warmly received by the leadership and laity alike. At that time, the church boasted several thousand members.

Following the service, we met with the senior pastor and his staff of associate pastors. The meeting proved to be very productive. They appreciated what we were trying to accomplish, and we appreciated their pledged support.

After the meeting the pastor had one of the ministers to give us a tour of the facility. As we were led around the large, but not overly impressive structure, we walked into a basic looking dining room where members of the church stood in long lines to purchase food served up on disposable plates. With plastic flatware and paper napkins in hand, they sat down to at eight-foot long folding tables to eat their meals.

Later, our guide took us into another dining room in a different section of the building. My colleague and I looked in astonishment at each other. In this room, no one stood in line to purchase food. There were no paper plates or plastic forks and spoons. This was the room where the senior pastor and his pastoral staff (along with their wives and children) were being served. These people were seated in front of very costly fine gold trimmed China ware with gold flatware and golden goblets. They had linen napkins on their laps, and they received special treatment fitting of royalty.

It was interesting that the senior pastor and his family are transported to church and around town in a luxurious stretch limousine chauffeured by some of the men of the congregation who operate on a rotating volunteer schedule. There are also numerous other servant benefits that the pastor's family takes advantage of daily. Image that. As pastors, He calls us to servant leadership, and we do the exact opposite.

Now, before you convince yourself that it is your church and pastor that I am referring to, you should know that this could be any one of hundreds of churches and pastors across America. While, this real life example may appear to have plantation overtones, it is important that you know that race, national origin, gender or the size of the church are all irrelevant.

What is relevant is pastors from all categories around the world enjoy the benefits of royal treatment and free labor. They get cooks, chauffeurs, maids, housekeepers and nannies, all for free.

Because church members of their churches think it is the pastor's right to be served, they are glad to give of themselves in this manner. The pastor agrees that it is his right, and is glad to accept their gracious and generous offerings and submission.

To make a point, going back to the time when I had the opportunity to visit that church, their pastor was not a nationally televised celebrity minister, but just a common example of what can happen when a congregation is taught that a life of luxury is the pastor's God given right. In this case, there may have been some critical racial disparities, but most often race is a non-factor. This is an issue of entitlement, not of race, gender, national origin, religious persuasions or anything else. Just pastoral entitlement.

Your pastor is your example of Christ in the church, so he wants you to believe that materialism and a lavish lifestyle are a mandate for pastors and overseers.

> *"Do you not know that if you present yourselves to anyone as obedient slaves, you are slaves of the one whom you obey, either of sin, which leads to death, or of obedience, which leads to righteousness?"*
>
> Romans 6:16 (ESV)

I believe it is perfectly within the will of God for the people of the Lord to care for, and to lighten the load placed on the shoulders of God's preachers. Thus, easing their burden of stress and providing them a greater freedom to serve and minister to the needs of the church. However, ministers should be careful as to not take for granted or take advantage of the kindness of their members.

What's crazy is preachers use materialism to keep score, as if the ministry is some sort of game. With each preacher trying to outdo the other. The game can even involve bigger, costlier and fancier churches than their pulpit peers.

There are pastors who are spending so much on their luxurious lifestyles that the church's outstanding debts aren't being paid on time. In fact, some of the church's bills aren't being paid at all. What some preachers pay yearly for jet fuel is more than some of you will earn in ten to twenty years on your job. As of this writing, well known churches are, reportedly, at risk of losing their property through foreclosure, while their pastors are still living a life of overindulgence. With some of the smaller churches, this can represent an even more serious problem than it does for the larger ones.

Hey! Wouldn't it be something if the pastor shared the Lord's blessings with some of the church's more faithful and more dedicated members? For example, that sister who is dragging her five or six kids around on public transportation every time the church doors open. Don't you think she could be even more faithful if the Lord blessed her with a new seven passenger minivan from some of the funds in His storehouse at Bank of America or Citibank; or wherever?

Preachers like to tell you about your many blessings waiting for you in God's storehouse in glory, while they are living from the church's storehouse right down here on earth. The pastor would like for you to believe that if you had faith like her, you could have what she has. A greater truth would be, if you had access to the church's checkbooks and savings accounts like her... you could have what she has.

It doesn't take faith to write a check against a full bank account. Some of you single moms or unemployed fathers are living daily by greater faith than your pastor ever could. In one of my upcoming books, I will be explaining to you the real purpose behind the church's storehouse. This is something very few pastors will want you to read.

MORE LIKE JESUS?

Don't you think it's peculiar that pastors say they want to be humble and more like Jesus, yet their actions tell a very different story? What we really see is preachers who want to be popular and liked by everybody; especially politicians, celebrities and wealthy businesspersons. What they want you to believe is that they are popular because they are earnest and full of faith, like Jesus.

They say, because of their deeper than normal commitment to God, they are your examples of just how much God wants to bless you with material things. Therefore, you must prove your sincerity by bringing what you have into the storehouse. Okay, I see where they're coming from. There's a half truth to that.

The Thug's Dual Perception of... More Like Jesus—

Many pastors have two separate and very different teachings on what it means to be more like Christ. The first teaching relates directly to you, the pew member. He teaches you, to reign with Christ, you must suffer with Christ. To be blessed by Christ, you must sacrifice all that you have to Christ, by way of the church and the pastor. You must be willing to faithfully and freely give of yourself and of your possessions. To be more like Jesus, you must be willing to follow the commands of your pastor. Just do what you are told to do and don't ask questions. So, it seems being more like Jesus means a suffering and sacrificing way for the lay member.

The second teaching relates to what, "more like Jesus" means when it comes to the pastor. For the pastor, it doesn't involve the same suffering and sacrificing that he teaches for his members. For himself, more like Jesus, means he or she gets to live like a king. Yes, the people called Jesus the King of the Jews, but they didn't treat Him like a king. The crown they made Him, wasn't a 24 carat gold or diamond studded one. You're paying for gold and diamonds for the pastor. The only jewelry Jesus wore was a crown of thorns. Do you really think your pastor is trying to be more like Jesus?

Nonetheless, you take the church's finances, and you purchase a big beautiful home for the pastor and his family, with all expenses covered by the church or ministry. You call it the church parsonage. One church committee was sent out on a mission to find the biggest and most expensive home available in, or near their major metropolitan city. They succeeded. At that time, I had never seen anything like it. Everything about it was stunning, including the gargantuan pool house.

Did you know that church parsonages became popular, because on a pastor's salary, most pastors couldn't afford to buy a house of their own? Those were the days when you became a pastor because your heart was in it, not because the job pays well. Church leaders eventually realized that the pastor's single greatest expense was a home for him and his family.

They knew they couldn't always afford to raise the pastor's salary, but they could relieve him of his heaviest burden. The church could actually buy a home tax-free and use it to house their pastor. Even though the pastor's income was still low, he and his family could now have a greater purchasing power with their modest income.

This took a lot of stress off the pastor and the church leaders. It even helped ease his marital strain, which was the result of financial woes. Eventually, the house would be paid off and it would be completely owned by the church. It would always house whoever was their current pastor at any given time.

That's the way the parsonage used to operate. Today, for some churches the parsonage is just another way of overtaxing, already heavily taxed people. A pulpit thug would have you to believe that more like Jesus means, you buy the pastor and his or her family two or three expensive cars to drive. A lot of pastors collect cars, while some of you are walking to church or taking public transportation.

There are preachers who will jump into their Rolls Royce or Bentley, and drive right past you standing there at the bus stop, as if they didn't see you. With tithes and offerings sacrifices, you proudly grin as you buy them pleasure boats, recreational aircraft, his and hers motorcycles, $1,500 suits, $400 shoes, and so on. Then, you brag to your friends about how prosperous your pastor is.

During these pastors' lifetimes, they live a regal life. They enjoy a lifestyle that rulers of some smaller nations would be excited to live. Then, when these same pastors die, you spend unthinkable amounts of money to bury them like palace kings and queens. So, is this what your pastor calls... being more like Christ?

Where in the Bible does it teach that Jesus Christ lived a materialistic lifestyle? Where does this thinking even come from? Well, we may not be able to pinpoint when and where it all started, but we can clearly see who's responsible for continuing it.

Jesus talked most about Kingdom Building. Many of today's pastors talk most about prosperity, money, positive mental attitude, and a whole lot of nothing.

What must some of these departed pastors be thinking, as their remains lay there in the bosom of an extravagant and high praise funeral service? Do you ever wonder if the pastor even cares about a two or three hundred thousand dollar funeral at this point?

I suppose it also doesn't matter much, if they left here righteous or unrighteous. Either way it goes, they've got bigger and more important things than their funeral on their minds now.

The Real Truth Behind... "More Like Jesus!"

Let's see what being like Jesus Christ really represents. Well, for starters, Jesus was born in a smelly stable, not a billion dollar, high-tech, steam cleaned hospital. He slept in a manger (a feeding trough for animals) not a softly padded and climate controlled infant crib or see through, sanitized acrylic bassinet.

Jesus grew up to be hated and despised by the very people He came to save. He was the most wanted man on the planet. Jesus suffered painful atrocities far beyond that which the human flesh, the human will and human endurance were created to withstand.

Clothed only in untainted innocence, Jesus was beaten unmercifully. Then, murdered on a wooden cross like a common criminal. He didn't have an insurance policy for an imperial funeral. Nor, did He have dozens of people who would stand to talk about how great a man He was. In fact, when confronted about his relationship with Jesus, one of His closest friends denied Him; not once... but three times.

There were no flowers or condolences from the members of His mega-church or His supporters. How many twenty-first century leaders would be okay with the thought of that? There was no earthly celebration and no musicians playing. No one took up a collection to help cover the burial expenses.

He wasn't put inside in a finely crafted casket and entombed in a granite or marble vault. Truthfully, Jesus didn't even have a burial plot of His own. I guess he figured, "What's the point?" I'll only be in it for a moment. So, they placed His body in a borrowed tomb.

One day, while in Israel, I was standing inside that very same tomb. I was looking at the spot where they had laid Him. I thought to myself, "Can you imagine the nerve of Jesus?" Picture this..."Uh, Joseph! Excuse me Brother, but I'm going to need to borrow your tomb later today? I'll just need it for a few days. I promise to give it back to you by Sunday." I mean... who does that? Who borrows someone else's brand new, unused tomb? And, for only three days? Apparently, Jesus did!

More Like Jesus Means Giving... Not Taking!—

The example set by Jesus for His caretakers of truth did not include being served and catered to on every whim and desire, but it included serving and self sacrificing. Preachers, if you genuinely want to be more like Him, just as you say to your members, you too must be just as willing to suffer for Him, as He was for us.

How can you say you're trying to be like Him, when you and your family bathe in the sunshine of prosperity, while your members do all the suffering? You bear the riches, while you members bear the cross. When was the last time you looked over your membership to see if there was anyone within your own congregation who was in need of a financial blessing? Or even a simple word of encouragement?

Preachers, I'm not against you enjoying some of the finer things of life. I like finer things too. But, I am against you being unwilling to live without those things, just as many of your members are forced to. I am against your church going into foreclosure, while you continue to deplete the church's storehouse to subsidize your own pleasures. I'm probably also against your teenage son or daughter owning and driving their friends around town in a brand new car. A car that you paid for out of church funds, while some of your oldest and most faithful members are walking or using public transportation to get to church.

These are the kinds of things that go on, as loyal members continue to support this extravagance with their last dollar. This is what can happen when you are enslaved to someone; anyone. It's even worse when the person you are enslaved to... is a thug preacher.

"To Thine Own Self Be True..."

William Shakespeare

Chapter Nine

RECOGNIZING CHURCH ABUSE

*Church abuse comes in many forms… and
from many different sources and directions*

C hurch abuse comes in many forms and from many
sources. It doesn't matter whether the pastor is the
perpetrator or some other member of the leadership
committee. Abuse in the church is wrong. I've discovered that many
of those who endure years and years of ecclesiastical or spiritual
abuse, do so because they lack the ability to recognize church abuse
or church abusers.

Church abuse is manifested in so many ways that it may be hard for the untrained eye to spot it. Today's churches are the perfect target for abuse, because parishioners are taught to worship the creature rather than the creator. Your love and loyalty toward the man or woman in charge make it uncomfortable for you to question what your own mind and conscience tell you is wrong.

> Some churches seem to put more time and effort into their church anniversary and the pastor's birthday celebrations than they put into Kingdom Building.

Have you ever wondered about that anniversary celebration for the pastor? Did you know that in the months leading up to, and during the celebration, churches raise thousands, to tens of thousands and even hundreds of thousands of dollars for their pastor? That isn't the problem. That's wonderful if that is what the members want to do.

The problem is that in most churches where these types of celebrations take place, the leaders and members put more effort and energy into the pastor's anniversaries and the pastor's birthday celebrations than they put into Kingdom Building. Some churches work all year long raising money and preparing for these pastoral celebrations.

In so many Christian churches, the various auxiliaries and departments of the church work hard at trying to come up with elaborate gifts and large amounts of money in an effort to outdo one another. This can include expensive shoes, custom suits, jewelry, cars; even homes. I actually don't think it's wrong to be a blessing to your pastor. I don't think there is anything wrong with taking a day out of the year to make your pastor feel appreciated. Some preachers need that. I'm just wondering which day out the year your church sets aside to celebrate God or His Son with that level of enthusiasm.

Have you ever thought about how great it would be if churches could get excited about giving to the Lord the same way they give to the pastor? I'm not talking about the building fund or the church improvement fund-raising drive. To tell you the truth, I'm not talking about raising money to be spent on your church at all.

Here's what I'm suggesting to pastors and church leaders. First, plan to have an over the top "Appreciation Service" for Jesus. Just imagine putting all that high energy into raising money to celebrate the King of Kings and the Lord of Lords. Make Him feel really appreciated. Have the service and go all out for the Lord. Raise as much money as humanly possible. But, don't use one penny of the money for you or your church.

Next, prayerfully search out some little church whose God is bigger than their membership. Find a church whose heart is bigger than their building. It should be one that is majoring in teaching and preaching the unadulterated Word of God; and as God would have it, they are specializing in soul winning and Kingdom Building.

Now, here is where most of you will think I'm nuts. Pay close attention to what I'm about to say next. Here we go. Give all the money you collected for Jesus' appreciation celebration to that little church that He led you to locate. The key is not to use any of it on yourself or your ministry. You think I'm crazy don't you? Well, as crazy as giving it all away it may sound, it wasn't your money in the first place. It was Jesus' money from the start. That is, of course, unless you raised the money under false pretenses.

For some pastors or churches to do this, would be as difficult as it was for the rich young ruler that came to Jesus. It's like trying to get that camel that Jesus talked about through the eye of the needle.

"Again, I tell you, it is easier for a camel to go through the eye of a needle than for a rich person to enter the kingdom of God."

St. Matthew 19:24 (ESV)

Some of you have no idea what an impact your gift can have on some of the smaller churches out there. This may just be the break they just need to get them to the next level. I have another suggestion for your consideration. Just suppose, you use the money raised to buy a church van for two or three different ministries. Have their church signage painted on it, and deliver it during one of their Sunday morning services.

Can you imagine the impact this would have on their faith and trust in God? It could even be choir robes, or chairs or a sound system. You could pay their heating bill for the year, or donate a new refrigerator. The point is, brotherly love and selfless acts of kindness are what the eleventh commandment is all about.

> *"A new commandment I give unto you, That ye love one another; as I have loved you, that ye also love one another. By this shall all men know that ye are my disciples, if ye have love one to another."*
>
> St. John 13:34-35 (NASB)

EXAMPLES OF CHURCH ABUSE

It's time to talk about recognizing and identifying signs of church abuse. In this chapter, I will be spotlighting three typical examples of misuse in the church. These examples are Financial Exploitation, Reduced Self-esteem, and Inappropriate Sexual Behavior.

The order in which these examples are presented is immaterial. They can be listed in any order. What is relevant is that the actual list can far exceed the minuscule examples mentioned here.

Financial Abuse—

Perhaps, one of the most common and most recognizable forms of church abuse is financial exploitation. In today's economy, finances are very important to the church. Jesus declared that as caretakers of truth, we would be empowered to perform the works that He did, and more.

> *"Very truly I tell you, whoever believes in me will do the works I have been doing, and they will do even greater things than these, because I am going to the Father."*
>
> John 14:11-13 (NIV)

However, I believe the greater works mentioned in scripture may have been based on Jesus' foreknowledge relative to modern inventions and improved technology. For example, Jesus and the preachers in Bible days either walked or rode on the back of an animal to get from one city or village to the next. However, at age nineteen when I conducted my first revival crusade, I stepped onto a jet powered aircraft in Chicago, Illinois and stepped off about two hours later in Birmingham, Alabama.

During the two weeks that followed, I preached in four different cities in the state of Alabama. That same evangelistic trip would have taken one of the New Testament apostles months to complete. Now, with the advent of the worldwide Internet, I can sit in my living room and live-stream to the entire state of Alabama in an instant; or for that matter, to the whole world. When Jesus spoke of greater works, I believe He knew we would have the availability of modern transportation, radio, television, the Internet, computers, books, advanced technology and so much more.

Yes, these major developments are available to us, but generally, they come at a cost. For example, to deliver a weekly one hour, high quality, nationally televised church broadcast to the 48 contiguous American states for a year could run well into millions of dollars. So, unless the pastor is independently wealthy or very resourceful, to accomplish such an enormous feat requires the generous contributions of the church constituency, along with random friends of the ministry.

Obviously, there isn't anything wrong with a pastor or a Christian leader sharing the ministry's needs or asking for financial support to further the Lord's ministry. Where it becomes a problem is when asking turns into blatant extortion, bribery, trickery or deception.

For example, in an effort to influence the congregation to give liberal amounts of money, a minister may start the offering off with a larger than usual offering amount. Later, he will meet with a member of the finance committee to have his bogus offering returned to him. I saw a visiting minister do this at a spirit-filled church, but the deacons of that church refused to return his offering to him. They weren't playing his game of phoney baloney giving.

How many times have you witnessed ministers have all the tithers to step into the aisle with their envelope in hand? Some ministers will even suggest that the tithe givers lift their envelope up high for all to see. This tactic serves a two-fold purpose. First, it gives the attention seekers an opportunity to proudly showcase their giving. Secondly, it shames the tithes slacker into stepping up to the plate.

The same holds true when ministers tell impoverished people to prove their faith in God by stepping out into the aisle and forming a "special" offering line. Frequently, pastors and evangelists will ask people to line up in the aisle according to the amount of their donation. The members are told, if they trust God enough to give (for example) a $100 sacrificial offering, God has a special blessing for them. They carry on about how God will honor the giver's great faith, how He will multiply their offering and return it back to them.

Once they have convinced all the $100 givers to come forward, they then will start working on those who will trust God with a $50 sacrifice. Again, they stress how God will honor their faith, multiply their offering and return it back to them. Next, they move to the $20 sacrificial gift, $10 gift, $5 and finally, whatever you have.

The "special" offering line scheme is designed to dupe people into believing that this great, enthusiastic display of money given to the minister or the church will enviably generate an enormously larger return on the money they gave. The more they give, the more they hope to receive in return for their giving. This is no more than what investment brokers hope for concerning their clients. The hope is, the greater the investment, the greater the dividends.

This method of giving is not just wrong, it is outright anti-Biblical. This is exactly what Jesus has instructed us NOT to do! In the sixth chapter of St. Matthew, Jesus teaches us that when we give, our giving should not be done openly before others, but secretly. He goes on to say, when we give to be seen by people, we receive the praise and approval of people. Therefore, we already have our reward and should expect no further reward from our heavenly Father.

"Be careful not to display your righteousness merely to be seen by people. Otherwise you have no reward with your Father in heaven. Thus whenever you do charitable giving, do not blow a trumpet before you, as the hypocrites do in synagogues and on streets so that people will praise them.

I tell you the truth, they have their reward. But when you do your giving, do not let your left hand know what your right hand is doing, so that your gift may be in secret. And your Father, who sees in secret, will reward you."

St. Matthew 6:1-4 (NET)

It is also common to see preachers, usually evangelists, conduct a prayer line and offering line combined. The people form one or more lines leading toward the offering receptacles. As they drop their offering into the receptacle, the pastor lays hands and prays for them.

This is not always a bad sign. There really are pastors out there who aren't concerned with what you're giving. They're not watching who dropped an offering in the receptacle. They're too busy praying for the people. These are the ones who are more concerned about you and your needs, than your money. For some older pastors who have already been standing for over an hour or two to minister, for health reasons they (wisely) take a seat, while laying hands to pray.

Then, there is the flagrant confrontation. It has always bothered me when ministers openly confront people during the service and venomously demand that they give, or openly pledge a certain amount of money to the ministry or the minister. They even go so far as to try to talk individuals into believing that their financial struggles and problems at home are the result of the individual's level of giving. Usually, the pastor is referring to the dollar amount given, rather than the level of sacrifice to God.

"Jesus sat down opposite the place where the offerings were put and watched the crowd putting their money into the temple treasury. Many rich people threw in large amounts. But a poor widow came and put in two very small copper coins, worth only a few cents.

Calling his Disciples to him, Jesus said, "Truly I tell you, this poor widow has put more into the treasury than all the others. They all gave out of their wealth; but she, out of her poverty, put in everything – all she had to live on."

St. Mark 12:41-44 (NIV)

Even though the widow in the scripture had only given mere pennies (or less), Jesus said that she had given more than anyone else had given. What Jesus wants us to understand is, the amount of the gift is not important to Him, but what He Does care about is the sacrifice offered. Usually, a financially secure person will have no problem giving $500 in the offering, while an impoverished person may struggle to come up with $2 to give to the Lord's work. To Jesus, the $2 sacrifice outweighs the $50 easily given offering. The widow gave all that she had. It isn't how much you give, it's how much you have left after you give.

Other forms of financial abuse may involve pastors persuading their members to participate in any one of a variety of business ventures. These could include investments, pyramid schemes, network marketing, multi-level marketing, loans, etc. Many pastors have successively persuaded members of their congregations to participate in pyramid schemes or multi-level marketing programs.

The truth is, a few people (usually at the top) make money and a lot of people lose money. Pastors are commonly recruited into pyramid schemes because they have a built-in warm market base. Many pastors are naturally attracted to these programs because they know their members will believe almost anything they tell them, even if it sounds too good to be true.

Another reason so many pastors are drawn to pyramid schemes is recruiters will sometimes eliminate the pastor's risk by offering to sponsor him or her into the program at no cost to the pastor. Frequently, the pastor is only required to allow the use of the church for meetings, and to encourage her members to join in the alleged prosperity.

148

When it comes to very successful ministers of extremely large congregations, business opportunity recruiters are willing to set the pastor up risk free and work free. The pastor doesn't have to encourage anyone to do anything. In fact, she doesn't even have to provide a meeting space. The only thing required of the pastor is the use of her name. The recruiter only wants to say that a popular pastor is a part of his descending network. For the use of her name, the pastor is generously rewarded.

Some very annoying thugs are some of the late-night TV preachers. Late-night television is filled with religious hustlers peddling everything from sacred sand from the deserts where Jesus walked, to holy water from the Sea of Galilee, to blessed prayer cloths from the robe of Jesus, to straw from the manger... and to anything else desperate viewers will send money to get.

When you view these programs, it's obvious, that nearly the whole program time is dedicated to soliciting funds by offering various tokens of appreciation for your generous gifts. In nearly every case, the hustling thug does little to no preaching or teaching at all. Typically, they place more emphasis on the power of the article they're peddling than they place on the power of the almighty God.

Unbelievably, for many TV con artists, this has proven to be big business in impoverished markets. Desperate people will give their last dollar to the so-called man or woman of God, with the hope of getting out of their desperate situations.

I want to be unmistakably clear on the matter of giving. There is a tremendous expense involved in operating a church or ministry. Furthermore, larger ministries are forced to bear even greater expenses. Some very large ministries operate on budgets that reach into hundreds of thousands, to millions of dollars per month. It makes sense that the financial support must come from God's people. Moreover, we ought to give, even as God has blessed us. We should give freely and we should give gladly.

"You must each decide in your heart how much to give. And don't give reluctantly or in response to pressure. For God loves a person who gives cheerfully."

2 Corinthians 9:7 (NLT)

But clearly, it is a problem when the pastor asks for financial support to further the ministry, but the funding of his extravagant lifestyle comes off the top. I cannot help but wonder if the hundreds of millions of dollars spent by ministers on private jet planes, private yachts, stretch limousines and oversized luxury mansions could be better used elsewhere in the Lord's work.

Reduced Self-Esteem—

One thing that I have come to realize over the past several decades is that there is an overflowing abundance of people in churches across America and around the world suffering from incredibly low self worth. These poor souls have seemingly lost confidence in everything and everybody.

This self-devaluation can lead to stress, depression, anxiety, diminished spirituality and increased vulnerability. Some pastors may resort trickery to prove to you how insignificant you are. Like most abusive persons, they often remind you of how worthless you are without them in your life. When in fact, it is the opposite that is true.

Just as incarcerated thugs and gangsters are able to control their territory on the outside from within prison walls, ruthless pastors are able to control what goes on in the homes of their members without setting foot inside the home. They sometimes gain this control by turning one member of the household against another.

They may even cause the husband to become suspicious of his wife's level of commitment to the pastor's teaching, and to the church and its' doctrine. When the husband comes to the pastor for guidance, he may be advised that as a man, he must take charge of, and rule his home. The pastor may also tell him that he needs to put (and keep) his wife and children in check.

Now the man begins to rule his home with an iron fist as advised by his pastor. Confused, the wife feels diminished in personhood. The kids are all unhappy, helpless and confused as well. Of course, the pastor is sure to remind the husband or father that he is subject to his pastor. So, he continues to follow the pastor's bad advice.

Now, the pastor starts instructing the man on how a strong man controls his home. This misguided husband and father desperately tries to follow the pastor's advice, but there is chaos in the home. Now, the poor brother is no longer in control of his own home as he may think. The pastor has now taken over the control of that home.

In other cases, the thug pastor may even try to make someone else's wife feel that he deeply cares for her, and that he feels as if she is closer to him than she is to her own husband. As one would expect, this stirs up a hornets' nest within that home. Now, the husband is suspicious and begins to wonder if he can even trust his wife; and of course, the wife accuses the husband of being jealous of her pastor.

The husband now feels that he cannot measure up to his wife's evaluation of the pastor and his personal esteem drops to rock bottom. Now the wife feels that she is soaring above the clouds, but she attributes that to the pastor. She believes that, all the good that she feels about herself, is not attainable without the pastor in her life.

Reduced self-esteem victims frequently hear the words, *"After all I've done for you!"* freely spew from the mouths of their abusive leaders. In essence, what they are really trying to make their victims believe is, "You OWE me your blind allegiance and loyalty." This type of preacher usually stacks the deck the member by offering to do favors for them. Once that member begins to accept the help from the pastor, the member has put himself in a very vulnerable position with the pastor. Now, this thug pastor can honestly say, "You owe me!" To accept any form of gifts or favors from this type of individual is like selling your soul to the devil.

Sexual Exploitation—

The matter of sexual exploitation is perhaps, the broadest forms of exploitation in the church. It can cover so many unrelated areas, from sexual harassment to rape. Sexual exploitation can involve a deeply emotional relationship or a series of one night stands with total strangers. Not always, but in many instances, sexual abuse is a coldly and carefully calculated scheme masterminded by the thug pastor. Although, in other situations, the pastor may have stumbled into an ungodly relationship that he does not know how to escape.

Often, where the victim is of consensual age, the sexual indiscretion is the result of a calculated scheme; perhaps by both parties. It could start with either one testing the waters first. Usually, it begins with verbal kidding and joking around, which later turns into vague flirtation. The flirtation gradually leads to subtle touching, which opens the door to disaster. Once personal boundaries are compromised and no objection has been raised by either party, they both believe they have been granted probable grounds for exploration of intimacy.

In other scenarios, the pastor may be a sincere, God-fearing leader with no ungodly thoughts whatsoever toward anyone other than her own husband. Still, she may find herself entangled in a web of adultery and deceit. Very often, this relationship may have its' initial beginning in the context of sincere counseling or crisis consolation. It could start with something as innocent as a concerned and supportive embrace. Far too often, innocent embraces charged with emotions, spiral out of control; eventually transcending professional discipline.

When, and where intimate compromise is established, both parties may feel trapped in a situation for which they were unprepared. Now, they must decide what to do with this huge problem that the sincere pastor and his member are intellectually, emotionally and spiritually unequipped to handle.

Either way it goes, whether calculated or purely unintentional, both sets of circumstances are wrong in the sight of God. While this book is written to shed light on the corrupt practice of charlatanism in the church, it remains the responsibility of all concerned parties to ensure that even sincere crisis comforting knows its boundaries.

Again, I must stress that the examples in this chapter are only a few examples of the numerous types of abuse that exist in the church. While, these examples may not be typical of your church, the list could easily, far exceed the few examples cited here.

Turn the page to take a surprise quiz to see whether the church you are attending is a spiritually healthy church; or a potentially spiritually unsafe one.

HOW SPIRITUALLY HEALTHY IS YOUR CHURCH?

This is a quick quiz that may help you determine just how spiritually healthy or safe your church is. While the quiz may not be fool proof in determining your church's potential for the spiritual progression and growth of its members, it may give you a basic idea of how spiritually healthy and safe your church is. Be sure to take your time and really think through each question.

Quiz

1. Does your pastor believe his or her teachings and interpretation of the Bible is the final authority for discerning Biblical truth and God's will for you and the other members of your church?

    Yes ☐   No ☐

2. Does your pastor make you feel uneasy about asking questions regarding his or her doctrinal teaching?

    Yes ☐   No ☐

3. Does your pastor discourage questions from the members regarding his or her governing of the church?

    Yes ☐   No ☐

4. Does your pastor speak often of being constantly persecuted by other believers because of his or her stand for God?

    Yes ☐   No ☐

Quiz

(Continued)

5. Does your pastor demonstrate rude behavior toward members who disagree with him or her?

    Yes ☐   No ☐

6. Does your pastor at times seem flirtatious...especially when his or her mate is not around?

    Yes ☐   No ☐

7. Does your pastor sometimes seem mean-spirited to people for no apparent reason?

    Yes ☐   No ☐

8. Does your pastor use public humiliation and embarrassment as a means, of shaming and controlling the members?

    Yes ☐   No ☐

9. Does your pastor require that members obtain his or her permission before visiting other churches or sitting under the teaching and preaching of other ministers?

    Yes ☐   No ☐

10. Does your pastor make the members feeling that leaving the church to join another church is the same as leaving God?

    Yes ☐   No ☐

Quiz
(Continued)

11. Does your pastor require that members obtain his or her permission before they can leave your church to join another church?

    Yes ☐   No ☐

12. Does your pastor discourage members from associating with, and maintaining a friendship with ex-members of your church?

    Yes ☐   No ☐

13. Does your pastor speak negatively of members who have left your church to worship elsewhere?

    Yes ☐   No ☐

14. Does your pastor discourage members from associating with Spirit-filled Christians who are not members of your local church congregation?

    Yes ☐   No ☐

15. Does your pastor discourage the members of your church from marrying Christians who are members of other churches?

    Yes ☐   No ☐

16. Does your pastor and church leaders conceal the business of the church from the members of the congregation?

    Yes ☐   No ☐

Quiz
(Continued)

17. Does your pastor seem more worldly and carnal than spiritual?

Yes   ☐   No   ☐

18. Does your pastor's vision seem to be directed more toward building a personal empire, than toward building the Kingdom of God?

Yes   ☐   No   ☐

19. Does your pastor promote hard work and faithfulness to him or her, as well as to the church, more than salvation through the blood of Jesus Christ?

Yes   ☐   No   ☐

20. Does your pastor claim to be the authoritative voice of God?

Yes   ☐   No   ☐

Quiz Totals

Okay. Now it's time to tally up your quiz results.

 Make sure you took your time and really thought through every question and each corresponding answer before you tally your "Yes" and "No" results. Try to be as accurate as possible. Don't guess! If you're not sure, answer the question with a no.

Total Number:

Yes [ ]   No [ ]

Next, turn the page to see the results on the spiritual healthiness of your church. You just might be surprised at the results. Let's see what all those questions and answers mean.

Final Results

Your results will only be as accurate as your answers. In other words, if your answers were off, your results will be off as well. On the other hand, if you were thorough, honest and spot-on in your answers, your results should be pretty accurate.

Grab your totals from the preceding page and hold on to your chair.

Okay... here we go! —

- If you earnestly answered "NO" to all 20 questions, you are probably in a spiritually healthy church environment. This should be a great environment for spiritual growth and nourishment.

- If you answered "YES" to 7 or more of the questions, your church may not be a spiritually healthy environment. There may be reason to wonder if this is the best place for your spiritual growth and development. Be prayerful and test the spirit of the church using the Bible.

- If you answered "YES" to 12 or more of the questions, your church is clearly not a spiritually healthy environment. You might want to seek guidance from a minister who you believe better fits the profile of a healthy minister.

- If you answered "YES" to all 20 questions in the quiz... *"Run for Your Life!"* Your church is really messed up.

"If the devil can't keep you from being saved, he will try to keep you from living 'victoriously' saved."

Frank Jackson

Chapter Ten

WHAT YOU SHOULD DO IF YOU ARE IN AN ABUSIVE CHURCH

*I think my pastor may have the signs of a
thug preacher— Now What?*

﬩

Okay. So, you completed the test, and now you're starting to suspect that you may be in an authoritarian or abusive church environment. You're not completely sure, but you're a lot more concerned than you were before you began reading this book. The all important question on your mind right at this moment is, "What do I do now?"

Well, this chapter addresses what you, the follower, can do if you suspect that you are in a church that is pastored by a reclusive thug or gangster type preacher. However, before I discuss what you should do in this situation, I believe it is essential you know that there are some things that you should definitely NOT do.

WHAT YOU SHOULD "NOT" DO!

The office of the gospel minister should be respected. Whether, they are true or false, accusations waged against a pastor can bring down a ministry faster than the Jericho walls. To make a mistake here could lead to devastation for the church. The damage done is often irreversible. I have listed a few things that you as the follower, should definitely not do.

Do Not Rush to Judge—

The first, and foremost advice I would offer anyone who believes that she or he may be in a thug preacher led church is to refrain from being in a hurry to judge. There is usually no reason for haste when dealing with the suspected negative actions of a leader. Slow down and follow Biblical principles for addressing issues of this nature and at this level.

The fact that a pastor may appear to be following some of the gangster tactics mentioned in this book does not necessarily prove him or her to be a thug or gangster. As it is with many preachers, your pastor may believe that leading with an iron fist is the Godly example of strong leadership. This may be the only example that he has seen throughout his tenure in the church. He may not know any better.

As I said earlier, most pastors simply lead, as they were led. Also, there are many cases where a pastor in his senior years is grooming a younger minister to take charge of the ministry. The elder minister may stress to his young apprentice, the importance of maintaining total control over the church operations, the church members… and the finances of the church.

The same is true when many senior pastors are preparing young ministers who feel that God has called them to start and build a new church. Very often, the apprentice minister is taught that if she learns to exercise absolute power over the congregation, she will be successful as a pastor and financially secure for the rest of her life.

Now, for me things were different from many young pastors coming along in the ministry. I did not have an authoritarian pastor as my example. What I did have was a loving and caring leader. Those who were close to him, knew Bishop H.W. Goldsberry, as a gentle and soft-spoken man of God. When Dad Goldsberry (as I called him) was alive, he lived very well. He lived in a beautiful well furnished home and drove a beautiful automobile.

Because I spent so much time with him, I was there to witness and learn many things about him that most people wouldn't know. People who have visited his home would be shocked if they knew that most of the furniture in his home was high quality, previously owned furniture that he purchased from estate sales and auctions. I was always impressed with the level of respect he received whenever we walked into a building where an estate sale was taking place.

I remember meeting Dad Goldsberry at his home at 7:10 one morning, many years ago. We were going to buy him a new car. We were supposed to leave his house at 7:00 in the morning. He was concerned that I was ten minutes late, as if the salesperson was going to send us home without the car because we were late. But, considering he was a man who had worked at one company for thirty-nine years and eleven months without ever being late for work, I understood his mind-set.

So, we went out to the garage, where I climbed behind the steering wheel of his big, beautiful, tan Cadillac, Fleetwood. He slid into the passenger seat. I thought we were headed to the dealership to trade in this car on the new one, but he wanted to stop at the credit union first.

Because my pastor was a punctual man, we arrived at the credit union at 7:30, and sat there for an hour and a half, waiting for them to open for business at 9:00. Now, he was okay with that, just so long as we weren't late. Secretly, I thought to myself, I could have gotten at least another hour of sleep, maybe even two extra hours. On the bright side, whenever we were together like that, he was always an overpowering hydrant of information, and I was a thirsty young minister with an unbelievable ability to process and retain information.

Once, he completed his business at the credit union, we were finally, off to the dealership. When we arrived at the dealership, they treated us like heads of state. As he asked for my thoughts on his next car, it felt good to know that my opinion mattered to Dad Goldsberry. I will never forget how proud I was that he had me to drive home before he had driven the car himself. I wanted everybody to see me driving that big beautiful Cadillac. Oh, by the way, it too was previously owned.

Bishop Goldsberry was an incredible steward for God. He was more concerned about the people of God than he was about things. He even put a ceiling on the amount of compensation that he would allow the church to give him. He always believed that, if his household needs were being met, additional monies should be used to pay off the church's mortgage, and to further the ministry.

Even though I had an exceptionally rare leader as my example of a pastor, everywhere else, I looked, everywhere else I read and everything else I heard suggested that a pastor should be tough. Because of my upbringing at home, and my examples in the ministry, I always felt uncomfortable about putting demands and unreasonable expectations on the people of God.

Do Not Judge a Pastor Based the Opinions of Others—

Another important thing is to be sure not to judge a minister's sincerity based on how others react to that minister. In other words, don't think that just because people render high praise to a leader that the leader is trying to steal God's glory. Some leaders, neither solicit, nor want, the praise of man. Somehow, people just seem to, instinctively, praise the creature over the creator.

I remember being at an international church conference some years ago. There was a quiet little jurisdictional bishop sitting on the rostrum that night. With thousands of people in the auditorium, and all the obvious hustle and bustle going on around him on the platform, he just sat quietly there.

At a certain point in the program, another bishop stood to introduce the modest little bishop. By today's standards, he wouldn't have been considered a celebrity preacher. He wasn't known for mountaintop preaching. He was just a mild mannered, gentle man of God.

> **He had led over 35,000 souls to Christ. Of course, it is impossible to calculate how many more souls were won by the 35,000 converts.**

As his name was announced, before he could stand up, the people in that auditorium went crazy! The whole audience rose to their feet to give him the loudest standing ovation I had ever witnessed for a minister. He approached the podium and tried to bring a calm to the audience, but they weren't having it. This expression of appreciation continued for several minutes.

As an ordinary man, this little bishop was just a meek and humble servant of the Lord. But, as the man of God, he had reached a good chunk of the world for the Lord. He had built and established churches in foreign and remote areas, where other leaders of that same organization had failed to realize the need.

At that time, it was documented that he had personally led over 35,000 souls to Christ. It's impossible to calculate how many other souls were won by the 35,000, and the others who followed them. Plus, these were just the ones that they had record of. His far reaching accomplishments in the ministry continued until God called him home. It is also impossible to know how many souls have been touched through him over the many years.

I was amazed at the audience's response to him, and quite frankly, so was he. Most of them had never met him. In fact, most of the people in that auditorium that night, had never even laid eyes on him. Nonetheless, his fame preceded him. Though they had not seen him before, they knew and associated his name with the great works that the Lord had performed through him.

THUG PREACHERS by Frank Jackson

He did not seek the attention he received, but the people recognized spiritual prominence in the room. Jesus said we should make sure that we do our good works not to be seen and praised by men. He promised that He Himself would see our righteous deeds and bless us openly.

> *"Take heed that ye do not your alms before men, to be seen of them: otherwise ye have no reward of your Father which is in heaven. Therefore when thou doest thine alms, do not sound a trumpet before thee, as the hypocrites do in the synagogues and in the streets, that they may have glory of men.*
>
> *Verily I say unto you, they have their reward. But when thou doest alms, let not thy left hand know what thy right hand doeth: That thine alms may be in secret: and thy Father which sees in secret himself shall reward thee openly."*
>
> St. Matthew 6:1-4 (KJV)

Do Not Instigate or Encourage Gossip About a Pastor—

Have nothing to do with gossip about a minister of the church, regardless of the reliability of its origin or transfer source. The spread of gossip is more harmful than the gossiper thinks it is. Most gossipers don't put much thought into the harm that could be caused by their words. People who gossip do so because they enjoy it. Not only does the juicy gossip of the day give people a connection with one another, it also gives them something to talk about, even if it is not true.

According to a "Woman's Day" article, Nicholas Emler, Ph.D., professor of psychology at the University of Surrey in England, shared his results of a 2009 study on gossiping. He says, "80 percent of everyday conversations are purely personal, with more of them being gossip, rather than anything else." In the same article, Frank McAndrew, Ph.D., a professor of psychology at Knox College in Galesburg, Illinois, is reported to have given his professional opinion regarding gossip and gossipers. According to Dr. McAndrew, "It's irresistibly fun."

When you participate in idle gossip about the pastor, you run the risk of doing great harm to the sincere souls who may have accepted Jesus through the ministry of that pastor or his local church. Countless individuals have realized the hurt inflicted by their gossiping words and have gone so far as to apologize. Sadly, apologies do little to stop the spread of damage caused. You can blow out a match, but you cannot blow out the mighty forest fire caused by that one little match.

In the illustrated story, "The Pastor's Pillow," David Brandt Berg talks about a woman who had spread very damaging rumors all over town about the pastor. Eventually, the woman came to realize that she was wrong for what she had done. In tears, she went to the pastor's house to tell him how sorry she was and to ask for his forgiveness.

After listening to her apology, the pastor told her that he would forgive her, but he needed her to wait while he stepped out of the room to get something. When he returned, he was carrying a feather pillow under his arm. The pastor who took the apologetic woman up into the church's bell tower. From the four open sides of the tower, they could feel the wind gently blowing upon them.

Without warning, the pastor raised the pillow up and ripped it open to allow the soft breeze to carry the feathers all over the village and far out into the countryside. They watched as the feathers drifted onto rooftops, under cars, into backyards, and into play areas where children were having fun.

As they stood high up in the tower watching the feathers float completely out of sight, the pastor asked the woman if she would now go and pick up the feathers. "How can I possibly pick up all those feathers?" gasped the woman? The dumbfounded woman told the pastor that his request was impossible. There is no way to know all the places where they have landed. "Exactly!" said the pastor. "Those feathers are like the lies you told about me. You may be sorry now, but there's no way to completely clean up the mess that you've made."

Cleaning up gossip is as equally challenging. You may be able to straighten out your chaos with some people, but you will never know the far reaching damage caused by your words. Some of God's best and most effective ministers are no longer working in the ministry because of the things that people have spread about them. Things, some of which may have even been true, but the harm done is not only to the targeted minister. People who trusted the ministry may suffer an even greater damage. Because of disappointment in man's infallibility, they may leave the church, vowing never to return.

Do Not Misinterpret the Preacher's Right to Be Blessed!—

Often, the many preachers who live prosperous lives also live under the microscopic condemnation of judgmental individuals who target them simply because they live the life that most believers would like to live.

Honestly, I'm not so sure that all the preachers who have been targeted by authors, writers and Internet bloggers even belong on the dirty preachers list. A minister's prosperity is not necessarily an indication of wrongdoing. In fact, sincere Bible believing preachers should represent the power of God to bless and to provide for His church. Owning or living in a big beautiful home, driving a luxury car and wearing fine clothes is not a sin.

Furthermore, the last time I checked, being a celebrity preacher is not a sin. I don't think we should set out to become celebrities through the ministry, but when you're on the air across the United States or around the world, it's tough not to become well known.

> "The blessing of the Lord brings wealth, without painful toil for it."
>
> Proverbs 10:22 (NIV)

However, it is a sin to target these anointed men and women of God simply because they have the faith and spiritual tenacity to trust God's Word. To judge these preachers as false or pretentious, based solely on the fact that they are prosperous and blessed is just wrong.

170

Now, preachers who are guilty of exploitation of the church of our Lord and Savior are a different story. To obtain and maintain a luxurious lifestyle through illegal means or by misusing and taking advantage of our brothers and sisters in Christ is a sin.

If you have been reading this book, you should know by now, I am totally against preachers using church funds for their own personal use. I do not believe in vanity jets, vanity boats, vanity motor homes or vanity anything else. Owning a bunch of big toys just so you can showboat and brag is wrong, especially when you purchased it with the ministry's funds.

There are many preachers who would resort to both illegal means, and cold hearted exploitation of the church to get what they want in life. There have always been, and perhaps always will be, those who prosper by breaking the law, as well through misuse of the people of God.

Likewise, I know pastors who made a decision to trade down on their lifestyle, to please the members of their churches. Some, sold their luxury vehicles and replaced them with ones that are more economical. A few, have moved out of their beautiful homes and into less plush housing.

Now, that may be what God has placed on their hearts to do. It's possible that some of those ministers fall into the category of individuals who cannot handle prosperity. For some individuals (preachers included) success, high social or religious status, money and materialism can be hazardous to their spiritual walk. These things can lead to pride taking control of some people, whether in the church or not. Additionally, as the Bible says, pride can lead many believers away from the principles and will of God.

Accordingly, for those preachers who cannot handle being abundantly blessed, getting rid of their possessions may be a good thing. Our chief purpose of establishing and building a relationship with Christ should not be prosperity, anyway. Although, there are millions of preachers who teach and preach prosperity and materialism as their main doctrine, prosperity is just a by-product of our Godly connection, not the central reason for it.

171

Still, we should all know that God has no problem with you having and enjoying the finer things in life, including material things. God is okay with you possessing riches. What He is not okay with, is… riches possessing you!

> *"If you give food to the hungry and satisfy those who are in need, then the darkness around you will turn to the brightness of noon. And I will always guide you and satisfy you with good things. I will keep you strong and well. You will be like a garden that has plenty of water, like a spring of water that never goes dry."*
>
> Isaiah 58:10-11 (GNT)

On the other hand, what many Christians don't realize is, what you call a luxury, is actually a necessity for hard working men and women of God. Many in the church think ministries should not own jet planes. You probably see that as a luxury, but you could be so wrong. For large ministries, a private plane may be necessary. When I think of the canceled flights, flight delays and the aircraft mechanical issues I've experienced, I'm almost tempted to believe we ought to give a private jet to every Bible-based, global ministry.

Many Fortune 500 chief executive officers don't have to worry about getting from point A to point B in an expeditious manner. They understand that time is of the utmost importance. For them time represents money; lost or gained. To the busy chief corporate officer, a fast jet is a tool of the trade. I believe I heard Billionaire, Donald Trump, say his 100 million dollar Boeing 757 jumbo jet is actually a money maker for him.

To the man or woman of God, time represents millions of souls won because we got to them with the message or life in time. It could also represent souls lost because we were stuck in an airport somewhere around the world, waiting for the airlines pilots' union strike to end.

Furthermore, when you really think about it, people make a bigger deal about preachers flying in private jets than God does.

When you are accustomed to dealing with a budget of two or three hundred thousand dollars yearly, the thought of a jet plane may seem extravagant to you. However, there are ministers who are empowered and entrusted by God with budgets of hundreds of millions of dollars. A brand spanking new jet plane is within their realms of possibility.

You can't just say, it's not God's will, because of the expense. If you're flying around the country only about three or four times a year, it would be insane for you to even think about purchasing a private jet for your ministry, unless you are financially independent.

Maybe your time is yet to come, but for now, please understand that there are men and women who are doing things for God on a far greater level than anything that you can go to sleep and even dream about. They dream big and they work bigger for the Lord. This is why they are where they are in the Lord, and in the ministry of the Lord.

Yes, some of them are on the dirty preachers list that seems to be so popular in the Twenty-First Century. To those of you, who cannot see the power of God in the lives of these anointed vessels just because the Lord has seen fit to bless them, shame on you. He will bless you too if you are willing to pay the price, as others have done.

To God, a jet plane is just a bunch of metal and wires strung together. He doesn't see a jet powered aircraft, a beautiful home, fine clothes or a luxury car, the same way we do. To God, these are all just things. To God, when it's acquired through honesty and integrity, it's no big deal. He places a greater value on your soul than He places on your things. He examines the motive behind these things. If your reasons for wanting these things are pure, He wants you to have them.

When you work for any major corporation, one of the first things you learn is, they invest heavily into their business. They spend big money to get the job done quicker, and more efficiently. Well, not only is God smarter than all the Fortune 500 board directors combined, He's also richer!

If a jet will get a preacher to a mission field safer and quicker, then that's what Jesus was talking about when He said, "Greater works shall you do!"

"Very truly I tell you, whoever believes in me will do the works I have been doing, and they will do even greater things than these, because I am going to the Father."

St. John 14:12 (NIV)

If financial security will take some of the indescribable stress off the man or woman of God, so they can focus on the business of winning souls, all the best to them.

I think, when it comes to reaching the masses for the Lord, people need to either put up or shut up. Ask yourself; "How quickly am I trying to reach the lost for Christ?" Or... "How many souls have I intentionally planned to win to the Lord this year?" Or... "If these men and women of God stop to listen to my mumble jumble, how effective would they be for the Lord around the world?" Lastly, ask yourself, "If they are involuntarily slowed down or hindered, due to airlines issues, am I willing and qualified to pick up the slack?"

I have had flights departing from airfields abroad that only fly to certain destinations once each week. If you truly believe Jesus is soon to come, do you really want the man or woman of God stuck in an airport waiting, while aircraft mechanics try to piece a plane back together? Or in a hotel room waiting until that certain day of the week, when their flight will be departing for their destination?

You should want to know that souls around the world are being reached as quickly as possible. No global minister has any business standing, sitting or sleeping around some cold and stuffy airport waiting for a plane to show up. God's business is too important and too urgent for that!

Now, of course, I realize that only a few ministers are able to even consider such an expense at this time. So, if mass transportation is all that is available to some ministers, thank God for what He has provided. This is when we praise Him for the airports and airlines, and even, coach buses. As our ministerial needs grow, we should trust God that our provisions will also.

However, for those ministries who can afford to provide private and safe transportation for their leaders, let's not fight them. What price can you put on a soul?

Safety is a whole other issue entirely. I have been on planes that were so old and so beat up, that the narrow escapes I've experienced were inevitable. There were flights that were so bad that the passengers all cheered when they heard the wheels of the plane actually touch down. There are some preachers reading this book who know what I'm talking about. God's cream of the crop ought not to be subjected to such nonsense.

When I flew with my team on a mechanically questionable flight from Amsterdam, Holland to Addis Ababa, Ethiopia, in East Africa, I wasn't surprised when A mechanic, who worked for that same airline, told me the next morning, that the plane I flew in on was unfit for flight. Thank God, from day one, I've laid hands, in the name of Jesus, on every plane that I've ever flown on... including that one. Nonetheless, there is a point to be made here. We should realize how important it is for the people of God to have their own tools and equipment.

> *"And my God shall supply all your need according to His riches in glory by Christ Jesus."*
>
> Phil 4:19 (KJV)

When we raise the matter of heads of state flying on the best cars and safest aircraft available, people say, that's different. They say these individuals are great and powerful people, and heads of state represent great nations. They're doing important things, so they are entitled to the best.

So, what are you trying to say? Are you saying, God's business is not as important or as urgent, as that of an ambassador or prime minister? Are you saying presidents of nations deserve safe travel, but caretakers of truth do not? Are you saying the running of America is more important than winning lost souls to Jesus Christ? I don't know of any job that is more important or more urgent, than saving lost souls from a fiery hell… as swiftly as possible!

No financially secure and prosperous preacher should feel forced to live the life of a lesser blessed or non-blessed individual, just to please the skeptics. If he can handle being blessed without allowing pride to take over, he is the true example that God wants and needs at the helm of the ship. He is indeed what God wants all of us to be. He is living the life that God wants you, and all born-again believers in Christ to live.

In fact, this type of minister should really serve as a tremendous source of encouragement and unquestionable evidence of the power of God to bless. God's blessings are intended to serve as an indictment against the preacher. Blessings, are not an indication of wrongdoing on the part of a leader. Do not be confused about a preacher's prosperity, or about his right to blessed by the Lord.

WHAT YOU SHOULD DO!

Now that we have explained what you should not do if you suspect you are under a thug preacher, let's move on to what you should do. The Apostle Paul realized and acknowledged that a bishop, apostle or pastor could possibly find himself in an unholy set of circumstances. Therefore, in 1 Tim. 5:19, Paul gives clear instructions on confronting ministers regarding their actions. Corrective actions against a minister should begin with witnesses to the accusation.

> *"Do not receive an accusation against an elder, except on the basis of two or three witnesses."*
>
> 1 Timothy 5:19 (NASB)

The Apostle Paul says, we must have two or three witnesses; not two or three people with an opinion about what they think might have happened, or what they heard someone say happened. Most dictionaries define a witness as, "One who, personally sees or hears something." Gossipers are unyielding when it comes to, spreading bad news, but a gossiper is not necessarily a witness. Avoid getting involved in the rebuke or correction of a minister based on gossip.

Test the Spirit of the Pastor—

One of the first things that you should do is found in 1 John 4:1. We can actually test the spirit behind the workings of the leader through the Word of God. Hoodlum pastors often do and say things that are in direct contradiction to the scriptures.

What may be a tell-tale sign of a thuggish leader is not just whether he is trying to lead as a dictator, but how he responds when presented with the truth of what God's Word has to say about lording over the very people that God has trusted to his care.

> *"Beloved, do not believe every spirit, but test the spirits to see whether they are from God, because many false prophets have gone out into the world."*

> 1 John 4:1 (NASB)

Take special notice of how certain pastors attack this book. If a pastor would rather fight than to conform to the Word of our Lord that should serve as a red flag warning. Thug preachers will always try to bypass Biblical efforts to hold them responsible for their words and deeds by misusing and misquoting the scriptures. When they want to back people off, they commonly use scriptures like:

> *"Touch not mine anointed, and do my prophets no harm."*

> 1 Chronicles 16:22 (KJV)

A caring and concerned pastor should be open to God's thoughts on the pastor's role in the church. On the other hand, a thuggish pastor's chief goal may be maintaining and expanding his or her, self-made (or inherited) empire. Always remember, just like any other type of abuser, hooligan pastors abuse people, simply because they can. They do it just because the opportunity is there.

GETTING HELP IN BREAKING AWAY FROM BONDAGE

Falling down into church bondage may prove to be a lot easier than climbing up out of it. This may be the hardest thing you have ever had to do in your entire life. Escaping from an abusive church environment can sometimes be tantamount to disassociating yourself from a street gang. It probably won't go down well. Thugs don't hide it; they don't want to let you go.

Very often, a nasty confrontation ensues. They take it personal. It's as though you've done something to them. So, instead of letting you live your life as you see fit, expect them to come out swinging.

Prayerfully Seek Guidance—

Finding the right guidance may be difficult. Approach it cautiously and prayerfully. Use the test in chapter nine of this book to get an idea as to how spiritually safe or unsafe your church is.

If you feel you are in a spiritually unhealthy church environment, expect most of the members of your local church to disagree with you. They will undoubtedly see you as wishy-washy. They may call you a flake, but who cares what people think? You must be willing to take uncomfortable steps to save your own soul. With God's help, breaking free may be easier than you could ever think or imagine. God has droves of qualified people available to help you through this sensitive period in your life. Pray specifically for direction.

Find Yourself a New Church Home—

Leaving is not always easy. The pastor will usually try to make you feel guilty. Now, brace yourself for the pastor's ultimate guilt trip phrase… "After all that I've done for you!" Yet, when you really think about it, he has done nothing for you without an ulterior motive that has always leaned toward his own best interest, not yours or your fellow parishioners.

The pastor might even try to make you believe that your leaving the church will deeply affect her and that it will break her heart. What the pastor is really hoping is that you will care so much about her, that you fall for this baloney. She is also hoping you feel guilty enough to change your mind about leaving.

On top of that, you have a history with this church and its members. Most of the people who you have regarded as your friends over the past five, ten or twenty years, are loyal members of this church. You have an emotional attachment. It may even feel like you're leaving family behind, but leaving is necessary.

Sometimes, an individual may need help from outside the abusive organization to break free. It is doubtful that anyone within the organization will be able (or willing) to help you. In fact, when you decide to leave an abusive church is when you discover just how many friends you really "don't" have.

> **Anyone looking for a new church home, should never join a church on the first visit. This could turn out really bad.**

Resist the Urge to Join a Church on Your First Visit—

My suggestion to anyone looking for a new church home is, never join a church on the first visit. This could turn out to be a bad decision on your part. Sure, you may have been stirred by the pastor's emotional message, and now you believe deeply in your heart that this is the church where God wants you to become a member.

We have all been there. Perhaps you are right. Maybe this is the church that God wants you in, but nothing will be lost by you visiting a few more times... just to see if the church has a spiritual steadiness or Biblical consistency. Remember, finding the right church home for you and your family is one of the most important things that you will ever do in life.

Sometimes, a person looking for a church home may visit a certain church for the first time, only to find that the speaker for that particular service is a guest pastor from another church. The preacher stands and presents a deep, soul searching message that convicts your inner spirit, and even persuades you to make "right now" decision for Christ.

When you find yourself in this situation, be extra careful NOT to join that church yet. You still have not been exposed to the ministry and message of the pastor that you actually came to hear. Come back again when the pastor is speaking. You may find that his ministry is nothing at all like the ministry of his guest speaker.

After a few visits, if you discover the ministry of this church is not one that you are comfortable with, you may want to check out the church where the visiting pastor was from. Perhaps, God had him to visit on that specific day just for you. Even if you decide to visit him, remember the rule. Never join a church on your first visit. Wait a while. Anything genuine will withstand the test of time.

If you have children, find out if they have a ministry that reaches children in the age range of your children. Sit in on their children's ministry. Don't just use them to baby-sit your children. Make sure that they are reaching your children at their level of understanding with the message of Christ.

Check to find out if they have programs to engage your kids. Most of all, inquire about the youth leaders. Who they are and what their background credentials, strengths and shortcomings are. These are your precious children.

You are responsible for both their Christian education and their safety. Ask your children questions about what happened during children's church. Instruct them to report to you anything that doesn't look, sound or feel right. Also, find out what they like most about the children's ministry.

Evaluating the depth of the church and the pastor's ministry isn't hard at all. Pastors are usually transparent in what they do after their message has concluded. Be sure to take note of two things. First, whether there is a call to action. Secondly, if there is a call to action, note what that action is.

Most empire builders will end their message with an invitation to visitors to join their church. Seldom do they make a sincere appeal for the spiritually deprived to repent of their sins, or to give their lives to the Lord. Remember what I said earlier. To the pulpit thug, people in the pew represent money.

So, makes sense that the more people the pastor can get to join, the more money he stands a chance of raising for the church and for himself. Kingdom builders understand that too, but their priority is on getting people saved. I suspect, to fly under the radar many of them will change their technique after reading this book.

Trust Your Instincts—

You are wiser now. Never again, will you have be that poor unsuspecting target with the bull's eye on the forehead. By now, you should know all the red flags and the warning signs. Trust your instincts. Don't ignore your gut feelings. If it doesn't feel right, it probably isn't. Above all, remain prayerful and by God's grace, you will do just fine.

With the guidance of a seasoned Christian, this book may prove to be an invaluable resource. Even without the help of others, if you are genuinely sincere, you should be able to use this information to help you find the strength and courage needed to break free and to stay free.

Always remember, you have this lifetime guarantee..."We have an amazing promise, from an amazing God, to broken people, living in broken places everywhere." For He has promised us, that His grace is sufficient.

> *"And he said unto me, My grace is sufficient for thee: for my strength is made perfect in weakness."*
>
> 2 Corinthians 12:9 (KJV)

"Our obedience must be to the Lord first. But, to obey the Lord, we must learn to submit voluntarily to His appointed leadership in the church."

Frank Jackson

Chapter Eleven

WHY YOU REALLY SHOULD SUBMIT TO GOOD, HEALTHY CHURCH LEADERSHIP

God actually does have genuine pastors who understand, respect and appreciate their God-given role in your life

 כ

After reading this book you may easily believe that I am against submission to leadership in the Christian church… and you would be wrong. In light of everything that I have written in this book, I still believe in submission to God appointed leadership. I pray that you're one of the many individuals who have been blessed enough to find a diamond in the rough. I hope you've found a spiritually healthy church and a true man or woman of God who genuinely understands and appreciates his or her God appointed, and God anointed role as your pastor.

This type of pastor isn't out to build a personal empire, but to build the Kingdom of God. He has been placed there by God to help you reach your ultimate plateau in the Lord. He always has an ear open to the will of God for the congregation, its' individual members and for himself. Very likely, you can trust his advice and guidance for direction in your life. He cares deeply about you and your well being.

But, with all this talk about whether one should obey the church's pastor, you may be wondering what your response to your own pastor should be. After all, you're one of the blessed ones. You have a good Bible centered servant pastor. Yet, you're confused about if you should obey him.

Please allow me to clear up the confusion. I think the word "obey" (even in its' best interpretive form) has an uncomfortable undertone. Aside from a populace of misguided church folk, it's hard to find an adult who enjoys obeying another person. Employees don't like obeying their employer; children buck at having to obey their parents; and brides cringe at the thought of vowing to obey their new groom.

Toward the end of the twentieth century, the word "obey" became a negative four-letter word. In those days the woman vowed to love, honor and obey her new husband for the rest of her life. These days, many couples are requesting that the word "obey" be removed from their wedding vows. Now, they just vow to love and honor him. By the way, some couples are also omitting, "Til death do you part" or "So long as you both shall live."

More recently, they are removing the phrase, "honor" and "obey." The new vow is just to "love" him. I'm not judging whether either way is right or wrong. I'm just talking about what marrying couples are doing these days.

Indisputably, people have a real problem with the word "obey." This may have something to do with the fact that to some persons, the word "obey" suggests following the slave master commands of another person; even against your own will. That certainly isn't what

God requires of us. Repeatedly, throughout the Holy Scriptures, God gives us choices, and He admonishes us to decide for ourselves which path we will take.

I don't believe the Bible encourages blind obedience to anyone but the Lord. However, I am fully persuaded that if you are under spiritually healthy and spiritually safe leadership, you should "submit" yourself to that pastor and his Godly vision for the ministry; and His God appointed guidance toward you. A common Merriam-Webster dictionary definition for the word "submit" suggests:

> "To stop trying to fight or resist something; to agree to do or accept something..."

It's impossible for unpretentious men and women of God to effectively lead and pastor a group of people who are resistant to the pastor. Even though your pastor is grounded in servant leadership, it's vitally important that you recognize that it isn't just the pastor who needs to practice servitude. The members should also learn how they fit into God's plan of servitude for the enrichment of the church.

Your pastor has a tough job. It isn't easy leading a group of highly opinionated (and often unappreciative) people from all walks of life. If your pastor is operating as a good shepherd, he deserves your respect, commitment and dedication. In the case where he is still learning, if he is not abusive, you should work with him, not against him.

For the nearly twenty years, or so that I served under my pastor, Bishop H.W. Goldsberry, I knew that God was preparing me for leadership. Because of the close bond I had developed with Dad Goldsberry, there were many things I learned from (and about) him that he didn't talk about openly. It was during those priceless moments that I learned to respect him for being more than the great leader that he was. I discovered that long before his leadership days, he had proven himself to be an even greater follower.

Throughout the many precious years that I spent learning from my mentor, I totally submitted myself to his wise counsel and spiritual guidance. I didn't regret it then... and I don't regret it now.

He taught me exactly how a good follower, under a good pastor, is supposed to respond to good leadership. It was a joy to serve under him. Had God not called me to be a pastor, I would have stayed under Dad Goldsberry's pastoral ministry until his last breath.

He taught me that as a shepherd, it is my responsibility to lead the flock. The beauty of sheep is, the shepherd leads, and the sheep follow. When we have a Christ centered pastor over the church, we can feel content in following him as he leads. Jesus refers to us as His sheep, or His flock. A group of sheep is called a flock, while a group of cattle is called a herd. As the pastor (shepherd) leads the flock by example, the sheep will follow that example.

A major difference between sheep and cattle is, sheep are led, but cattle are driven. As the shepherd walks in the direction that he wants the sheep to go, they will walk in the same direction. Godly members of the congregation should do the same thing. Where their true shepherd leads, they should follow.

On the other hand, just as all pastors are not real shepherds, all members of the congregation are not real sheep. Some members are like cattle. You won't be able to lead cattle by just walking ahead of them and demonstrating a righteous example for how they should conduct themselves. You may get caught in a stampede and end up trampled by them. You will soon learn that for some, it is pointless to expect them to follow the example you set, for how they should conduct themselves. They will generally do as they choose, despite your example.

Have you ever watched an old western movie where they talk about a cattle drive? To get cattle to move in a particular direction, cattle drivers get behind and on the sides of the herd and make a lot of noise. They crack whips, they shoot their guns into the air and they shout as loud as they can. It's as though they're trying to scare the herd into submission.

While it may seem like a lot of craziness, it gets the job done. The cattle conform to the wishes of the cattle drivers (or cowboys) and ultimately they end up where the cattle drivers wanted them to end up. In the church you have sheep… and you also, have cattle.

186

Some members respond well to a kind, gentle leader. Others respond best to a hard-nosed, cattle driving pastor. We all know people in the church like that. If a cattle driver is necessary in order for you to follow the Word of God, the problem may not be with the pastor only. It may also be with you.

Just to be clear, even though we find cattle throughout the church world, none of us are called to be cattle. Moreover, no man or woman of God is called or appointed to be a cattle driver. Pastors are called and appointed by the Lord to lead the flock; not to drive them. There are enough cowboys and thugs out there who would be more than happy to take care of the cattle.

Obedient children of God don't need a cattle driver; they need a shepherd. To the member, your obedience should be the Lord. To obey the Lord, we must learn to submit to His appointed leadership in the church.

"As we get close to God, He is going to reveal things in our life that aren't pretty."

Chip Ingram

Chapter Twelve

HOW YOU CAN TELL IF YOU ARE
AN ABUSIVE LEADER

*We must learn continually to examine and
cross-examine our own motives and actions*

T his particular chapter speaks directly to ministers. For the most part, it's directed to pastors. I suspect there will be concerned preachers who will read, or hear of this book and start to wonder if they might have any of the signs of a thug preacher. The only way to find out for sure is by being honest about who you are as a minister.

SELF-EXAMINATION

I'm sure most of us are familiar with the six long-standing words written by the astute and famous poet and playwright William Shakespeare. Shakespeare wrote, "To thine own self be true." What a powerful statement of conviction. We must first be honest with ourselves about who we are and where we are in God. We must learn to call our own moral and spiritual integrity into question; regularly.

> **Self-examination isn't easy. It requires you (the examiner) to look into your own life in a way that may be uncomfortable.**

Self-examination is an absolute necessity when it comes to evaluating where we stand in God and the Lord's ministry. In too many instances, huge egos often represent stumbling blocks in our ability to see ourselves as others may see us. While it may be difficult, it is necessary that we look deep into our own hearts and minds. Then, we should examine and cross examine our actions and our motives for those actions. Question yourself and your intentions the same as you would a member of your congregation.

In fact, it would be wise to place greater expectations on yourself than you might place on members of the church. As leaders, God requires more of us.

> "For unto whomsoever much is given, of him shall be much required."
>
> Luke 12:48 (KJV)

Self-examination isn't easy. It requires you (the examiner) to look deep into your own life, in a way that may be uncomfortable. You will need to recognize and challenge your own selfishness, self-centeredness, self-righteousness, cold-heartedness, and mean-spiritedness.

Sometimes, it's just a matter of you being willing to deal with your lack of understanding concerning how you should interact with the members of your congregation. You might also need to confront your own insecurities, stubbornness, rebellion against God and insensitivities to others.

Self-examination can be tough on the pride and ego. So of course, your pride and ego could be something else you may need to come to terms with. As pastors, none of us want to see ourselves in a negative light. But, in order for you to end the cycle of authoritarianism, church abuse or thug leadership, you have no alternative but to face the truth head on.

ABUSE OF POWER IS A TREATABLE CONDITION

Pastors who misuse the pulpit can be helped. The fact that you have discovered that you have abusive traits does not indicate that you are a bad person. The fact that you refuse to do anything about it, indicates that you are a bad person.

I believe many of you are very gifted individuals whose ministries could bring great healing, freedom and blessings to the people of the Lord. The abuse of pastoral power will not fix or correct itself. But thank God, abuse of power is treatable. It is a condition that God can help us with.

Treatment for ending the madness of abusing your own congregation involves several carefully executed steps. It may be a long journey to some preachers, and a simple mind change for others. Whether yours is a long journey or a short sprint, it must start with being honest with God and yourself.

Acknowledgement—

I'm sure some preachers will choose to stereotype the term "thug" to exclude or dismiss themselves from the problem. This could prove to be a big mistake. Perhaps, you already have a general profile in your mind of what a "street" thug looks, walks, sounds and acts like. And, based on that particular stereotype or profile, you believe you couldn't possibly be a thug. The fact that you don't match your own mind's picture or imagination of a "street" thug, does not automatically excuse you from the problem pulpit thugs.

The use of the word, "thug" in this book is in no way intended to suggest ethnicity, gender or national origin, but a specific style of pastoral leadership. Step one is always acknowledgement. It is

191

essential that you look deep within yourself and be honest about what you see. Without genuine truth in self assessment, you cannot help yourself. It is impossible to correct any problem without first acknowledging that there is indeed a problem.

In general, most individuals will seek medical or psychological help only when they believe they have a problem. Before a pastor will seek help for herself, she must first acknowledge that she needs it. If she doesn't acknowledge the need, she won't seek the cure.

Any authoritarian pastor must start out by honestly confessing to God that he or she definitely has an abuse problem. To dress up the problem by calling it strong leadership, tough love or anything else but abuse, is prideful and not a plea for help from God.

Empathetic Discovery—

It would be good for you to learn to put yourself in the position of those whom you've wronged. Think of how you would feel if someone were to treat you in the manner in which you treat others.

Of course, if you have always served under, or if you were trained and groomed by authoritarian leadership, this example may present some challenges for you. It may be difficult for you to see the wrong that has committed against you, and against those were a part of your circle.

Regret and Remorse Over Past Actions—

It's one thing to know what you are doing is wrong, but to be sorry for your actions is very different. There are always those who are more regretful for getting caught, than they are for what they were caught doing. If you're remorseful, you're sorry for what you've done or said.

True remorsefulness is an insatiable yearning and desire to turn back the hands of time. Though you may find forgiveness for your actions, you will always know that if you could go back in time, your choices would be very different. That's what Godly sorrow and true repentance is.

A woman apologized to my wife for a wrongful act that she had committed against my wife and our children. This woman also confessed that if my wife had done the same thing to her she would never have tolerated it. Her apology went something like this, "I'm sorry for what I did and that I offended you. If someone were to do the same thing to me, I would be very offended. But, if I had it to do over again, I would handle things the exact same way." That kind of thinking isn't anywhere close to godly sorrow. When you are really sorry, you wish you could roll back the hands of time, so that you could fix your wrong.

> The reclusive thug's method of selective preaching is not the same as strong, healthy Bible-based preaching.

Remarkably, most of the people who are being taken advantage of in the church, have no idea that they're being misused and abused. But the victim's personal knowledge of your wrongfulness against them has nothing to do with your own regrets. God has a record of your actions and He knows better than anyone, if you're sorry for what you've done.

Ask God to Forgive You—

God has made a promise to us that He is bound to honor. He says if we ask for His forgiveness for whatever we've done, He would grant it. Let's identify church and member abuse for what it really is. To mistreat anyone is sin, but when the mistreatment is by one member of the body of Christ perpetrated upon another member of the body of Christ, you give up your rights to Christian discipleship. Mistreatment violates the code of Christian love, and Jesus referred to our love for one another as the "single greatest" mark of a disciple.

> *"Everyone will know by this that you are my disciples—if you have love for one another."*
>
> St. John 13:35 (NET)

Pastor, if you will repent of your sins right now, and ask to be forgiven, God will restore you to a wonderful place in Jesus Christ. Experience a fresh anointing. You should pray to God for deliverance. Fancy mountaintop prayers are not needed here.

Just start out by praying this simple prayer:

"Lord Jesus, I acknowledge that I have committed sin against you and against the people you entrusted to my care. I'm sorry for hurting, abusing and taking advantage of those who believed in me and trusted me the most.

Lord, forgive me for my wrong. I pray that someday, somehow, those members for whom I caused so much pain, will find it in their hearts to forgive me as well. Now Father, give me a new start... In Jesus' name, I pray."

Now pastor, as you lift your hands and your heart toward glory, open your mouth and tell God, "Thank You!"

***You Must Be Willing to Forsake Your Abusive Way**s—*
Knowing that you are guilty of wrongful doing isn't enough. Even being sorry for your cunning actions, doesn't necessarily mean you're willing to change the way you do things. Remember what I said earlier about purebred thugs. These are people who know to do good, but choose to do wrong, they are willfully committing sin.

"Therefore to him that knoweth to do good, and doeth it not, to him it is sin."

St. James 4:17 (KJV)

Abusive and manipulative church pastors tend to rule their congregations through fear, shame and guilt. They bully them into submission. They also keep tight reigns by causing their members to be suspicious of other ministries, churches and leaders.

Pastor, the real evidence of true repentance is a changed life. As an authoritarian leader, you must be willing to give up the leadership lifestyle that you've grown accustomed to.

For some of you, this could involve you going before your congregation and confessing what God has recently revealed to you about yourself. You may want to tell them that you saw yourself in this book, and you were uncomfortable with what you saw.

The reaction from your church may be more positive than you might expect. But even if the response isn't as positive as you had hoped it would be, there's nothing better than walking in the perfect will of God. The result of unresolved church and member abuse is the same as the result of any other unresolved sin.

The key to your success at this point is that you stop doing whatever it is that you were doing to violate the trust of your congregation. The pastoral power that the Lord has so freely given you doesn't have to be abusive. There are many ways in which God's power in you can be used or expressed to set God's people free.

Seek Godly Counsel for Help in Staying Free—

If you need help, my suggestion is that you try as best as you can to find someone who can guide you in the right direction. God has a lot of good men and women of God out there who can provide excellent guidance and support. It's important to prayerfully, seek out someone you can trust to help you through this tough process of deliverance from member abuse.

Don't select a counselor on, the basis of church size, popularity or how skillful or entertaining the preacher is. Frankly, your guidance may come from a barely known preacher who pastors a small church. He may not even be classified as a great preacher. The pastoral counselor you seek, should be seasoned and able to give qualified guidance and advice from a Godly perspective, and they must respect your moral and legal right to privacy.

I know what it's like to be in dire straits with no qualified and confidential support to turn to. I understand what "alone" feels like. Sure, there were experienced individuals in the ministry who I might have been able to speak with, but they lacked an appreciation for confidentiality. It would have been equal to broadcasting my personal message over the Internet.

If you are a church pastor and you've discovered a truth about yourself while reading this book, I want you to know you are not alone. Get help. There are other pastors who have been there, and who can relate to what you are feeling.

In some cases, you may be unable to find the support you need. This is why God has given me a special burden for the pastor who has no support system. If you cannot find a qualified minister to help you, I will try as best as I can to be here for you, to provide the help, guidance and confidentiality needed to get you through what may be a difficult time in your life.

Just know in your heart, I am here for you. Contact me on the worldwide web at: FrankJackson.org. I promise to respond within a reasonable time-frame.

"Broken People Need Trusted Leadership."

Frank Jackson

Chapter Thirteen

A WORD TO THE SINCERE PASTOR

"Broken people need trusted leadership"

This chapter is strictly to sincere, earnest men and women of God. It's directed to serious pastors, not your members. I want to share a brief word of advice to the sincere pastor who may have found herself or himself in a situation where you are now having to deal with formerly abused individuals. These wounded souls are now members of your church congregation. You need to know what to do. If you haven't been prepared, you don't just automatically wake up one morning, knowing how to deal with this situation and these people.

The key thing to know and remember is, they aren't broken because they didn't like a particular style of church. They are broken because church leadership has failed them, and preachers everywhere have betrayed them. If you forget everything else that I have said in this book, try to remember these five words, "Broken people need trusted leadership."

SOME CHURCHES SPREAD MORE DISEASE THAN CURE

One afternoon, while researching the spread of disease and infections in hospitals, I came across a very interesting article. It was a post by CNN Senior Medical Correspondent, Elizabeth Cohen. According to this article, Dr. Peter Pronovost, director of the Quality and Safety Research Group at Johns Hopkins University, announced, "About 100,000 people die each year from infections we give them in the hospital."

Dr. Pronovost went on to say, "About 65,000 of those deaths are the result of infections from ventilators and catheters." Here's how he breaks it down. There are about 5,000 hospitals in the United States. So, statistically each hospital in the United States gives these deadly infections to one patient every month.

PBS TV broadcast journalist, Ray Suarez joined the growing list of town criers who, like Dr. Peter Pronovost, are calling attention to this healthcare atrocity. Suarez says, "The numbers are sobering." He continues, "The federal government estimates that each year about 100,000 people die in the U.S. after acquiring one or more infections during their stays at a hospital."

Can you even imagine 100,000 preventable deaths actually occurring in the U.S. each year? This number is inconceivable to me, but if there is an ounce of accuracy here, this gross negligence ought to be regarded as criminal, and criminals should be prosecuted.

The death toll from the 911 terrorist attack in New York was roughly around 3,000. That one massive attack shook up our nation and the world. Now, if my calculations are accurate, it would require terrorists repeating 911 about every 11 days to equal the number of the alleged deaths caused by hospital workers in a single year.

Of course, terrorists would have to do the same thing all over again each year to keep up with the reported annual death toll caused by our hospitals. So, who are America's real terrorists? Then again, that's a whole other story.

There have been a number of investigative news reports, all adding up to the same thing. The fourth major cause of deaths among Americans, behind heart disease, cancer and strokes is hospital infections. Infections resulting from unsanitary hospital conditions and unsanitary hospital personnel take more lives yearly than fires, automobile accidents and drowning combined.

The fact that hand washing saves lives is not exactly "Breaking News." More than 150 years ago, Dr. Ignaz Semmelweis, a greatly accomplished Hungarian born doctor, working in the Vienna Hospital, proved that his dirty handed medical staff members were responsible for the high death rate of women after childbirth.

When Dr. Semmelweis, insisted that his fellow doctors and medical students wash their hands before delivering babies, the death rate plunged from 13% to 2% among new mothers in just one month. This proves that the spread of disease in hospitals is by in large, avoidable.

Christians and Suicide—

Now, you might ask why I spent so much time talking about hospital deaths and the terrorist attack that took place on U.S. soil on September 11, 2001. The reason is simple. Because, hospitals and churches parallel one another. Both are places where people go, in search of life altering help. Both are also places where people can leave in worse shape than when they arrived. And both are places where only some of the workers truly care.

If all the hospital staff members really cared about their patients, we wouldn't have 100,000 avoidable deaths in America's hospitals each year. Likewise, if all the members of the Christian church really cared, we wouldn't have millions of people suffering from loneliness of the soul. Nor, would there be so many people dying and passing into eternity, without God.

So, if you can understand the dynamics of this problem from the healthcare viewpoint, you should be able to understand the spread of infectious disease problem in the church. As with the hospital, you should be able to go to the church to find a cure for what's bothering you, but this is not always the case.

> According to a "Christianity Today" article by Al Hsu, every fifteen minutes, someone in the United States takes his or her own life.

The fact that reaching out to broken people saves lives too, is also not "Breaking News." Millions of wounded individuals and hurting victims of spiritual abuse, enter churches weekly, expecting to be helped. But, too often they end up dying spiritually, mainly due to indifferent church workers, thoughtless pew members and thugs in the pulpit. Unfortunately, most churches are much like some hospitals around the world. When suffering individuals who view you and your church as their last hope, are poorly treated, the results can be horrendous. The outcome can range from feelings of rejection, to suicide.

I have discovered that the available information on Christians who commit suicide is difficult to come by, and much of what is available is inconsistent. However, what we do know is Christians are committing suicide at an alarming rate. Christian Feminist Today once published an interesting article written by Cliff Williams, Ph.D. of Wheaton College in Illinois. Appropriately, Mr. Williams titled his article, "When Christians Contemplate Suicide."

In his article, he talks about the shame that suicidal people, at large, live with. Cliff Williams says, "When shame and a low sense of self-worth are combined with an overpowering hopelessness, along with little support from others, the results can be deadly." According to Mr. Williams, some Christians experience these same exact feelings, including thoughts of committing suicide.

In 2013, Christianity Today published an article by Al Hsu, entitled, "When Suicide Strikes in the Body of Christ." According to this article, every fifteen minutes, someone in the United States takes his or her own life. Now, if those figures are true, 35,000 people kill themselves in America each year. That number could be higher when you consider the many suicides that are ruled or disguised as accidents. Al Hsu goes on to say, "Sadly, suicide occurs among Christians at essentially the same rate as non-Christians."

Hsu also says, "Each suicide leaves behind on average six to ten survivors, including husbands, wives, parents, children, siblings, other close friends or family members. Every year, hundreds of thousands of people, including many of our church members, will grieve the loss of a loved one to suicide."

Hate Is Not the Opposite of Love, but Indifference Is—

I know from my experience in working with suicidal individuals, many of these lives can be saved. I have had numerous suicidal subjects call my broadcast while I was yet on the air. There have been several who have called me while in the actual act of committing suicide. Many of these poor souls tried, but could not find the much needed help and comfort in the church. Often, it was because, to the church, they were not important or popular enough to matter.

That's how it is in many churches. If you're not a part of the "in crowd," no one has the time for you. As if, non-members are not worth their time. Non-members require unwarranted effort on the part of the "real" (as they like to say) members of the church, who are too busy enjoying one another. Too often, unfortunate individuals are left with feelings of very low self-worth, which may border on self-hate, and self-hate can lead to suicide. This should not be happening in the church, but it's happening all the time.

As I have already stated in an earlier chapter, the opposite of love is not hate, as most people seem to think. The opposite of love is indifference. Most church people don't hate or love the people they come in contact with daily at work, or school, or those who come to their churches for help each Sunday. In fact, they have no emotions toward these people whatsoever. They just don't care about them. This is what many desperate people who try to go to the church for help soon discover. The church just doesn't care.

Your members may not want to admit it because they enjoy hanging out at church with their friends and they prefer not to stop. It is easier for them to pretend they don't see the problem than to fix it. You may ignore it, but it's happening right under your nose practically every week. Yes, the church is filled with indifferent people who are more concerned with themselves than with others.

Disease is Easier to Spread than Cure—

Disease is a lot easier to spread than cure. The spread of disease requires no special training or expertise. It doesn't require a medical degree from the Harvard School of Medicine to be a spreader of disease. Anyone can do it. Infectious diseases spread faster, and can travel much further than cure.

Likewise, some churches spread more disease than cure. When you or the members of your congregation are insensitive or unkind to their visitors or new members, or when they practice a double standard among the members of the church, this is the same as spreading an infectious disease.

When they band together with another member, or even a visitor, to tear down or to destroy the pastor and his reputation, they are spreading disease. Whether the pastor, or any other leader or member of the church is the guilty party, it is infectious, and like any other disease, it must be stopped.

When your members tell people, who are survivors of previous church abuse, that it was their fault, they spread more disease. Because, infected members of the church are highly contagious, it would be best if those who are vulnerable would avoid them.

It can be dangerous to the ministry to have contagious individuals in positions of influence or authority. Infected ministers often find ways to destroy or split churches. They tend to whisper about the pastor's shortcomings and the flaws in his individual ministry. To them, his sermon is usually off point. They sometimes create and circulate rumors about the pastor, where none existed. They are never satisfied with the pastor's triumphs and accomplishments.

Sooner or later, the new convert or the new member finds himself caught up in this whirlwind of church discord. After a while, they begin to wonder if being in the church is worth it. They may even start to believe that there is no point in trying to live flawlessly for God since no one else seems to be doing it.

These days, people in need of spiritual help, can actually find themselves in worse shape than when they first joined their church. It is your job to make sure that this does not happen! If your church is not qualified to help these people, you owe it to them, to direct them to someone or somewhere they can be helped

CREATING A RESTORATIVE ENVIRONMENT FOR HEALING HURTING AND BROKEN PEOPLE

To achieve definitive success in bringing about inner healing for broken and shattered members within the congregation, the sincere pastor needs to know the importance of creating and establishing a solid base or atmosphere for helping delicate and hurting victims of church or pulpit abuse.

There must be a positive and strategically designed environment for producing spiritual healing. This must not be left to chance. Much prayerful thought must go into creating a healthy environment for curing brokenness.

The Entire Medical Center is Part of the Cure—

When a person goes to the hospital, it is not just the doctors who work toward curing the patient. There is a fully trained team of medical personnel who are involved in the physical restorative process. There are doctors, nurses, nursing assistants, lab technicians, X-ray technicians, janitors, etc. From the hospital administrator to the cleaning personnel who sanitize every part of the building, each person is a part of the cure. The entire hospital is an environment for medical diagnosis and treatment.

Here's an example. Not long ago, I was diagnosed with a massive macro adenoma. Just to give you an idea of what that is, a massive macro adenoma is a very large tumor most commonly located on the adrenal or pituitary glands at the base of the brain. It was determined that surgery was required to remove the tumor.

Here are the facts, as they were explained to us. Some years ago the survival rate was 50/50. Fifty percent of the people who underwent the surgical procedure for removal of the tumor died during surgery. Now, only twenty percent of patients die during the procedure. Of the eighty percent who survive, we're told that only fifty percent of them come out of the surgery with normal brain functions.

> I went into the hospital for brain surgery on Monday morning, and by Friday, I was back home.

I did consent to have the surgery. The neurologist said the surgery would take roughly six and a half hours. There were three doctors in the operating room; two surgeons and the anesthesiologist. The first surgeon and his team had the task of cutting through, and creating access to the interior of my skull, while opening a pathway leading directly to the macro adenoma.

Once this had been accomplished, the first doctor stepped out of the way, so the neurologist could take over for the actual removal of the tumor. He placed surgical instruments through that newly created access point and removed the tumor. About three hours after the surgery had begun, both surgeons walked together, back into the family waiting room, and by the grace of God, informed Liz that the surgery was successfully completed, in about half the expected time.

Once the surgery was finished, I was moved to recovery where another team of professionals were waiting to help with the recovery from the anesthesia. From there, I was moved to the Surgical Intensive Care Unit, where another team of specially trained personnel were waiting for me. I felt no signs whatsoever of having had surgery. A few hours after surgery, I was sitting on the side of my bed placing a call to my sister.

The nurse walked in the next day, as I was sitting on the side of my bed eating breakfast, she said to me, "Wow! You're already six weeks ahead of everybody else who comes through here." From there they had expected to move me to a regular patient room, but because I was doing so well, I was discharged to continue my recovery at home.

Throughout the process, there were X-rays, CAT-scans, MRI's, endocrinologists, nurses, aides, phlebotomists, dieticians, etc. At each step, I was met by trained medical professionals. Each one of those people served a pertinent purpose toward my treatment, healing and recovery, not just a single surgeon. I'm sure you get my point.

I'll be right back after this special news report!

Folks, let me break in here to tell you about God. His hand was on me the whole time. I was blessed to have had prayer warriors from around the world, touching in faith and believing with me. I can't begin to tell you how much that meant to me. I went into the hospital for brain surgery on Monday and was back home on Friday.

However, they wouldn't discharge me without a certain prescription. We were told, that once they disconnected the IV, and the intravenous medication that was already in my system, wore off, the pain would be unbearable. So, I sat around waiting for them to track down the doctor who could write the prescription.

I don't know what that was all about. It's been over a year now, and I haven't needed that medication yet. In fact, I don't even know where it is. I haven't felt even the slightest bit of pain, from the time I waked into the hospital to have the surgery, to now. What a wonderful God we serve. Somebody, shout "**Hallelujah!**"

We now return you to our regularly scheduled program...

It takes All of the Church for All of the Cure—

Just as with a holistic medical center, the whole church should be a spiritually holistic environment where hurting people, as well as the unsaved, can come to find forgiveness, hope and healing. No church can effectively operate around a solitary individual. The entire church needs to be a part of the restorative process. It cannot be the pastor working alone.

The trained specialists should consist of the ushers, the deacons, the Sunday school teachers, the choir members, the musicians, the associate ministers, the members of the congregation, and so on. Everyone has a specific role in the ministry of the church.

Pastor, you should learn how to determine where your members fit into the inner-healing process of others. Then, make sure that those members receive qualified training to ensure that they are the absolute best at what they do.

Every believer, even the new ones, should be able to share a word of hope and encouragement. Or, at least one verse of scripture from the Bible. For me, it was the scripture that led to my salvation, Romans 10:9.

"If you confess with your mouth the Lord Jesus and believe in your heart that God has raised Him from the dead, you will be saved."

Romans 10:9 (NKJV)

Because, I was able to passionately share this one verse from the Bible with hundreds of individuals, many became born-again believers. A great number of those who accepted Christ into their hearts, were members of my own family. It just goes to show, that for your members who have lived through bad occurrences of abuse, the mere telling of their stories of survival may help others find hope too.

At the very least, they should be able to offer a blind Bartimaeus testimony. When questioned about Jesus, this (once) blind man did not know very much about Jesus at that time. However, what he did know was, until Jesus came along and touched him, he had lived his life in visual darkness… and now, he can see. So, his personal testimony was what he talked about.

"He answered, "Whether he's a sinner or not I don't know. One thing I do know: I was blind, now I see."

St. John 9:25 (NET)

God Uses Some of the Most Unlikely People—

You might be surprised to discover that God uses some of the most unlikely people in the church to bless us, and to lift us up in Christ. For me, it was the janitor. When I first gave my heart to the Lord, my greatest source of inspiration was Brother Frank Evans, the janitor at my home church. In fact, even after I became a minister, Frank Evans continued to play a major role in my walk with Christ.

Because, I was blessed to live only one city block away from the church, I spent many hours there on an almost daily basis. Those hours were spent learning the Christian life from Brother Evans. Although, this was his job, not just his church, he never turned me away. And he always completed his job in an immaculate way. Many times I would help him with his work, just so I could spend time learning from him.

> Today's Church has become one big social club where people go for social interaction and exchange.

I could never repay Frank Evans for what he has meant to me, from my spiritual infancy, all the way through my development and enrichment in Christ. Nor could I repay him for the much needed and welcomed encouragement he provided.

Personally, I have traveled the world for the Lord, Frank Evans has not. However, the strength that he instilled in me over the many years has found its mark in countries throughout Asia, Europe, Africa, South and Central America, etc. I have been truly blessed to have had the right people in my life, at the right time.

It doesn't matter what a member's position is in the church. As in the case of Brother Evans, your members don't have to be church leaders to be used by God. He can use anyone. They don't have to hold a prominent position in the local or jurisdictional church if you can just teach them to make themselves available to God. Within the body of Christ, every position is prominent.

THE CHURCH MUST LEARN
TO PROMOTE CURE, OVER DISEASE

Seeing as how pulpit abuse and spiritual abuse are products of the church, it would be reasonable to think that the solution to this problem would also be found within the church. Unfortunately, the church of today is a big social club. It is where church people go for social interaction, or where singles go to meet other singles.

It's where church folk go to be entertained by great singing and mountaintop preaching.

Some church people even go to church to invest or gamble their hard earned money, under the disguise of sowing seeds, with the expectation of getting greater financial or material returns than what was actually invested or gambled (or supposedly sowed). Many of them do the same thing at the casino.

It's also, where radicals meet up to band together in the fight for social causes. Nearly everyone has his or her own agenda or reason for going to church.

Most People Go to Church for All the Wrong Reasons—

It's too bad, but most people do not go to church for reasons that God considers most important. They don't go to church with the expectation of helping some dejected soul find their way home. They don't go to church fasted up and ready for a battle with demons and devils over lost souls. They certainly don't go to church prepared to pray the preacher through, so God can pour out His anointing during the service.

They don't even go to church looking for a supernatural breakthrough from God. They go for carnal reasons, and when our reasons are carnal, our results will be carnal.

Sincere pastors should make sure that they themselves are not just great preachers. They should also make sure that they are, in particular, trained and qualified to deal with victims of church abuse. It is equally important that the members of the church, who assist in the restoration process of hurting people, are trained and qualified to deal with these special needs casualties of spiritual cruelty. It is not enough to be a good Sunday school teacher.

Training Should Be Ongoing—

The church should have an ongoing, never-ending training program. Everyone who comes in contact with visitors and new members should be trained, or at the very least, they should be in the process of being trained. The training should encompass how to greet and meet new people from the moment they walk through the door, to helping them reach a place of steadfastness in Christ. They should also have a separate training program for dealing exclusively with handling victims of spiritual or church abuse.

CHURCH ABUSE VICTIMS ARE NON-TRUSTING

If visitors enjoy your main worship service, they may want to participate in some of your other church services or meetings. Encourage their involvement in healthy functions around the church. Make them feel at home by including them in your conversations and discussions. Do not talk over their heads by using a lot of church jargon or terms that are unfamiliar to them. Try hard to avoid lengthy dialogue about people or things that may be known to the church, but not to your visitors. Learn how to have discussions that will not make your visitors feel out of place.

When your members come together as a prayer group or Bible study group, some visitors or new members may wish to talk about their experiences with abuse, others will shut completely down if the subject leans in that direction. Do not make them uncomfortable by pushing too hard.

Be sensitive to their lead. Additionally, if they do feel comfortable enough to share their experiences, you must not make them feel as though you are judging them. Allow them to share their thoughts. Abused people usually have a lot of pinned up feelings inside.

Let Them Tell Their Stories—

They are dealing with a roller coaster of emotions. Past and present victims of church abuse do not know whether to feel disloyal or violated and betrayed. They are straddling the fence between angry and guilty. They are not sure if they should be afraid or enraged.

When they get an opportunity to tell their story in a healthy private or group setting, they discover that disloyalty, fear and guilt are not options. They must realize that they did nothing deserving of the abuse they lived through. They must be made to see and understand that they are not traitors, but victims. This helps them to find the presence of mind and the freedom to deal with the reality of what has happened to them, rather than to deny it.

When in a group discussion, if you discern that they do want to open themselves up to the group, about their past mistreatment, let them freely speak. Do not interrupt or talk over them. Do not compete with them for the floor. Sit back and listen as they speak.

Show empathy. Acknowledge from time to time that you clearly heard what they have just said, but let them get it out. This may be their only opportunity to unload. You can acknowledge by simply nodding your head, as an indication that you are listening. You may periodically, echo their words. Sometimes, when the person who is baring their soul hears you repeat their own words, they feel as though you are paying attention, and that you really are interested in what they're saying.

Some years ago, I had just concluded ministering to the Chicago White Sox baseball team, when a very renowned member of the team approached me. Out of respect for his privacy, I will not mention his name, but most baseball fans would know him. He wanted to talk about domestic issues in his home. Without interruption, I listened.

When the time was right, I addressed his concerns. He was happy that I listened and allowed him to unload what had been on his mind and heart for a long time. Then, he asked if I would speak with him and his wife together, to help bring about healing in their marriage.

This experience has repeated itself time after time. The wounded want your help, but they have a need to tell their stories. Sometimes, telling the story is all that is needed to bring about healing. I read a "Psychology Today" article, written by Dr. Lissa Rankin, OB/GYN, author and founder of Owning Pink Center, a women's health practice in Mill Valley, California.

According to Dr. Rankin, telling your story, while being witnessed through the loving attention of others who care, may be the most powerful medicine on earth. She says, telling your story causes you to turn off your body's toxic stress responses and it causes you to turn on relaxation responses that release healing hormones.

They are Just Learning to Trust Again—

If you create the right environment for broken people to speak up, you will quickly discover that it isn't just your new members and visitors who need to be healed of their past. In most churches, there are people throughout the congregation who are still suffering from inner hurts and wounds sustained at some point in their former church history. This kind of atmosphere also makes it easier for members to talk about different or other types of painful experiences in their past or present.

It doesn't matter if it's spousal or elder abuse, at home or in the church. Nor does it matter if it's harassment in the workplace or at school, the ice is broken for anyone to pour out his or her heart.

People are not always looking for a response from you the listener. They just want to get it out there. They need to express themselves without feeling condemned, ridiculed, unaccepted or rushed. They may have been carrying a heavy burden for a long time, and they want to unload somewhere. God may have picked you and your group for such a time as this.

Respect and Protect Their Confidentiality—

These stories should not be talked about with other members of the church, or people outside the church. These cell group members should be trained to protect the confidentiality of the person sharing their life's experience.

On the other hand, if previous abuse victims, desire and feel comfortable enough to speak with you in confidence, they need your genuine assurance that it is okay for them to speak freely. As, they trust and reveal to you secretively, God is holding you particularly accountable for protecting that individual's confidentiality.

If you do not believe you can protect their privacy, there is no need for you to feel bad about it, just tell them so. Then, refer them to someone who can. You must understand; these are wounded people, who are just learning to trust again.

213

Counseling the Person Whom You've Hurt?—

Pastor, I realize (unfortunately) that it isn't out of the realm possibility that you may have played a part in someone having been hurt or abused. If this is the case, I hope and pray that this is now indeed a part of your past, not your present life. We all have a past, even men and women of the cloth.

Nevertheless, you have repented for your wrongful deeds and have accepted God's cleansing for your sins and His delivering power from the unclean forces that led you to commit your transgressions and iniquities. It is a wonderful thing that you are now prepared to meet the Lord when that time comes. However, there may still be a hurting victim out there who must be treated and healed in this present life.

Because you (at least in part) caused the hurt, it is just natural that you would want to help bring about healing for that person. It isn't unusual that a genuinely repentant person would want to fix the problem he or she created. Most people would give anything for the opportunity to right a huge wrong. What a wonderful second chance at making the right choice this could be.

You may feel that you owe it to God, and you owe it to the wounded person. Especially, since you pulled the trigger that caused the wound. While they may need an abundance of emotional and spiritual counseling, I strongly advise against you being the one to take on that role.

Pastors who are trained counselors face many challenges and special issues when working with people who have suffered moral mistreatment, or spiritual neglect. Like most people, counselors become upset or angry when they hear about vulnerable persons being hurt or being taken advantage of. But, as a counselor it is even worse when the person hurting, was actually hurt by you.

Some pastors or Christian counselors may find themselves in a professional situation where they may have to confront their own acts of abuse and neglect against another individual. It isn't only the victim who has been devastated, but the perpetrator as well. Even though the pastor has repented and moved on in God, he will still have to deal with the impact that his wrongs have had on his own life. And, I can tell you, from personal experience, that even pastors must suffer the harsh reality of reaping what they have sown. No one is above the Word of God.

In general, some survivors of abuse may already pose many relational challenges to the counselor; but especially if the abuse was of a sexual nature. These former victims are often mistrustful, while at the same time needing a trustworthy relationship. Because church abuse reflects a fundamental violation of trust, it is doubtful that the pastor who created the problem, will be able to establish the deep level of trust needed to bring about complete spiritual and emotional healing.

On the other hand, the client's history of having been hurt by the counselor who is now seeking to help them, in certain rare situations, could very well present a unique opportunity for healing. All the same, I would still advise against it.

"By this everyone will know that you are My disciples, if you have love and unselfish concern for one another."

St. John 13:35 (AMP)

Chapter Fourteen

A WORD TO THE SINCERE MEMBER

The member's role in reaching out to spiritually wounded people

נ

This chapter isn't to the pastor. It's to his members. It isn't about the church reaching out into a spiritually deprived community. It's about the church reaching inwardly to spiritually abused victims in the church. Encountering former victims of pulpit abuse isn't nearly as complex as you might think. They're actually all around us. Hurting people come in many forms. They come as visitors, new members, existing members, charter members, church leaders, preachers, teachers… even pastors.

This is why earnest believers are so important to the church's growth and development. Sincere members can reach where the pastor cannot always reach. They can see what the pastor cannot always see. Every member is crucial to the church, and to the progress of the church.

When visitors show up at your services, please try to understand, this visit isn't always by coincidence.

It's like being in a hospital, surrounded by ailing patients. You may not be able to perform open-heart surgery, or repair a severed leg, and no one expects you to. However, what you can do is wipe away a tear, or speak an encouraging word or two to a suffering patient.

"Do not neglect to show hospitality to strangers, for thereby some have entertained angels unawares."

Hebrews 13:2 (RSV)

Some of what I say here may be offensive to some readers. However, I believe if you can receive these words with an open heart, you may in fact benefit from them. Most people who have never been to church before, have a false sense of what to expect.

Often, they think church people are very different from themselves. What people who have never been to church expect to find in the church are caring, loving and kind people. They think of church people as a cohesive and unselfish group of individuals, willing to stop their own world to help anyone in trouble or in need.

When they think of what the church must be like, they think of the "Good Samaritan" and they imagine someone willing to give his last dime to help a stranger, if need be.

"But a Samaritan who was traveling came to where the injured man was, and when he saw him, he felt compassion for him. He went up to him and bandaged his wounds, pouring oil and wine on them. Then he put him on his own animal, brought him to an inn, and took care of him. The next day he took out two silver coins and gave them to the innkeeper, saying, 'Take care of him,

and whatever else you spend, I will repay you when I come back.

St. Luke 10:33-35 (NET)

So far, I'm not seeing anything in the expectations of the unchurched individual that Jesus isn't expecting from all members of the body of Christ. Unfortunately, what they consistently find is totally opposite of their expectations. When they visit, they often find a group of people who are selfish, moody, temperamental, judgmental, angry and disagreeable. This is why sincere believers have their work cut out.

OUR STUDY ON "FIRST TIME" VISITORS

During the research phase of Thug Preachers, with help of my staff, I conducted several church studies. Because of our need to assess the level of compassion and kindheartedness that exists in U.S. churches, two things were considered. First, we sat down and brainstormed among ourselves, as to what our own experiences have been when visiting a church for the first time, over a specific number of years. We also wanted to be sure that we made the distinction between American churches and churches outside the United States.

Next, we discussed what we could remember regarding what we have observed, as it relates to what we have witnessed other new visitors run into, whether positive or negative. Then, we decided to conduct our own painstaking experiment to understand and appreciate the dilemma of first time visitors to a church.

The study involved us visiting various churches around the United States. To appreciate what we experienced, you should know that our children were also very much affected throughout this research period.

During this "first time" visitors study, we were able to obtain enough research data to draw a definite conclusion. In this chapter, I share a few examples of what we experienced. The stories told may be somewhat lengthy, but we wanted you to feel exactly what we felt as first time visitors to these houses of worship.

THE VISITOR'S FIRST EXPOSURE TO YOUR CHURCH

When visitors attend your services, you need to understand that it isn't always by coincidence. There are times when God has led them directly to your ministry. They may not even know it's by divine order. You "MUST" meet their expectations, from their first exposure to your church, all the way through their final experience.

Other than in the case where a member invited them, the ushers are usually the visitor's first contact or encounter with your church. They are much more important to the church than people realize. It is imperative that all ushers be trained in more than locating seats and delivering notes to the pulpit.

Usher or Gatekeeper?—

Your ushers should be trained to understand that many visitors are very delicate. Some ushers see themselves in a narrow position of power, and they like that. They can sometimes be very tough to deal with, even downright rude. Unfortunately, the tough guy act doesn't always work with spiritually fragile individuals.

Ushers need to be proficient, but flexible. If a visitor is more comfortable sitting next to the aisle, don't force him to sit in the center of the pew when there are available seats next to an aisle. No visitor should be forced to leave the service over seating. I have seen ushers drive people away from the church by being inflexible. It's the usher's domain and she's not bending her rules for anyone, or for any reason.

Some years ago, my family and I decided to visit a prominent church in Northwest Indiana. I don't know if it can be considered a mega-church, but it was pretty close. This was our first time visiting the church. Since service had not yet begun, there were hundreds of empty seats all over the auditorium.

As we were walking down the aisle toward a cluster of vacant rows near the front, an obviously frustrated usher rushed up to us. In a huff, she told us that we could not sit up front with a baby. We advised her that we had never had problems before with any of our children in church, but she wasn't having it.

So my wife said, "Where would you like for us to sit?" Without responding, the usher turned toward the rear of the sanctuary and started walking. We assumed she wanted us to follow. She led us to the back row, behind obstructions. We suggested to her that there were plenty of the empty seats between the front and back rows. Pointing to the last row, she told that if we wanted seats, this is where would have to sit with a baby. Now, keep in mind, although we were trying to remain pleasant toward her, she was still angry with us. We never really understood why.

Ready for battle, the usher stood there staring at us, as if we had just kicked over their communion table. Impatiently, she said "So, what are you going to do?" Since church building involves encouraging visitors to feel at home in the services, I wondered what she would do if a visiting family of five potential church members considered leaving to go to another church.

So, I said to my wife, "Why don't we just go somewhere else?" The usher responded with, "That's your prerogative!" We wished her a nice day and headed out to the lobby. A woman in the lobby who had warmly greeted us as we entered the building just minutes earlier, asked us why we were leaving. Once we explained what had just happened, she replied, "Oh, yeah. That is the rule."

As we were walking down the sidewalk toward the parking lot, the same woman from the church lobby approached us again. This time, she suggested that if we put our baby in the church's nursery, we might be able to get better seating. We thought that was an odd suggestion, since the baby was only six weeks old. To us, that wasn't a viable option.

Now, in fairness to the pastor of this church, I don't think he knew about our unpleasant experience. Initially, we thought perhaps, people with babies were penalized over those without. However, in talking with members of this church, we've discovered that this particular church seems to set rules that take precedence over common courtesy and Kingdom Building.

We also learned that had we entered the sanctuary through a different door, we would have not encountered this particular usher, and our experience might have been much different. We were told, because of her unpleasant disposition, many of the members avoid entering the sanctuary through her door.

Most, already troubled visitors would not subject themselves to such "gatekeeper" treatment, and they shouldn't have to. For crying out loud... it's a church! It's not a private, members only country club! This kind of tactlessness is a poor example of what the church is supposed to represent. It can seriously damage people who were already bruised upon arrival. This anti–Biblical treatment may cause fragile victims of pulpit and church abuse to give up on the church; or even on God.

Let me give you an example. If you ever suffered a serious heart attack, paramedics will probably be summoned to your aid. When the ambulance arrives, paramedics will immediately put their life saving skills into action, and those skills continue all the way to the ER. As you pull into the ER ambulance entrance, a team of trained medical professionals meets the arriving ambulance.

With only the attending paramedic speaking and explaining his findings, he hands you off to the ER physician. While yet in motion, the doctor asks a few more questions of the paramedic, while taking over the patient. Fortunately, with all the hospital's resources working on your behalf... you survive to full recovery.

Let me ask you, when do you suppose the cure began? Some would say, from the moment you arrived at the hospital. That's a good answer, but a wrong one. If you think it began when the paramedics arrived, that would be another wrong answer.

The truth is, the healing began from the moment the trained 911 emergency operator answered the call. From there, trained paramedics were dispatched. Through God's grace, they kept you alive long enough for you to reach the hospital, where doctors and other hospital workers took over. Usually, the cure begins with the first responder. Here, it was the 911 dispatcher who responded first.

The whole church should be taught to provide a loving and caring atmosphere for the spiritual, emotional and mental treatment of its arriving victims. Often, the first responder is an usher.

The ushers should welcoming to your guests. They must be trained to handle visitors delicately, and to keep them holding on long enough to be handed off to the pastor or some other skilled personnel within the ministry.

This is crucial if the healing process is to take place. In critical situations, we must get it right the first time. We aren't guaranteed a second opportunity. There is no margin for error. There is no place in the church of Jesus Christ for harsh gatekeepers who block doors and turn away distraught sufferers.

AMERICAN CHURCHES ONLY CLAIM TO BE FRIENDLY

Once the visitor gets past the usher, another problem exists. American churches "claim" to be friendly. In reality, most of them are friendly to one another, but unfriendly to visitors. Some churches have the nerve to call themselves, "The friendly church where everyone is a friend, and no one is a stranger!" Mannn! What a bunch of garbage!

What thousands of first time visitors experienced last Sunday was, they arrived as a stranger, they sat though the service as a stranger, and when they left… they left as a stranger. Not a soul approached them. This is exactly what happened last Sunday; and it happens all the time.

New Members Wanted…"By Invitation Only!"—

There was something else that our study uncovered that we didn't expect. You don't have to be a first time visitor to get the cold shoulder in church. My family and I visited and financially contributed to an alleged "friendly" church for two years, and during that entire time, less than a half dozen people bothered to speak to us. Of the ones who did speak to us, we usually started the dialogue.

The pastor only spoke to us two times. The first time was after two years, and only because we approached him to introduce ourselves. At that time, what he did say to us, however, was he had noticed that we were regularly attending the church. The second time was a casual greeting as we were passing each other at church.

That's just how some pastors are. If you're not making a big deal over them, you don't really matter to them. This is why it is so important that the members pick up the slack. Visitors should not have to feel like a fifth wheel. If the pastor gets around to meeting guests of the church, that's fine. If he does not, and you're doing what God requires of you, your guests probably won't notice.

What were able to observe, was when a visitor would come as the guest of an established member of the church they were well received by the membership. You know, kind of like an organization or network that accepts new members at the invitation of an established member only.

My impression is, you would not be able to just drop in at one of their church services or meetings and expect to be part of the warm fellowship crowd. It's almost as if, to be accepted you would need to have been invited and endorsed by one of the members. The church should be open to all people, and all people should all feel welcomed.

> *"Opening his mouth, Peter said: "I most certainly understand now that God is not one to show partiality..."*
>
> Acts 10:34 (NASB)

Guess Who's Coming to Dinner?—

A few years ago, my family and I attended a special church event. At the event, they announced that there was a fellowship dinner right after service, "and everyone is welcomed!"

We thought this might be an opportunity to meet some of the members. As we walked into the dining hall of the church, we passed within six feet of the pastor, who was sitting at a table laughing and joking with the members as they entered the room. Upon seeing my family, he greeted us with a simple, "Hello." We returned the greeting.

My family took a table in the dining hall. With all the fun going on around us, we thought surely we would be meeting new people, and our kids could have fun with kids from the church. We were there for two hours watching the excitement, but other than the pastor's casual hello, and the people serving up the food as we walked by with our plates, no one else even said hello.

How does this happen? How can a whole family sit in the middle of a "CHURCH" fellowship dinner and go unnoticed by ALL the members of the church, while they are busy enjoying the fellowship of one another? And with the pastor sitting right among them!

> If you can't figure out how to take care of God's business first, "over" church business... then you need to close your doors!

You might think to yourself, "Well, Pastor Jackson, why didn't you speak to them first?" We did, and any reply they gave was short and direct. Then, they returned to their merriment. Like many others, these people call themselves "the friendly church." Who cares about how friendly you are, if you're only friendly to one another? If only the church would grow up and demonstrate Jesus Christ in more than just great singing and mountaintop preaching.

Before they made the announcement that they were having a fellowship dinner, we had already planned on going out for dinner after service. Then, they announced that the fellowship was for everyone. Now, I "reaaaally" wanted to stay! I wanted to observe how they would interact with their visitors in a fellowship setting. I was interested in seeing just how far they would carry their unfriendliness toward non-members.

Now, most wise and amiable pastors would not have continued to clown around with their members, while visitors are left alone; especially in a "fellowship" gathering. They might have engaged their guests in conversation.

Perhaps, they would have tried to get to know us, or at least something about us. Like, "Hi, I'm Pastor John Doe, and you are...?" It also makes sense to know if the guests live nearby, "Wow! It was great having you in our service today. Do you live in the community?" It's always good to know how people found out about you, "How did you find out about our church?" Since, your church operates a fun Children's Ministry and an excellent private Christian school, "How old are the kids? And what school do they attend?"

225

A cordial pastor might have talked about regular services and upcoming events at the church. Words like, "I would like to personally invite you to be my guest..." goes a long way when it comes from the pastor. In a church where friendliness is natural, it would have been unlikely that we would have been ignored for so long.

In cases, where the pastor instills hospitality into the hearts and minds of the membership, the pastor could have given some of them a signal and they would have gotten the message that we have guests in the room who we should be welcoming to our church.

By the way, let me say one last thing about this. When you serve up a church dinner with hot dogs, chicken wings, chili and cake as your menu, don't be stingy with your guests. My wife asked for two pieces of the wings; one piece for her and the other for me. A server, very abrasively said to her, "You can only get one chicken wing! If your husband wants one, he'll have to come get it himself." Moments later, a group of young people sat down at the table next to us with their plates piled high with the same wings that their guests could only get one of.

That's backward thinking. The members of the church go out of their way to please other members, but they act as though visiting individuals or families don't matter. Seemingly, new people have to earn the right to receive kind treatment from the church. It doesn't look or feel good to visitors, to be treated like beggars. As a matter of fact, it can be embarrassing to a person who is already feeling uncomfortable as a visitor. That's only because we treat them like outsiders.

We like to say, "We're in the ministry." Well, that means we're in the "people business!" Or, in the business of reaching souls for Jesus Christ. Sometimes pastors and church leaders are too busy with church business to take care of God's business. Anytime you're too busy for God... "you're too busy!" If you can't figure out how to take care of God's business, over the business of your church, or your choir, or your youth ministry, or your pastor's aid committee, or whatever... then you need to close your doors!

The Friendly Church Where No One is a Stranger!—
One Sunday morning, I decided to visit a very popular church alone. Although, the pastor and I knew each other at the personal level, I had never been to his church. Because, I had spent so many years on the radio, some of his members might have recognized my voice, but I don't think anyone there knew me on sight. So, I walked into the sanctuary and sat at the back of the room.

About a half hour into the service, I realized the pastor was out of town on this particular day. A guest minister had been invited to bring the morning message. While sitting in the pew observing everything, they had the appearance of a very friendly church. They said all the right things, and they did all the right things.

I enjoyed the service, the choir, the guest minister's sermon and everyone who participated in the service. What was interesting was, at the conclusion of the service, I stood around the sanctuary for about ten minutes and no one greeted me. There may have been a nod or two, but that was about it.

Next, I walked out to the lobby and stood there for about ten minutes. The members were very enthusiastic with each other, but no one said a word to me. I began thinking, there might be a hurting visitor here who needs to feel God's love. This was not a good sign.

I wondered if I could get them to reach out to an unfamiliar visitor if I gave them a gentle nudge. So, I approached some of the members who were standing in groups. As I gave a friendly hello to them, most were kind enough to return the greeting, but nothing more. Finally, I walked outside. It was a beautiful day. Some of them seemed to enjoy the sunshine, but still no one came near me to welcome me to their church or service: not even a church leader.

Because I was visiting alone, I didn't have anyone to chat with. It was a very uncomfortable feeling for me. I stood around the church for at least half an hour. I felt invisible. I thought to myself, this is how a solitary visitor must feel at an unfriendly (to visitors) church.

I wondered, what might have happened had I actually come to this church with an expectation of meeting a group of believers who could point me to Jesus Christ. Would things have been any different? I doubt it.

The next day, I spoke by phone with the pastor of that church. I don't remember if he called me or, if I called him. I told him that I had stopped by his church while he was away. He responded, "You did? No one told me you were there!" That was when I shared with him what it was like to attend his church as a first time visitor. He was ashamed. He thanked me for telling him of my experience and assured me he would report to the church what my visit was like.

A Friendly Church Retains Its Visitors—

Most of the churches in the U.S. that build in part, from guest visitation, do so because the visitors enjoy or admire their pastor, not because of friendly members. If you notice, many of your repeat guests will leave right after the message or at the close of the service. They have given up on expecting interaction with the members.

Christian churches in the U.S. ought to take pointers on friendliness from some of the Christian churches in other parts of the world. I'm not saying churches abroad or in the other countries are exempt from pulpit thug issues. They have their hard-core thug preachers just as we do. The point is, if churches in the continental U.S. were only half as welcoming as many of the Christian churches in other nations, they would have no trouble building up their ministries.

Most American churches seem to acknowledge their first time guests as a part of their regular order of service. It's even printed in their church bulletin or program. They usually have a planned spot in the service where the pastor or a designated greeter will stand to acknowledge the presence of their first-time visitors. Then on cue, the members will applaud their guests. Some members may even walk around to greet and shake hands with the guests (as if they really cared) during this deliberate stop set in the service.

The visitor makes the mistake of thinking these people are happy to see her. However, as the service ends, the friendliness seems to end too; when it matters the most. This is why millions of people who visit churches in the United States each year, do not return. For many, this was their first (and possibly last) time attending church.

How would you feel if you went to the hospital for help, and the entire staff of medical professionals ignored you? Suppose you were a patient in a hospital, and you could hear the staff talking loud and laughing together all night long, as you lie vulnerably there in need of their help.

> **The church has become a big social club, where church people go for social interaction and exchange.**

Can you imagine going to a hospital with the anticipation of receiving healing, and this is what you get? Who would come back to this hospital? Clearly, some of the staff members seem to have so much fun interacting with one another that they are less sensitive to the fact that suffering people have come to them for help.

The church has become a big social club, where church people go for social interaction and exchange. Like these healthcare workers, church people have been having so much fun, for so long, until most of them have forgotten that everyone isn't there for the fun.

Some people have come to you because they are suffering. They come expecting help. We cannot allow ourselves to get so caught up in the social aspects of the church that we forget what the passion and crucifixion of Jesus Christ represent to spiritually alienated and depressed people.

This is what hundreds of thousands, to millions of broken-hearted visitors all across America experience in our churches each Sunday. They check themselves into your church for an hour or two. They place themselves under the care of you and your pastor for treatment. What do they get in return? They get ignored by everyone from the pulpit to the back pew. That's not what God wants for them.

"The Lord is close to those whose hearts have been broken. He saves those whose spirits have been crushed."

Psalm 34:18 (NIRV)

No wonder their hearts are broken and their spirits are crushed. Your (so-called) "friendly" church has failed to provide the help or healing that they so desperately needed. Why should they come back? Would you?

Time and again, I have heard pastors and church leaders give the same old tired excuse for why people who visit their churches, don't come back. Preachers have the audacity to stand and proudly shout from the pulpit, "We have who God wants us to have in our church. If God wanted this church full... *He would fill it!*" Now, that's just pathetic. What a sorry excuse for not caring enough, or for being unwilling to work hard enough to reach out to, and retain your visitors. If you think God doesn't want His precious church filled, you must have missed St. Luke 14:23.

"And the lord said unto the servant, go out into the highways and hedges, and compel them to come in, that my house may be filled."

St. Luke 14:23 (KJV)

In this passage, God is telling the church to reach both urban and rural regions of the world, and to constrain people to come into the body of Christ, so His house will be filled. In the fulfillment of the Great Commission, it is just expected, that if you're filling the church, you are leading the people to the Lord too. This is what God's objective is really all about.

For those unsaved or unchurched people who visit your church, your job is to take the time to help lead them into the born-again experience. In contrast, as it relates, to existing believers in the body of Jesus Christ, who are also previous abuse victims, God could have sent them to any one of hundreds of churches in your area, but He chose to send them to your church. So, stop goofing off and take care of the Lord's business!

Now, God understands that you cannot always identify a hurting or broken victim on sight. Sometimes, they look just like any other visitor of your church. So, He has a foolproof remedy for this set of circumstances. His remedy is, when first time guests show up at your church, you receive everybody with the utmost Christian hospitality, courtesy and consideration. Treat them all the same way you would want to be treated and received. Who knows? You might just be receiving an angel.

"Do not neglect to show hospitality to strangers, for thereby some have entertained angels unawares. Remember those who are in prison, as though in prison with them; and those who are ill-treated, since you also are in the body."

Hebrews 13:2-3 (RSV)

Be extra kind to every visitor and new member. After all, we are supposed to be examples of Christ. No mature Christian believer should ever put church socializing over the real purpose behind the Lord's ministry. Remember these words... if you cause further hurt to God's spiritually wounded children, He will hold you accountable for your lack of Christian compassion and your insensitivity. The church needs to grow up and understand what God's true intent for His church is.

You Have a Mission Field at Your Church Door

Many churches are raising tons of money so they can go out somewhere on a foreign mission trip. Why concern yourself with foreign missions at this point in time? Right now, I'm speaking straightforwardly to some reader.

How are you going to evangelize the world outside your four walls, if you can't even hold on to the hungry and thirsty souls that God brings to your front door? Next, He drags them through the door and down the aisle. Then, He plops them down into your pew, and you still aren't reaching out to them. Yet, you think God is calling you to the foreign mission field? For what?

Let me guess. You want to do foreign missions work in Jamaica, Belize, Hawaii, the Bahamas or the U.S. Virgin Islands, huh? Who are you kidding? I've been on the foreign mission field. I know what it's like. It's not a walk along the beach under a moonlit sky.

Unless, you have a strong team of workers laboring with you, it can involve hard physical labor. It can be tough, demanding and draining work. It can affect you, physically, emotionally and spiritually. But, if you can't reach out to the people who visit your church, you have no business whatsoever on the mission field.

231

By the way, in case if you weren't paying attention, Hawaii and the U.S. Virgin Islands aren't foreign territories.

If you want to go to Honolulu, Hawaii that's fine. Take your family on a vacation to Hawaii, but don't call it a mission trip. Usually when I see pictures from mission trips to nations like Belize or Jamaica, I am amazed at the amount of touring and sightseeing that goes on.

> An unfriendly church is as worthless as a swimming pool full of empty peanut shells. They serve no useful purpose.

Belize is a great place for tourists to visit, but don't call it mission field; and yourself a missionary. However, I suppose if you look hard enough, you can find a disenfranchised populous in any nation, especially the United States. But, you don't need to worry about going out on foreign mission fields until you've done right by the mission field coming through the front door of your church.

An Unfriendly Church is a Worthless Church—

Also, I want to be clear on something. A packed church is not necessarily an indication of a friendly church; neither is it an indication of the presence of the Lord. Your friendliness meter is not activated by how many people are in your congregation, but by how many of your visitors are attended to. Often, even the pastors and the associate ministers are not friendly to the visitors of their church.

These days, so many pastors are struggling with the fame that goes along with having a popular or very prominent church. In the past, we were honored that God trusted us to reach out to the lost on His behalf. Now, the congregation and pastors alike give the impression, that it's the visitor who should feel honored to walk through their prestigious doors.

It doesn't matter how many services you have on Sunday, or how packed your services are, to spiritually aching people, an unfriendly church is as worthless as a swimming pool full of empty peanut shells. They take up a whole lot of space, but they serve no useful purpose.

A Standing Room Only Crowd—

My family and I were visiting a church in sunny Arizona, several years ago. This was the Sunday morning just before Christmas. My wife had originally been invited to the church by a recent acquaintance of hers. We thought we were early enough for good seating, but apparently the service began earlier than we expected. Upon our arrival, nearly every seat was either already occupied, or being held by a member of the church. It seems, they were presenting a special holiday service. As far as I could tell, the church's membership had come out in full force for this special pre-Christmas celebration.

We spotted two seats down near the front of the room. So, I asked my wife and children to take those seats. We had our newborn baby and two older kids with us. Of course, my wife held the baby in her arms, while my teenager and pre-teenager shared the second seat.

Seemingly, each empty seat that I walked toward was being held for someone. As a visitor, I felt uncomfortable roaming the aisles during the service in search of a vacant seat, only to be told that it was already taken. To be honest, I thought once one of the ushers saw a visitor standing, they would surely seat me. After all, isn't that what the ushers do? And, there were certainly plenty of them.

Unfortunately, they looked at me, but none of them offered to locate a seat for me. So, I placed myself in clear view of the ushers at the rear of the sanctuary, hoping they would spot me standing there as an eyesore to their decor, and decide to find me a seat.

While standing there, I watched as an array of singers performed. Next, came the praise dancers. By now, it had already become apparent, that me and that back wall were going to be spending a very long time together. After the dancers came more singers.

It was quite some time before the pastor took his place at the pulpit podium. When he finally stood to speak, he seemed to look right at me standing there against that wall. This was not a mega-church. It would have been hard to miss my 6' 3" and 250 pound statue. I was happy when he looked at me. I was naïve enough to think he was going to ask someone to find a seat for a guest. That was probably just wishful thinking on my part, but as the old saying goes, "Like sheep... like shepherd." Which means, the sheep are usually a reflection of their shepherd.

This was the embodiment of poor hospitality. It didn't have to be a problem at all. Any member of that church could have resolved this issue in less than two minutes. Sadly, when your church is not naturally kind to outsiders, this is a prime example of what can happen. I promise, by the end of this chapter, I'll share with you several things that could have been done to easily fix this problem.

As the service continued, the pastor spent a good amount of time wishing the congregation a Merry Christmas. Periodically, he would glance back at me standing there, but that was all. They had a packed house that day. The congregation seemed very happy. After all, it was Christmas time. They were having a blast. There were happily fellowshipping with each other, and exchanging holiday greetings, but other than the woman who had invited us, no one bothered to speak to us.

Even the person who invited us, didn't bother to introduce us to anyone, nor did she spend any time with us. Just a quick and generic greeting and she was on her way to fellowship with the other members. Oh, wait!... There was one other person who did speak to my wife. This was the woman who gives out the visitor cards. My wife made a mistake while filling in our card, and asked for another one. That didn't go over too well. For some reason unknown to us, this woman seemed very upset with my wife for asking for a new card. Believe it or not, like so many others, they also call themselves "The friendly church, where everyone is a friend and no one is a stranger."

Before you rush to judge this church or any of the churches mentioned in this chapter, I suggest that you spend a few weeks observing how visitors are treated at your church. You just might be surprised. Most of the churches having this problem, don't realize it. That's because, very few church people even notice their visitors after the service. The members are having such a great time with their friends until they think everybody is having a great time.

234

Now, in all fairness to churches and pastors around the United States, our experience at this particular church is not typical of what we encounter at most of the churches we visited. Actually, when I think about it, I've never experienced such poor hospitality at any church, anywhere in the world.

While it shouldn't matter, as a seasoned minister, most established pastors usually recognize me and acknowledge my presence right away. So, their members seem to handle my family and me a little more gingerly than what we experienced at this Christmas service. However, my clergy status should be a non-issue.

I'm not as concerned about how churches treat me, as I am with how they treat people who come to them for help. For some broken individual, this could have been the last straw before walking away from the church completely. We don't want to risk that happening.

No First Time Visitor Should Ever Be Left Alone

When we visit churches around the country, we usually make it a point to observe who the visitors are when they raise their hands during the traditional visitors' acknowledgment portion of the service. Later, if we see any of these visitors standing unattended for long periods, it has become commonplace for us to walk up to them to introduce ourselves to them.

We believe they should feel noticed and important enough to matter. They matter to us and they matter to God. I know what some of you may be thinking. You're thinking, we're visitors too; and that may be true when comes to these particular church families. However, we're certainly not visitors to the family of God. My point is, if the church is to convert unchurched visitors into born-again believers and members of their local church congregation, friendliness is an absolute must!

In some churches, after the service has concluded, a team will take the visitors off to the side or into a separate room to welcome them to their church and to explain the key points of the church's ministry to them. This might be the right thing to do, but perhaps, not the right time to do it.

Side-room meetings are great for acquainting visitors with an illustrated version of the church's love for the community, but nothing can replace the personal touch of friendly members. Instead of immediately removing the visitors from the sanctuary, it would be far better for the membership to, enthusiastically acquaint themselves with your guests. This gives the visitor a chance to meet some of the people they will actually fellowship with, should they decide to unite with your church.

The church needs members who are outgoing enough to approach visitors after the service, to help them feel more welcomed and appreciated. I don't mean, "Hello. It's nice having you in our service today. I hope you come back again. Bye!" I'm talking about striking up a conversation to make the visitor feel important enough to have been noticed. Once you meet them, introduce them to some of the other members of your church, "especially if you were the one who invited them!"

Sure, you would like to enjoy the fellowship of your friends and kinship; the same people you normally make a straight beeline to after each service. Not only can they wait until the visitors are attended to, but they should be greeting visitors as well. Tell the visitor a little bit about yourself. Find out who they are. Don't talk over them, but listen to what they say to you.

Invite them and members of their family to a special service or program, an event, a birthday party, mom's night out, teen's night out, etc. It also makes sense to include their kids in whatever it is the church is doing or planning. Inviting them to something other than your regular church worship service makes them feel accepted, more comfortable, and already a part of what's going on in your church. If they feel as though they are already a part the church, they will keep coming back, and they will bring others.

The Target Approach to Welcoming Visitors—

The entire church should make visitors feel at home. Whenever possible, use the target approach in meeting and greeting your visitors. I realize, most churches cannot always match teen for teen, or senior for senior, but whenever you can, you should do it.

When it comes to teenage visitors, they almost always feel weird when visiting a church for the first time. You can fix that immediately! The church's teenage believers can welcome the visiting teens to your church. This causes them to feel less weird. As teens, there's nothing wrong with you wanting to hang out with their regular church friends. That's perfectly okay, but involve the visiting teenagers in the fellowship.

It works even better when the teenagers approach visiting teens as a group. Enthusiastically, tell them about the teen population in the church, the fun things you do and the big plans for the youth of the church. Use power phrases like, *"You're really going to enjoy it here!"* This makes the visiting teens feel as though, you've already accepted them as part of the group. The church's teens take care to represent the and their Christian testimony well, and the teenage visitor will rave about it to their parents, all the way home.

You should also involve your younger children whenever possible. This should no problem, given how easily young kids bond. Parents of very young children like to know that there are other young children in the church for their children to enjoy. You would be surprised to know how excited visiting parents get when they see their kids enjoying themselves at church with other youngsters of the church.

Tens of thousands of people join churches weekly because of the youth or children's populous at those churches. Everyone has a purpose in the ministry of the church; even the precious little ones. Remember these words of Jesus:

> *"Suffer little children, and forbid them not, to come unto me:*
> *for of such is the kingdom of heaven."*

St. Matthew 19:14, St. Mark 10:14, St. Luke 18:16

If you are a single parent, and you heard one of the visitors say they were a single parent, go to them and let them know you are too. If they came as a couple together, you and your spouse should approach them together to introduce yourselves to both the husband

and the wife. Seniors play a major role too. Whenever senior male members of the church greet senior male visitors, they strike a common chord. the same applies to senior women. So, can you see how everyone really can be a part of the process?

The point is, no visitor should ever be left standing awkwardly alone, to fend for himself or herself. The main thing our "first time visitor" study taught us is, in a strange land… "Alone feels bad!" Don't leave it all up to the pastor. Roll up your sleeves and get down to business for God, and for your church. If the church does its part, God is bound by His infallible Word to do His part.

Now, Here's How They Could Have Easily Resolved That Little Seating Problem at the Christmas Program

Okay! Do you remember the story about the church Christmas service? I promised you that I would tell you what they could have done to solve that little seating problem. Even if every seat in the room was taken, the seating issue could have been easily resolved. Actually, there were a few things they could have done.

Let's review some of them:

1. Two of the church's kids could have shared a chair. Remember, my teenager and my pre-teenager shared one chair together.

2. The teenage young men in the church should have already been taught to relinquish their seats to an older person… especially a visitor.

3. An attentive usher or a considerate member of that church, could have brought in a chair from another room and given it to their guest. There were even extra chairs in the hall. Some were just outside the sanctuary door. As a guest in someone else's house, it would have been inappropriate for me to move items around. However, any one of their members could have brought in a chair from as a gesture of good hospitality.

238

4. Since, the ushers spend much of their time standing, there was no need for them to have individual chairs. Under the circumstances, they could have seated a visitor in one their chairs. Then, they could have taken turns with the remaining seats.

5. Perhaps, the best solution would have been to have the members who were holding seats for others, to remove the coats and other objects that were being used to tie up those seats. In fact, some of the people held seats through the entire service for individuals who never showed up. So, many of those reserved seats were never used. What a disappointment.

6. This last solution may have been the most difficult of all to achieve. The pastor's chair was not on the platform, but just ahead of the front row of audience seating. While the pastor was up announcing, greeting, presenting awards, singing and preaching, his seat was vacant the entire time. That was more than two hours.

Now, because so many of today's pastors suffer from what I call OPS... "Overwhelming Pride Syndrome," the last suggestion would have been the most unlikely solution of all. What I found interesting was, there was a table set up between the pastor and his wife's chairs, and to me it looked like that was where the drinks and other goodies were stashed. I guess they must have missed the sign in the lobby that said... *"No food or drinks allowed in the sanctuary!"*

Frankly speaking, I could be wrong but I believe, had the pastor known I was a visiting pastor, he would have made sure that I was seated. Perhaps not in his seat, but seated nonetheless. However, the fact that I was a visiting minister should have had nothing to do with whether guests receive first class hospitality in the house of God.

As a man of God, I would be less likely to be hurt by their shameless treatment than a less secure visitor. That's what troubled me the most. I could have been a wounded abuse victim or a lost soul. I didn't see concern for what mattered most to Jesus— *souls!*

A FINAL WORD REGARDING OUR "FIRST TIME" VISITORS STUDY

I want to say one last thing about the study we conducted. There will be some people (pastors and church leaders included) who believe the study to be an invasion of one's right to privacy. These people believe they should have been made aware that a study was going on, so they could have prepared their congregations. They seem to think that advance notice would have made a difference.

I want to start out by saying, there is nothing private about an open and public church service. Now, about that advance notice, if you really think about it, you were given advance notice. We all were. Your notice was sent out over 1,900 years ago, through the book of Hebrews. The writer tells us that we must make a conscious effort to treat everyone with kindness and proper hospitality. You never know who it is that you are entertaining.

"Stop neglecting to show hospitality to strangers, for by showing hospitality some have had angels as their guests without being aware of it."
Hebrews 13:2 (ISV)

Church-tainment Cannot Fulfill the Greatest Need of the Soul!—

One thing that our study revealed is that the average Sunday worship service is just wrong. What most modern or traditional churches call a worship service is all messed up. It has become a big theatrical performance. The "Church Show" must stop!

During the study, we all witnessed church members, seemingly floating on a cloud as a result of the pastor's message or the choir's performance. They were all thoroughly entertained, but too naïve to realize that was no real worship of God had taken place. It's about time for the church to grow up, and start practicing what we've been preaching and singing about.

While it may feel good, "church-tainment" cannot fulfill the soul's greatest need. The greatest need of the soul, is a real relationship with God! There's nothing wrong with us enjoying the service. It's okay for us to experience that wonderful tingling feeling that some of us get in the presence of the Holy Spirit. However, when the whole program is focused on our own entertainment, enjoyment, emotions and feelings, rather than on "sincere" praise and worship of God, it contradicts the basis for "actual" praise and worship.

If you pay close attention, you'll notice that the average church service isn't even planned to offer worship to God. Furthermore, in many of the miniscule settings where it is, worship isn't the central theme of the program. Of course, for those of you who don't understand the Biblical premise for worship, you might find my critique difficult to appreciate.

Yes, you should enjoy church, but you should not plan God out. When was the last time, while in church you thought about, whether God was enjoying the service as much as you and some of the others around you? I'm not asking, when you last felt or thought about God during service. I'm asking when you last thought about whether He was enjoying the service too.

God's thoughts and ways are above ours. He knows that time is winding down. He's more interested in us taking advantage of the gathering, to draw souls to Him. He's more interested in souls than songs. Souls saved, is what God enjoys. In fact, souls saved, is what all heaven enjoys.

> *"So He told them this parable: "What man among you, who has 100 sheep and loses one of them, does not leave the 99 in the open field and go after the lost one until he finds it?*
>
> *When he has found it, he joyfully puts it on his shoulders, and coming home, he calls his friends and neighbors together, saying to them, 'Rejoice with me, because I have found my lost sheep!' I tell you, in the same way, there will be more joy in heaven over one sinner who repents than over 99 righteous people who don't need repentance."*
>
> St. Luke 15:3-7 (HCSB)

Let me tell you what I believe. If we spend less time entertaining one another, and more time in "GENUINE" worship and "REAL" praise to "GOD," the results in our services and throughout our

241

churches and ministries would be very different. There would be a spiritual fallout upon the worshippers, and upon the church. It would be like a nuclear fallout. You can't ignore it.

Of course there will always be true brothers and sisters in Christ, who are not necessarily dependent on the church for worship and praise. They have their own personal time, or joint times with their families where they offer sincere praise and worship to God. I'm not saying they don't need church. I'm just saying if the church chooses to stay messed up, these people will survive. However, the truth is most people in the Christian church aren't quite there yet. So, the church assemblage presents a great opportunity for getting them together, and for getting them there.

Now, to the churches we found who really do get it, thank you for making our time with you, a very pleasant experience. We had a great time, and we met a lot of wonderful brothers and sisters in Christ during the study. The biggest blessing for me, is that I have established some rock solid friendships that I will probably cherish for the rest of my life. It's our prayer that as we share our findings throughout the upcoming years, the church of Jesus Christ will wake up and receive the best that God has for us.

As for those of you who take issue with our "first time" visitors study, don't get too worked up over it. Nor should you allow yourself to be bothered by the fact that you weren't made aware that our team was gathering research while at your church. Our study isn't the one that really matters.

What you really should be worrying about the most, is the fact that God had already been conducting His own study on your church… and churches around the world, long before we showed up.

"You are God's child. You are fearfully and wonderfully made. And He wants you to prosper... in all areas of your life.

Psalms 139:14

Chapter Fifteen

GOD'S PERFECT
PLAN FOR YOUR LIFE

*Your life can be made totally "Brand New"
within the next few minutes!*

In this chapter, you will learn how you fit into God's perfect plan for humankind. It doesn't matter where you've come from, who your parents are, or even what your level of education or social status is. God has a purpose for every single one of us. Although, we are unworthy of His undeserved favor toward us, we are not worthless in God's eyes. When it comes to God's great plan for humanity, we matter to Him.

THE ETERNAL SOUL OF MAN

God's perfect plan begins with soul salvation. We are made up of body, soul and spirit. The spirit and the soul are the parts of man, which dwell within the housing known as the body. Most Christian preachers teach that the righteous will live forever and the unrighteous will not.

Now, here is where we get into a theological riff. I fail to see the soundness in this teaching, concerning physical or spiritual death. Now, I realize that the commonly accepted belief among Christians is, the soul of the righteous will live forever, and that the soul of the unrighteous will die.

Of course, the Bible teaches that the body of both, the righteous and unrighteous will die, but that's just the physical death. Your body is only the housing for the soul, and yes, the body will die, but your soul does not end there. Your soul is the inner you. Despite what theologians teach, whether you are saved or unsaved, your soul is the part of you that will exist forever.

> *"Finally, the poor man died and was carried by the angels to be with Abraham. The rich man also died and was buried, and his soul went to the place of the dead. There, in torment, he saw Abraham in the far distance with Lazarus at his side. The rich man shouted, Father Abraham, have some pity! Send Lazarus over here to dip the tip of his finger in water and cool my tongue. I am in anguish in these flames."*
>
> Luke 16:22-24 (NLT)

God outdid himself when He created the human body, but still, the mortal body will not last forever. Regardless of how well you care for your body, it is going to die. Now, don't get me wrong; we should take care of our bodies. The Bible tells us that the body of the believer is the temple of the Holy Spirit.

> *"What! Know ye not that your body is the temple of the Holy Ghost?"*
>
> 1 Corinthians 6:19 (KJV)

We should be good caretakers of the Holy Spirit's dwelling place. However, we shouldn't concentrate so much time, effort and energy on the structure that you neglect the tenant or resident living inside that structure. The body will die in its own time. Strength training and vitamins won't stop death.

Plastic surgery and a hairpiece may take ten or twenty years off your appearance, but they cannot stop the clock from ticking on your body, neither can they prevent physical death. God doesn't care if your body is pampered, toned or beautiful. He doesn't care whether you are short or tall, fat or skinny, weak or strong, black or white, but He does care about your eternal soul.

We've all heard people talk about how willing they are to die for the Lord, but God isn't looking for anyone to die for Him these days. What God really wants is someone who will "live" for Him. He's looking for someone who is willing to be a living sacrifice for Him. There's no need to get in a rush to die for the Lord. He's more interested in finding people who will "live" for Him.

> *"I beseech you therefore, brethren, by the mercies of God, that you present your bodies a living sacrifice, holy, acceptable to God."*
>
> Romans 12:1 (NKJV)

Your time to die may come sooner than you think. In due time, your body will die and lie dormant awaiting the resurrection. We all have at least one appointment with death.

> *"It is appointed unto man once to die, but after this the judgment."*
>
> Hebrews 9:27 (KJV)

When that time comes, your body and soul will separate from one another. Your body will go into its grave, but your soul will continue to exist... somewhere. Your body is the soul's house, but your soul is you. It is who you really are! Your soul is the part of you that was made to live forever.

THERE ARE TWO ROADS TO ETERNITY

The Bible talks about the two roads in life. Both roads lead to eternity. One is a broad (or wide) road; the other is a narrow road. Every one of us has to make a choice to travel on one or the other. You must choose between the broad road and the narrow road. According to Jesus, the wide road is easy to find. Just follow the crowd! Most people find the broad road to be exciting. Some people would kill for the opportunity to travel the big road. Some people actually do.

> *"Enter through the narrow gate. For wide is the gate and broad is the road that leads to destruction, and many enter through it. But small is the gate and narrow the road that leads to life, and only a few find it."*
>
> Matthew 7:13-14 (NIV)

Both Roads Are "One-Way" Highways—

Both roads are one-way streets; each moving in one direction, toward its own separate destination. The broad road only goes down, dead ending at a place of eternal destruction and damnation. There are no traffic lanes, roads or highways leading out of hell. If there were, you would have a traffic jam that defies human imagination.

Think about it. All wide road traffic leads to hell, but have you thought about the fact that there is no traffic leading away from hell? Wow! Talk about putting the accent on the word, "Final!" However, in contrast… there is also no traffic leading from eternal life. Why should there a road leading out of heaven? What sense would that make? Who would use it?

Let's look at some of what you're guaranteed to find on the wide road are travelers from every walk of life, including church folk of all faiths. Because it's so heavily traveled, you'll find that it's overloaded with traffic jams, road rage and fighting all the time. You're also likely to find droves of preachers traveling the wide road every day. In fact, some preachers even use the broad road for family trips. They're leading their whole family down the wide road.

Now, let me tell you what you will not find on the wide road. You won't find pulpit or church abuse. You won't discord among the travelers, or those who sow the seed that causes it. You won't find cheaters, thieves or liars on the wide road. I'll tell you what else you won't find. You won't find racial profiling or religious or gender discrimination; or inequality based on national origin. You also won't find police or military abuse and partiality, racial privilege and special majority entitlement.

> Granted, I've never heard anyone talk about it before, but did you know that the wide road is actually a toll road?

Everyone is treated the same. Every traveler is welcomed and gladly accepted. The right to travel this road is highly respected and protected.

It can definitely be fun, but there is just one problem with the broad road. Granted, I've never heard anyone talk about it, but did you know that the broad road is actually a toll road? Although, no one is turned away, you do have to pay to travel the wide road. Of course, you don't need any cash or remote devices, when you reach your final destination, your toll (soul) will be thankfully collected! And there won't be a thing you can do about it.

The narrow road, on the other hand, is not as easy to find. Comparatively, there are actually very few people traveling along the narrow road. Sadly, many of the lights on the narrow road are not as bright as they really ought to be. This is one of the reasons it is so hard to find. For those of us traveling on the narrow road, Jesus wants us to let our lights shine brightly. Use your high beams. It makes the narrow road easier for others to find.

"Let your light so shine before men, that they may see your good works, and glorify your Father which is in heaven."
St. Matthew 5:16 (KJV)

Contrary to what people may tell you, the narrow road can actually be very exciting to travel on too, but you have to know where to look to find the excitement. It's for members only; not church members, or club members, but members of the body of Christ. Like the broad road, the narrow road is also a one-way street.

The great thing about the narrow road is, if you stay on it long enough, you'll run into streets paved with gold. The narrow road takes you up, not down, and it eventually leads to eternal life with Jesus Christ.

Every person reading this book is on one of those two roads at right now! You don't need a doctorate in Sacred Theology to figure out that, after you die, your soul is going to continue to exist forever— *somewhere*. Either you are on the road to heaven, or you're on the road to hell. It's that simple!

> When I saw my cousin Lois, sitting in the back of that Cadillac Limousine with a pretty pink baby's casket on her lap, I suddenly realized... caskets come in all sizes.

Caskets Come in All Sizes—

As a youngster, I thought only older people needed to concern themselves with preparing for the reality of death. At age 17, dying never crossed my mind, until my 8 month old cousin died in her crib. I watched as the baby's grandmother sat in the back of that Cadillac Limousine on the way to the cemetery, with a tiny, pink baby's casket resting on her lap. I realized then, caskets come in all sizes.

A woman recently shared with me that her father just told her that he's not going to worry about picking a road anytime soon. He says he's going to have as much fun as he can right now, and when he gets much older, he'll make his decision on which road he will travel on.

You may be thinking the same thing. Perhaps, your plan is to have your fun first. Then, when you're ready, and in your own time, you'll make your choice on which road you will take. Nevertheless, you're not going to let some preacher or religious fanatic force you into making a decision before you're ready. The bottom line is, you want to take your time in choosing your road.

Unfortunately, it's not that easy. If you are breathing, and warm blood is running through your veins, you have already chosen a road. Regardless to whether you want to accept it, you are actually traveling on the road of your choice right now. Either you have chosen the wide road or you have chosen the narrow road. But, you have definitely made your choice.

To reject one road, is to automatically choose the other one. If you've rejected Christ, you've chosen the multi-lane expressway to hell, and there's not a thing you can do about where you end up when you travel on this road.

Your only hope is, while there is still time, that you turn right at the junction ahead, and change roads. Have you ever been traveling cross-country on the highway, and you're exhausted? You're tired of the fast lane and you want to pull off and rest. You're trying to find a nice, peaceful hotel, but you aren't sure which one is right for you and your family. Suddenly, you see a hotel's sign or billboard that seems to shout the hotel's name right out at you. You just know it's the right one. Then, in big bold letters, you see these words on the sign, "Exit Now! Then, turn right, and go straight."

When you see "Exit Now!" You might find yourself steering your vehicle across four lanes of traffic to get out of the fast lane, and off that wide highway. You pull off and turn right... onto a quiet little narrow road. You keep going straight, and you finally reach your destination, where you find the rest you were looking for.

GOD'S WONDERFUL PLAN OF SALVATION

If you have discovered that you've been traveling on the super wide, fast paced highway to hell..."Exit Now! Turn Right, and continue straight until you reach your destination, where you will find rest for you soul." If you desire, you can change roads right now. Make a decision to travel the narrow road, and you've made the perfect choice.

If you never have been saved before, I can relate to where you are at this point in your life. One of the hardest things I have had to do in life was accepting Jesus Christ as my Lord and Savior. The process wasn't hard at all, but I didn't know that at the time. I wasn't resisting being saved. Once I heard the good news of Jesus Christ, I really wanted to be saved. However, I could not grasp the concept of receiving something as significant as God's gift of salvation without having to do something extraordinary to get it. As a result, it was a great mental effort for me.

It wasn't hard for God. He was prepared to save me. It was hard for me to believe, that to accept Christ through faith could be so easy. I had to condition my mind to receive through faith. I didn't just sit back waiting for my mind to condition itself. I fasted and prayed, I searched God's Word and I consulted with a minister. I later discovered that what I thought was so tough, was actually very easy.

Throughout the years, my testimony has blessed hundreds, to thousands of prospective converts who like me, could not understand the words, "Just believe." Because, I recognize what they are struggling with, I'm able to meet them at their level of understanding.

We Must All Acknowledge That We Have Sinned—

No one is saved or forgiven of their sins without first recognizing that they have sinned against God. You start out by being honest about yourself as a sinner. It is okay to come to God as a sinner. He already knew who you were, before you knelt to confess that you had sinned. Every one of us is a sinner. Some of us are sinners who are saved by God's grace. Others are sinners in need of the redeeming grace of our Lord. The point is, we have all sinned, and we have all had to come to terms with ourselves and with God regarding our sins.

> *"For all have sinned and come short of the glory of God'."*
>
> Romans 2:23 (KJV)

According to scripture, any man who says he has not sinned is a liar. The Word of God declares that every one of us is a sinner. Either we are sinners in need of salvation, or we are sinners who have accepted His wonderful plan of salvation.

> *"If we claim to be without sin, we deceive ourselves and the truth is not in us."*
>
> 1 John 1:8 (NIV)

I said the same thing to a young man one day. He agreed with me that he needed to get right with God, but he said he had a few things that he wanted to do first. This way, when he gives his heart to God, it will be for real. He felt that if he did it in his own time when he was ready, it would be easier. He promised me that he would one day give his life to the Lord, but later, not today. What captured my attention was he actually seemed to be excited at the notion that one day he would give his heart to God.

Within weeks of our conversation, I got the news that he had been walking down a stairwell, when a group of young gang members shot him at close range and blew the back of his head off. Sadly, the time he thought he had to get things in order before getting his heart right with God, had run out.

As I stood over his casket to deliver the eulogy, I looked around the sanctuary. It was filled with promising young men and young women who might have been thinking the same thing this young man thought. I shared his story with the audience, and one by one people began to stand up all over the room. While I was yet speaking, they were coming forward to give their lives to Jesus Christ.

This may be your last opportunity before God calls in the marker for you. Maybe you're thinking like that young man. He admitted that he needed Jesus, but he just wanted to get a few things taken care of first. Don't make the same mistake he made. The clock is ticking for all of us. Don't wait until it is too late.

Perhaps You Previously Accepted Christ as Your Savior—

Now, to the person who has already accepted Christ at some point, but for some reason or another, you have decided to go back out into the world, this next appeal is to you. God loves you, and He wants you back. He can give you the strength to overcome backsliding.

> "I will heal their backsliding, I will love them freely: for my anger has turned away from him."
>
> Hosea 14:4 (KJV)

God is not angry with you because you are a backslider. He views backsliding as a sickness or disease that can only be cured through His divine power. You don't have to live another minute as a backslider. God can heal you from your backsliding ways right now.

"Let the wicked forsake his way, and the unrighteous man his thoughts: and let him return unto the Lord, and He will have mercy upon him; and to our God, for He will abundantly pardon."

Isaiah 55:7 (KJV)

We Cannot Hide Our Sins from God—

There is also another individual that I want to reach out to at this time. You are faithfully involved with the church, but you are struggling in your spiritual walk with the Lord. You appear to be a spiritual powerhouse in front of the congregation. You may even be one of the leaders in your church, but your life is not exactly what others in the church may think it is. This message is to you. You can hide your transgressions from the pastor and the other members, but you cannot hide your sins from God.

He is the great eyewitness to everything you've ever done and to everything that you have ever thought. He has seen every deed you have committed and heard every word you have spoken. Hidden sins are condemning sins. The road to hell is paved with hidden sins. You can continue down the road you're traveling, or you can change roads now. It does not matter if you are the son or daughter of the pastor or a high ranking leader in the church, we must all travel the same road if we intend to reach heaven. No one gets a free ticket or a clergy pass. There are no shortcuts to heaven.

We Must All Confess Our Sins to God—

Let's face it. We have all sinned at one time or another, and God knows that truth better than anyone. Don't beat around the bush with God. You cannot afford to straddle the fence when it comes to, confessing your sins. People often pray, "Lord, if I have committed any sins, please forgive me." The word "if" is not an option in the sincere prayer of repentance. You need to lay it all out there.

In the book of St. Luke, Jesus tells a story of two men who went to the temple to pray. One was a Pharisee and the other was a publican (tax collector).

"The Pharisee stood and prayed thus with himself, God, I thank thee, that I am not as other men are, extortioners, unjust,

adulterers, or even as this publican (tax collector). I fast twice in
the week, I give tithes of all that I possess."

St. Luke 18:11-12 (KJV)

They both went to the temple to pray. The Pharisee stood to pray. Jesus said he stood alone (by himself.) While others were kneeling in the presence of the Lord, or lying prostrate on their faces in total humility, the Pharisee proudly stood upright and erect. He was too good to kneel as a common sinner. He even had the nerve to insult the other worshippers in the Temple, including the tax collector.

Jesus, the great storyteller, tells us that the Pharisee actually used his prayer time to boast to God (and all those in earshot) about what a great man he was. "I thank you Lord!"He bragged... "I'm better than all these lowly sinners around me, especially this thieving tax collector!" Now, the tax collector didn't feel worthy enough to raise his face up toward heaven. With his head bowed, he struck his own chest with his fist and cried out, "Lord, have mercy on me for I am a sinner!"

"And the publican, standing afar off, would not lift up so
much as his eyes unto heaven, but smote upon his breast, saying,
God be merciful to me a sinner."

St. Luke 18:13 (KJV)

This parable plays out in church all the time. Boastful leaders, and members alike, stand in the house of God to toot their own horns. We cannot earn God's mercy, but we can sincerely ask for it. If we seriously ask for forgiveness, God will forgive and save us. Confess to the Lord that you have sinned. Don't think you're going to shock God with your hard news report. God is un-shockable!

To be forgiven, you must confess that you have sinned. Earnestly confess to Him what you need Him to forgive you from, and to free you from. Don't pretend with God. You can only be forgiven if you confess that sin is present in your life. You cannot be forgiven if there is nothing to forgive.

Although both men went to the temple to pray, it was only the tax collector who received God's blessing that day.

"If we confess our sins, he is faithful and just to forgive us our sins, and to cleanse us from all unrighteousness."

1 John 1:9 (KJV)

We Must All Repent of Our Sins—

You must be godly sorry for your sinful actions. To be godly regretful is the same as wishing you had never committed those devious acts of corruption. Have you ever done anything so horrendous that you wish you hadn't done it, or that you could undo it? That's what repentance feels like.

All over the Internet and in libraries and bookstores around the world, we read that repentance means to turn from sin. It's preached in most every Christian church. However, the word repentance in the Bible simply means, to be so sorry for your actions. It means to be so sorry until, if you had it to do over, you would not make the same mistake. Repentance is not the same as turning to God. Nor is it the same as turning from sin. In the New Testament, coming to God is a two step process. Staying with God involves a third step. The first criteria for being saved to repentance. The next step is to turn to God.

"Now repent of your sins and turn to God, so that your sins may be wiped away."

Acts 3:19 (NLT)

Here, in Acts 3:19, we see two things. First, we must repent of our sins. Next, we must deliberately turn to God; and that's just to prepare us for having our sins forgiven and washed away. The third step is to turn from sin, which I thoroughly cover later in this same chapter. But, because the matter of repentance is so crucial to your salvation, I want to make sure that I do my best to help you understand it. Here's one more example of what true repentance should feel like to you.

All America, and other parts of the world, were watching the end of a NFL Super Bowl championship game. The score was tight between the two teams. There were just seconds left on the play clock.

The fans had already decided the winning team, when the quarterback did the unbelievable. He threw the ball directly into the hands of a defending player, who easily backed himself into the end zone. Of course, the team who was expected to win at that point, wound up losing that championship contest.

Do you suppose that quarterback ached for the opportunity to live those last few moments over again? You bet he did. That's what real repentance feels like. He was troubled by his actions. He wasn't comfortable with his mistake. He wanted, somehow, to make it right, but of course, the Super Bowl championship game for that particular year was over. For him, time had run out on the play clock before he could correct his error.

You don't have to let your play clock run down, before fixing your past mistakes. The quarterback had an advantage that none of us have. He could, at least, see how much time he had left. We aren't afforded that luxury. For us, time could run out at any moment; without advance warning.

The forsaking of sin is the cornerstone of true repentance. Repentance leads to a change of heart (mind). Changed minds lead to changed lives. If you change your mind and attitude regarding sin, you're more likely to turn from it.

> *"And do not be conformed to this world, but be transformed by the renewing of your mind, that you may prove what is that good and acceptable and perfect will of God."*
>
> Romans 12:2 (NKJV)

A transformed or changed mind allows you to have a clearer perception of right and wrong. Through a changed mind, you have a better understanding of who Jesus is, and what we must do to walk with Him. While turning from sin may not be the true meaning of repentance, it is indeed the evidence of true repentance. When a person is genuinely sorry for their actions and their rejection of Jesus Christ, the result will be a changed life.

We Must All Ask for God's Forgiveness—

If you are truly sorry for the sins you have committed, you must ask God to forgive you for what you've done. This is where we must rely on the Lord's mercy. We don't deserve His forgiveness, but because He is a faithful and just God, He has promised to forgive us, when we just ask. Thank God, He gives us what we need, not what we deserve.

> *"Whosoever shall call upon the name of the Lord shall be saved."*
>
> Romans 10:13 (KJV)

Thank God, He doesn't give us what we really deserve. What we really deserve is to burn eternally in a Godless hell. We don't deserve His forgiveness, but because of His Grace, and because He is the only faithful and just God, He has promised to forgive us when we ask.

This promise is not based on our love for Him. It is based on His immeasurable love for all humankind. God's unprecedented love is the central focus of redemption.

> *"For God so loved the world, that he gave his only begotten Son, that whosoever believeth in him should not perish, but have everlasting life."*
>
> St. John 3:16 (KJV)

We Must All Accept Jesus and What He Did On the Cross—

You must accept the death, burial and resurrection of Jesus Christ as atonement, redemption and full payment for your sins. Jesus gave His life on the cross at Calvary, which was His way of paying for the sins of humankind. He sacrificed His life so we would not have to.

Adam introduced sin into the world. This resulted in all humanity, being born into a sinful world, with a natural inclination toward sin. Just as one man alone caused all to become sinners, because of one man alone (Jesus), many are made righteous.

> *For as by one man's disobedience many were made sinners, so also by one Man's obedience many will be made righteous."*
>
> Romans 5:19 (NKJV)

Now, all that is necessary is for you to accept His sacrifice as payment for your own sins. You don't have to carry the burden of your sins or guilt any longer. Accept Jesus Christ and be set free. To accept Jesus is a simple act of faith. It would be the same as if someone were to stretch forth their hand to give you a brand new Bible.

> You don't have to carry the burden of your sins or guilt any longer. Accept Jesus Christ and be set free.

What would you need to do to receive it? You're exactly right. You would reach out to accept the Bible from that individual. This is the same way you receive or accept Jesus Christ. By faith, you reach out and accept Him into your life and into your heart.

"That if thou halt confess with thy mouth the Lord Jesus, and shalt believe in thine heart that God hath raised him from the dead, thou shalt be saved."
Romans 10:9 (KJV)

In the above scripture, I purposely highlighted in bold, the three things that jumped out of this scripture to me, when I was struggling to accept Christ by faith. Those three things are:

1. **Confess**
2. **Believe**
3. **And Be Saved!**

It's just that easy! Now, you can always feel free to pray and say whatever you wish. He will always know and understand your heart, even before you open your mouth to pray.

"It will also come to pass that before they call, I will answer; and while they are still speaking, I will hear."

Isaiah 65:24 (NASB)

For those who may feel a bit intimidated or uncomfortable in the beginning, you may choose to use the following words as a suggested prayer of repentance.

"It will also come to pass that before they call, I will answer; and while they are still speaking, I will hear."

Isaiah 65:24 (NASB)

A Prayer of Repentance

Lord Jesus, I come before you today as a sinner. I acknowledge and confess that I have sinned against you. I'm sorry for every sin I've ever committed.

I ask for your forgiveness through my Lord and Savior, Jesus Christ. I ask that You would cleanse me of my sins, and set me free right now in my spirit.

Make me over again. Lord, make my life brand new. This, I ask in the name of Jesus Christ. Now, I thank you, Lord.

Amen

Now, Take a Moment to Thank the Lord for Saving You!—

Hallelujah! Because of your decision to accept Christ, all of Heaven is rejoicing. Heaven is a joyous place when a sinner repents and accepts Jesus, as his or her Lord and Savior.

"There will be more joy in heaven over one sinner who repents than over ninety-nine righteous people who have no need to repent."

St. Luke 15:7 (AKJV)

Even now, at this very moment, as you read these words, just know this... because of you, the angels in God's Kingdom are rejoicing! Well, you might as well join them. Lift your hands and your heart up toward heaven right now and tell God, "Thank you for saving me!"

We Must All Give Up Our Sinful Ways—

Now that you are saved, what's next? Well, let me be the first to tell you, being saved is only part of the plan. You've taken a step that less than ten percent of the world's population has chosen to take. It feels good, doesn't it? Well, there's a little more to the plan of salvation than that.

260

St. John, the disciple of Christ, gives a powerful report of a condemned woman. The woman was accused by the scribes and the Pharisees and charged with committing adultery. She was surrounded by stone wielding fiends bent on stoning her to death for her devious act.

They brought her to Jesus while He was at the temple teaching. This was an attempt to put Jesus on the spot. The crowd is shouting, "This woman must be stoned; it is the law." As if He wasn't aware of what was going on, Jesus bends down to the ground and starts to write on the ground with His finger. They must have thought, "This guy is a basket case for sure." Someone probably may have thought, "Maybe He has an attention disorder."

Well, they weren't about to give up that easy. They continued, "What about it Jesus? After all, it is the law!" Jesus raises Himself up from the ground to agree with them.

To everyone's delight, He looks at the woman, then He says to the crowd, "Yeah, I suppose you're right. Every one of you is right. It is the law. Now that we're all in agreement, let's get on with it."

Suddenly, Jesus turns His attention away from the terrified woman and focuses in on the crowd. I can almost hear Him now... saying, "Let's destroy this adulterous woman. But, wait! Let's do it in style. In fact, let's all take turns stoning her. I think the honor of throwing the first stone should go to... hmm, let's see now. Oh! I've got a great idea! Why don't we have the person among you who has never committed a sin, to throw the first stone? Please step forward!" Jesus calls out. "Move to the head of the line. If you're ready to throw the first stone, step up! Who will be first?"

Then Jesus stoops back down to the ground. The crowd of self-righteous hypocrites began backing away as Jesus continues to write on the ground with His finger. Moments Later, Jesus stands back up and looks around. The only ones left were Jesus and the accused woman. He asked the woman, "Where are those who condemned you?" When she replied that there was no one left to condemn her, Jesus said, "Then I don't condemn you either. Now, as you leave this place, remember you must also leave your sinful ways."

"Jesus straightened up and asked her, 'Woman, where are they? Has no one condemned you?'...'No one, sir, she said.'... 'Then neither do I condemn you,' Jesus declared. 'Go now and turn from your life of sin."

John 8:10-11 (NIV)

Being saved is not enough. Now that you're saved, you must learn to stay saved. Staying saved is the key. To remain saved, you must turn from your sinful ways.

Welcome to a Brand New You!—

Here's the fun part. The new you must now live in such a manner that represents the image of Christ within you. There are more books than I care to read, where the writer is talking about walking in newness of life. This may be easier said, than done. For this to become reality, there are some things you will need to know.

One of the main enticements pulling new converts back into their old life is peer pressure. If you hung out with a partying, drinking and promiscuous bunch of friends, your new life with Christ is likely to be short lived unless you change your circle of friends and acquaintances.

Unless most of your friends were already in the church when you accepted Jesus, your friends probably won't be as excited about your new life as you want them to be. They won't try to encourage you to study the Bible, pray and spend time in the fellowship of the people of God. They would much rather have you spend time with them, doing what you have always done together.

Surround yourself with people who you can draw from spiritually, not people who drain the spiritual life out of you. Hang out and have fun, but hang out with some of the more spiritually grounded and established members of the church.

"Do not be mismatched with unbelievers. For what partnership is there between righteousness and lawlessness? Or what fellowship is there between light and darkness?"

2 Corinthians 6:14 (NRSV)

Don't forget the importance of spending time in Bible study and prayer meetings. Learn from them, and in time, you will find that your desires and interests will begin to change and mature spiritually.

If you find yourself making mistakes in your new Christian walk, that's okay for now. Just don't get discouraged and give up. The Bible tells us that we should grow in God's grace. Things that are tough for you to handle will become easier in time. With the Lord's help, you can become the perfect example of what a born again follower of Christ should be.

The primary evidence of salvation is a changed life. When your old friends see the peace, joy and happiness in your life, that may be the greatest demonstration that some of them will ever witness of the redemptive power of God in action. Your old friends, associates, co-workers and family members will see a "Brand New You!"

Be an Example to Your Family and Friends—

For me, it has been exciting living for the Lord. I have seen and done wonderful things that would never have been possible had it not been for my new birth. It has been an incredible journey. I think the greatest blessing for me has been, just knowing that multitudes of my own relatives have given their lives to the Lord. It started with me accepting Jesus into my life. Little did I know that this would be the catalyst for my family members giving their lives to the Lord. As I lived the life of a believer, they saw Christ in me. For some, it has been a direct impact from my life, others have been indirectly impacted. One by one, they began coming to Jesus Christ.

If you want your family members saved, don't rely on someone else to win them to Christ. You can be the Christian example that influences them to accept the Lord. The Christian journey is more than a good subject for singers and preachers to use for songs and sermons. For the believer, it is a way of life.

I ask you today… "If Jesus were to call you into eternity before you completed this book, can you truthfully say you would go to heaven to live with Him?" If the answer is "NO"…or if you're not sure, go back and read this chapter again.

"What man of you, having a hundred sheep, if he lose one of them, doth not leave the ninety and nine in the wilderness, and go after that which is lost, until he find it?"

St. Luke 15:4 (KJV)

Chapter Sixteen

USE "THUG PREACHERS" THE BOOK FOR YOUR CHURCH STUDY GROUP

Become trained and informed believers in the
"Ministry of Search and Rescue"

Unfortunately, it doesn't appear as though thug preachers are going anywhere anytime soon. If anything, the number of pulpit thugs seems to be increasing, rather than decreasing. So, it behooves us as children of God to prepare ourselves to do battle with the enemy to rescue our blood siblings in Christ.

Who can forget the rescue of former Iraqi POW, Jessica Lynch? I still get goose bumps when I think about the dramatic rescue of Pfc. Lynch, who (according to some reports) was badly injured and was recovering at a military hospital in Germany. In full battle gear, an American commando entered the hospital room, as the terrified POW had her bed sheet pulled over her head. Removing his own helmet so Pfc. Lynch could get a better look at him, her rescuer said, "We are United States soldiers, and we are here to protect you, and to take you home."

> Usually, despite how desperately and passionately church abuse victims tell their stories, their reports go unrecognized as a cry for help.

Can you imagine the emotions 19 year old Private Lynch had to choke down? How wonderful it must have been to know that somebody cared enough to risk life and limb to search for her, to rescue her and to bring her home.

Right now, there are frightened people out there who are in dire need of God's commandos to find them, protect them and take them to safety. This is not a call to set out on a campaign to tear up churches and tear down pastors. There's no need for that. In your normal everyday lives, you meet people who are looking for, and need your help.

Usually, despite how desperately and passionately church abuse victims tell their stories, their reports go unrecognized as a cry for help. These people are stuck in situations that they don't know how to get out of. This where you come in, but to be effective you must be trained, and you must be well informed.

Military search and rescue missions don't just happen on a whim. These missions are well calculated and strategically planned. Much research, reconnaissance, time and effort goes into planning each mission. As a well prepared and highly informed commando representing the King of Kings, it is your job to help church abuse victims find hope. God has made this important information available to you through this book, mainly because you come in contact with hurting people on a regular basis who need your help.

Of course, it isn't likely that you will be able to help anyone unless you are able to recognize the signs of abuse and the scars left on these poor souls. You must also understand that these individuals may not be as welcoming of your enlightenment as you might hope or expect.

You must know how to reach the soul of pain stricken and abused people… even against their own distorted sense of judgment and self-esteem. Together your study or prayer group will prepare for war against the strongholds that keep our suffering brothers and sisters in bondage.

This book, along with the Bible, will teach you and your Bible study or prayer group how to get involved in what I believe to be the single most ignored ministry in the Christian church. In fact, until now, I don't believe this concept of seeking out and helping victims of church abuse has ever existed. I've chosen to name it the "Ministry of Search and Rescue."

OPTIONAL STUDY GUIDE SUPPLEMENT

For those who wish to use, "Thug Preachers" for prayer group and Bible study purposes, the layout and continuity flow are ideal. Simply follow the chapters in their chronological order or pick certain chapters for a more targeted study.

I will also be making available an easy to understand optional study guide supplement. The study guide is the perfect complement to "Thug Preachers." With it, you are able to easily train your study group to better understand and identify abusive church leadership.

The study guide is user friendly, and is especially designed for Bible study groups when used alongside "Thug Preachers" and the Holy Bible. This soon to be released study supplement provides incredible, irrefutable, scriptural support on what we can expect of true men and women of God. It also gives conclusive guidance on how parishioners should respond to this widespread problem of church authoritarianism.

You and your study group members will find yourselves more knowledgeable on the matter of church abuse. As a team, you will be more sensitive to, and better prepared when dealing with new or existing study partners who are yet suffering from the effects of pulpit abuse. You cannot afford to pass up this opportunity to learn how you can seek and rescue broken people.

There are advantages to being armed with the information contained on these pages. For those who study this book, rather than just reading it, you will learn and understand the many sides of church abuse. You'll know whether the abuse is by design or the result of ignorance.

You'll be able to spot pulpit abuse from a distance. It would be next to impossible for you to ever become bamboozled by pulpit kingpins. You'll know the tell-tale signs of an abusive church leader, authoritarian environment or thug preacher.

You'll also know what signs to look for in a genuine sincere man or woman of God. You'll be armed with knowledge needed to prayerfully find a good, solid Bible based church home. You'll know how to find a church where you can be spiritually nourished.

There are literally millions of suffering victims of pulpit abuse around the world. Most of them don't even realize it. They know that it doesn't feel right, but they think to themselves, "This is the church and he is the pastor, so it has to be all right." Well, it isn't all right

With the help of the new study guide, your group can learn how to help these people without causing a disturbance within the body of Christ. If you choose to take advantage of the new optional, easy to follow "Thug Preachers" Study Guide, it may prove to be instrumental in getting you and your group prepared in a shorter amount of time.

If you cannot find the study guide in your local retail center or online store, you may place your order at: FrankJackson.org.

If you or your church is interested in obtaining information on successfully launching a "Search and Rescue" ministry, the Frank Jackson World Ministries team is conducting training seminars around the United States. These powerful workshops cover Search & Rescue, Kingdom Building, Witnessing on Target, Christian Leadership, Deliverance and Demonology, Creating a Healing Center and the Call to Ministry. To find out when and where these seminars will be taking place, please contact us on the worldwide web.

Also, if you are a pastor or church leader and you need help in setting up a "Search and Rescue" ministry at your church, you may also contact me to discuss sponsoring an individual training workshop/ seminar to be conducted at your own church.

Contact Frank Jackson World Ministries, Inc. on the web at:

FrankJackson.org

ABOUT THE AUTHOR

World respected husband and father, Frank Jackson is a leading expert on cults, occultism and spiritual warfare. He is regarded by both Christian and secular media. For several decades he has been the ideal confidant, providing spiritual guidance to, and helping Christian ministers across the United States. This former senior

pastor is esteemed by many church ministers as the "pastor's pastor." He has trained and mentored pastors, Christian leaders and church laity around the world.

Frank Jackson is the former, and founding, executive director of Missions International Inc. Recognized for his deep commitment to foreign missions, he places a heightened emphasis on short duration missionary projects, to third world countries.

This author is the creator of deep probing Bible study modules and Christian training programs. As a seasoned preacher and teacher, he leaves his audiences on the edges of their seats, as he so giftedly, unfolds the deeper truths in the Bible.

Jackson has formed, and presently sits on the governing board of four human-interest organizations... covering bullying of students by both teachers and other students alike; homeschooling for the committed Christian family; unjust and unconstitutional violation of American citizens everywhere; and domestic abuse against men.

Highly appreciated for having spent the majority of his adult life in radio and TV broadcasting, Frank Jackson has received numerous awards for outstanding performance and excellence in Christian broadcast communications.

In sports, he is a proven and persuasive speaker to both, American and National major league baseball teams. Included in his other writings are, The Four Majors Cults Affecting America, Witnessing on Target and Deliverance and Demonology.

If you would like to arrange a professional seminar, webinar, workshop, presentation, Internet, TV or radio broadcast interview, a church or special event speaking engagement featuring Pastor Frank Jackson… or if you would like contact us for any reason, visit us on the worldwide web at:

FrankJackson.org

APPENDIX I

It is generally difficult to write with accuracy, in the absence of the invaluable benefit of research. Research isn't just a conversation with an individual or two, but it usually involves hundreds, to thousands of hours of study, investigative probing and fact-finding. Both, the author and the publisher of "Thug Preachers" the book, wish to acknowledge the significance of the following individuals, organizations and institutions in the research, development and production of this book.

Dr. Chet Weld, Director of Pastoral Counseling at Casas Church
https://www.preachitteachit.org/about-us/the-team/chet-weld

Richard R. DeBlassie, The Counselor Privileged Communication And The Law
http://www.ascd.org/ASCD/pdf/journals/ed_lead/el_197604_deblassie.pdf

Ingela Ratledge, Woman's Day Magazine
http://www.womansday.com/life/a2230/why-we-love-to-gossip-114587

Nicholas Emler, PhD, professor of psychology at the University of Surrey in England.
http://www.surrey.ac.uk/psychology/people/nick_emler

Frank McAndrew, PhD, professor of psychology at Knox College in Galesburg, IL
http://www.knox.edu/academics/majors-and-minors/psychology/faculty/mcandrew-frank

Chicago Tribune
http://www.chicagotribune.com/news

Emrys Westacott, PhD, professor of philosophy at Alfred University in Alfred, New York, NY
http://las.alfred.edu/faculty/profile.cfm?username=westacott

APPENDIX I

Robin Dunbar, PhD, director of the Institute of Cognitive & Evolutionary Anthropology at the University of Oxford.
http://www.icea.ox.ac.uk/fileadmin/ICEA/staff/Dunbar_CV_Jun2009.pdf

Mark O'Connell, L.C.S.W., Psychology Today
https://www.psychologytoday.com/experts/mark-oconnell-lcsw

Nigel Nicholson, Ph.D., professor of organizational behavior at London Business School http://faculty.london.edu/nnicholson

David Berg, Family International, contributor of "The Pastors Pillow" http://deeptruths.com/treasures/pastors_pillow.html

District Superintendent, Harvey Burnett, COGIC, The Dunamis Word blogspot http://bethelburnett.blogspot.com/2011/07/gold-chains-crosses-rings-missions-call.html

John MacArthur, president of The Master's College and Seminary Santa Clarita, CA http://www.masters.edu/president

Richard D. Dobbins, Ph.D., Christian psychologist and minister, EMERGE Ministries, Christian Mental-Health Center in Akron, Ohio http://www.emerge.org/#!dr-dobbins-founder-of-emerge/cekv

Central News Agency
http://www.cna.co.in

Susan Hafen, PhD, professor of communication at Weber State University in Ogden, Utah
.http://www.weber.edu/Communication/SusanHafen.html

APPENDIX I

The National Domestic Abuse Hotline
http://www.thehotline.org/2014/07/men-can-be-victims-of-abuse-too

Asian News International
http://www.aniin.com/index.php Thaindian News

The Guardian - Domestic violence can't be a gender issue
http://www.theguardian.com/world/2001/nov/26/gender.uk1

Rick Nauert PhD, Domestic Violence Affects Men
http://psychcentral.com/news/2008/05/19/domestic-violence-affects-men/2309.html

Honora Gathings, ABC News - Another face of domestic violence- men
http://www.abc3340.com/story/28083806/another-face-of-domestic-violence-men

Mayo ClinicDomestic violence against men: Know the signs
http://www.mayoclinic.org/healthy-lifestyle/adult-health/in-depth/domestic-violence-against-men/art-20045149

The Scotish Government
http://www.gov.scot/Publications/2002/09/15201/9624

David Zimmerman, Church from a Visitor's Perspective |Church Marketing Sucks
http://www.churchmarketingsucks.com/2007/09/church-from-a-visitors-perspective

Psychotherapist-Patient Privilege (Supreme Court Standard 504)
http://jaffee-redmond.org/laws/rule504.htm

APPENDIX I

Steven Johnson, author - Counseling Christians for Mental, Emotional, Behavioral, and Spiritual Health
http://etherapycentre.com/counseling-christians-for-mental-emotional-behavioral-and-spiritual-health-rebt-and-spiritual-growth-series/

Clyde White, writer - Think the Bible - Mind Control
http://www.oori.org/Lessons/contending/contending04.htm

Lee Ann Rubsam, author, publisher and teacher
http://www.leeannrubsam.com/

Dr. C. I. Scofield, creator of the Scofield Reference and Study Bible
http://www.biblebelievers.com/scofield/index.html Clyde White, "Think the Bible," Lincoln, Nebraska

Dr. Joseph Mattera, Presiding Bishop of Christ Covenant Coalition and Overseeing Bishop of Resurrection Church in New York, NY
http://josephmattera.org/seventeen-signs-you-are-building-your-own-empire-but-not-gods-kingdom/

Henry Kissinger - Power is the ultimate aphrodisiac
http://www.independent.co.uk/news/people/profiles/henry-kissinger-a-diplomatic-colossus-who-is-still-a-key-influence-in-us-amid-syria-crisis-8815533.html

CBS News
http://www.cbsnews.com/news/pa-man-robert-leone-suing-state-police-for-alleged-brutality-during-arrest/

APPENDIX I

Weinstein's Federal Evidence, Second Edition
Psychotherapist-Patient Privilege (Supreme Court Standard 504)
http://www.fjc.gov/public/pdf.nsf/lookup/sciman00.pdf/$file/sciman00.pdf

Brian Croft, Senior Pastor of Auburndale Baptist Church in Louisville, Ky and
Founder of Practical Shepherding, Inc.
http://practicalshepherding.com/2012/12/24/how-much-does-a-pastor-share-
with-his-wife-in-regard-to-confidential-matters

Eugene Cho, author - Death by Ministry, Is pastoral ministry a dangerous
profession -
http://eugenecho.com/2010/08/11/death-by-ministry

Lissa Rankin, M.D - The Healing Power of Telling Your Story
https://www.psychologytoday.com/blog/owning-pink/201211/the-healing-
power-telling-your-story

Dr. Richard J. Krejcir - Statistics and Reasons for Church Decline
http://www.churchleadership.org/apps/articles/default.asp?articleid=42346&c
olumnid=4545

ABC News - Jessica Lynch Scared When Rescue Began
http://abcnews.go.com/Primetime/story?id=132433

Thaindian News
Men too "suffer psychological trauma from partner abuse."
http://www.thaindian.com/newsportal/health/men-too-suffer-psychological-
trauma-from-partner-abuse_100523538.html

APPENDIX I

Pastor Josh Buice - Private Accusations Against Your Pastor is a Sin
http://deliveredbygrace.com/?p=574

Dr. Joseph Mattera, Presiding Bishop of Christ Covenant Coalition and Overseeing Bishop of Resurrection Church in New York

"The Problem with Cheap Grace Churces and Preaching"
http://www.ephesiansfour.net/the-problem-with-cheap-grace-churches-and-preaching

Smith, Gambrell & Russell, LLP, Attorneys at Law
What the Attorney-Client Privilege Really Means
http://www.sgrlaw.com/resources/trust_the_leaders/leaders_issues/ttl5/916

Fast Facts about American Religion
http://hirr.hartsem.edu/research/fastfacts/fast_facts.html

Dr. Peter Pronovost, director of the Quality and Safety Research Group at Johns Hopkins University
Posted by Elizabeth Cohen, CNN Senior Medical Correspondent
http://thechart.blogs.cnn.com/2011/04/14/the-gruesome-math-of-hospital-infections

Todd Rhoades - Pastors: How much (confidential) information do you share with your spouse?
ToddRhoades.com

Hidden Hurt - Bible Verses on Abuse & Violence
http://www.hiddenhurt.co.uk/bible_verses.html

APPENDIX I

Steve Atkerson - Building Congregational Consensus
http://www.ntrf.org/articles/article_detail.php?PRKey=13

John Kampfner - The Guardian - The truth about Jessica
http://www.theguardian.com/world/2003/may/15/iraq.usa2

Richard R. DeBlassie - The Counselor Privileged Communication and the Law
https://www.google.com/search?q=Richard+R.+DeBlassie%2C+The+Counselor+
Privileged+Communication+And+The+Law&ie=utf-8&oe=utf-8

Nigel Nicholson, Ph.D., author, professor of organizational behavior at London
Business School - The New Word on Gossip - Psychology Today
http://www.psychologytoday.com/articles/200105/the-new-word-gossip

Goodreads quotes
http://www.goodreads.com/quotes/tag/spiritual-abuse

Mike Fehlauer, Pastor, Author, Director of Foundation Ministries, The
Christian Broadcasting Network (CBN) - Warning Signs of Spiritual Abuse,
Spiritual Life in God - Parts 1, 2, 3
http://www.cbn.com/partners/about/our-ministries
http://www.cbn.com/spirituallife/churchandministry/Spiritual_Abuse2.aspx
http://www.cbn.com/spirituallife/churchandministry/Spiritual_Abuse3.aspx

James L. Melton - How I Know the King James Bible is the Word of God
Published by Bible Baptist Church, Sharon TN
http://www.av1611.org/kjv/knowkjv.html

Investopedia
www.investopedia.com

APPENDIX I

Anno Mundi - Disciples called Christians in Antioch - Anno Mundi Books
http://www.annomundi.com/bible/disciples_called_christians_in_antioch.html

Cliff Williams - Published in CHRISTIAN FEMINISM TODAY -
When Christians Contemplate Suicide
http://www.eewc.com/Articles/when-christians-contemplate-suicide

Ingela Ratledge - Why We Love to Gossip - Woman's Today
http://www.womansday.com/life/why-we-love-to-gossip-114587

Eugene Cho, co-founder and executive director of One Day's Wages
http://www.onedayswages.org/profile/eugene-cho

Helen Fisher, PhD, biological anthropologist and Author of New York, NY
http://www.helenfisher.com

Kent R. Rieske, Ministry Director - Bible Life Ministry
http://www.biblelife.org

Francis A. Schaeffer - Why New Churches Fail
http://www.churchleadership.org/pages.asp?pageid=66941

What is Going on with the Pastors in America?
by Dr. Richard J. Krejcir
http://www.intothyword.org/apps/articles/?articleid=36562

Press Connects/Part of the USA Today Network/Press & Sun Bulletin
http://www.pressconnects.com/story/news/local/2015/05/19/vestal-robert-leone-lawsuit-jury-verdict/27577061

APPENDIX I

Out of Context scriptures, Martin Saunders/ CHRISTIAN TODAY
Contributing Editor
http://www.christiantoday.com/article/out.of.context.five.of.the.most.
misused.bible.verses/40647.htm

Please Convince Me, Aaron Brake
http://pleaseconvinceme.com/2013/a-text-out-of-context-2-chronicles-
714http://pleaseconvinceme.com/2013/a-text-out-of-context-2-
chronicles-714

Commonly Misused Bible Verses, Tim Chaffey
https://www.google.com/search?num=100&safe=active&rlz=1C1AFAB_enUS
460US460&q=commonly+misused+bible+verses&oq=Commonly+misused+
Bible+verses&gs_l=serp.1.0.0.144669.144669.0.145754.1.1.0.0.0.0.0.142.142.0j1.
1.0....0...1c.1.64.serp..0.1.140.zPtQ20V6BIc

Kent R. Rieske, Ministry Director - Bible Life Ministry
http://www.biblelife.org/bondage.html

The Robert Leone Story by Larry Hohol
https://www.youtube.com/watch?v=O5eOknaXgYU&list=PL32CF3CF
3F5890482

Macrohistory
http://www.fsmitha.com/h2/ch34-sa.htm

APPENDIX II

The complete list of the American English translations
of the Bible that are used in Thug Preachers

21st Century King James Version	(KJ21)
Authorized (King James) Version	(AKJV)
Amplified Bible	(AMP)
Contemporary English Version	(CEV)
Easy-to-Read Version	(ERV)
Good News Translation	(GNT)
King James Version	(KJV)
New American Standard Bible	(NASB)
New Century Version	(NCV)
New English Translation	(NET)
New International Version	(NIV)
New King James Version	(NKJV)
New Living Translation	(NLT)
Word English Bible	(WEB)

APPENDIX II

Biblical Linguistics and
Biblical Historical Research Tools

Interlinear Bible
http://www.scripture4all.org/OnlineInterlinear/Greek_Index.htm

Hebrew Interlinear Bible
http://www.scripture4all.org/OnlineInterlinear/Hebrew_Index.htm

Strong's Concordance with Hebrew and Greek Lexicon
http://lexiconcordance.com

Vine's Complete Expository Dictionary of Old and New Testament Words
http://www.ultimatebiblereferencelibrary.com/Vines_Expositary_Dictionary.pdf

Association for Diplomatic Studies and Training
http://adst.org

Greek Interlinear Bible
http://www.scripture4all.org/OnlineInterlinear/Greek_Index.htm

RESOURCES

Biblical Hermeneutics Stack Exchange
http://hermeneutics.stackexchange.com/

Academy of Homiletics
http://www.homiletics.org/

Bible Hub
http://biblehub.com

You Version
https://www.bible.com/bible

Open Bible
https://www.openbible.info/labs/cross-references

Bible Study Tools
http://www.biblestudytools.com

Online Dictionary
dictionary.reference.com

Bible Gateway
https://www.biblegateway.com/passage/

Study Light
studylight.org

Family Christian
www.familychristian.com/church-resources/bible-studies.html

RESOURCES

The American Church in Crisis: Ground breaking Research Based on a
National Database of over 200,000 Churches
by David T. Olson

Pastor Burnout Workbook
by Daniel Sherman
http://www.pastorburnout.com/pastor-burnout.html

Weinstein's Federal Evidence, Second Edition
by Jack Weinstein, Margaret Berger, and Joseph M. McLaughlin

Management: A Biblical Approach
by Myron Rush

Toxic Faith
by Stephen Arterburn

Healing the Scars of Emotional Abuse
by Gregory L. Ph.D. Jantz and Ann McMurray

Combatting Cult Mind Control
by Steven Hassan

What is Going on with the Pastors in America?
by Dr. Richard J. Krejcir
http://www.intothyword.org/apps/articles/?articleid=36562

Bible Gateway
https://www.biblegateway.com/passageGreek

284

INDEX

INDEX

INDEX

INDEX

murder 40, 87

N

newborn 70, 95, 227
New Testament 2, 9, 27, 30, 32, 44, 128, 141, 248, 264
Nicholas Emler 164, 264
non-biblical 4, 8
non-biblical system 4
non-denominational 62

O

obedience xxii, 1, 4, 30, 31, 32, 33, 38, 73, 82, 107, 119, 120, 132, 178, 181, 183, 250
obedience to God 4
obey 180
OB/gynecologist 93
offerings and sacrifices 4, 73
Old Testament. *See* Bible
organization xviii, 4, 5, 38, 55, 63, 78, 80, 87, 97, 101, 106, 111, 121, 163, 175, 218

P

Paprocki 28
parishioner 1
passages 9, 28, 29, 75, 76, 120
Pastor's Pillow 165
peitho 30, 31, 32, 33
physicians 94
Pilate 53, 54
political xviii, 4, 57, 90, 101, 113
power of God 2, 82, 118, 129, 166, 169, 172, 254

proistemi 29
prophecy 27, 28, 49, 71, 72
prophe-lied 71, 72
public humiliation 65, 107, 151

R

rage 64, 240
reinstating 70
religion 5, 7, 45, 55, 56, 59
religious obligations 82
religious structure 4
religious studies 89
responsibility iv, 7, 8, 14, 26, 37, 43, 70, 74, 148, 182, 200
restored 2
rule xvii, 1, 8, 9, 14, 15, 29, 30, 37, 38, 45, 59, 62, 64, 81, 92, 103, 118, 126, 146, 147, 176, 190, 215

S

sacrifice 4, 19, 73, 92, 142, 143, 144, 239, 250
scolding 68
selective preaching 75, 76
self-humility 14, 17
sexual abuse 147, 148
Shakespeare 186
Shakespeare, William 136
sheep 182
slavery 125, 126, 281
social 4, 90, 113, 127, 167, 203, 223, 237
solid food 70
South Africa 14

INDEX

THUG PREACHERS
by Frank Jackson

XAVIER PUBLISHING HOUSE, INC.

Made in the USA
Middletown, DE
19 August 2019